Using Time, Not Doin

Wiley Series in Personality Disorders

Series Editor: Professor Eddie Kane – Personality Disorder Institute, University of Nottingham

The Wiley Series in Personality Disorders publishes both single-authored and multi-authored books. The aim of the series is not merely to present critical findings and commentaries based in excellent science but also to ensure they are grounded in the realities of day-to-day practice and service delivery. The series seeks to draw together work from across the wide spectrum of professional disciplines that are essential to the development of well-balanced theoretical perspectives and truly holistic service delivery. Books in this series will be useful to clinical practitioners, lawyers, policy makers, ethicists, services users, carers and those who fund and manage the complex systems of health, social care and criminal justice.

Published

Using Time, Not Doing Time: Practitioner Perspectives on Personality Disorder and Risk
Allison Tennant and Kevin Howells

Forthcoming

Forensic Care for Personality Disordered and Psychopathic Offenders
Mark Freestone

Personality Disordered Offenders in a High Secure Setting: A Practitioner's Perspective
Neil Gordon and Phil Willmot

For all titles in this series please visit www.wiley.com/wiley-blackwell

Using Time, Not Doing Time

Practitioner Perspectives on Personality Disorder and Risk

Edited by Allison Tennant and Kevin Howells

A John Wiley & Sons, Ltd., Publication

This edition first published 2010
© 2010 John Wiley & Sons Ltd.

Wiley-Blackwell is an imprint of John Wiley & Sons, formed by the merger of Wiley's global
Scientific, Technical, and Medical business with Blackwell Publishing.

Registered Office
John Wiley & Sons Ltd, The Atrium, Southern Gate, Chichester, West Sussex,
PO19 8SQ, UK

Editorial Offices
The Atrium, Southern Gate, Chichester, West Sussex, PO19 8SQ, UK
9600 Garsington Road, Oxford, OX4 2DQ, UK
350 Main Street, Malden, MA 02148-5020, USA

For details of our global editorial offices, for customer services, and for information about how to
apply for permission to reuse the copyright material in this book please
see our website at www.wiley.com/wiley-blackwell.

Library of Congress Cataloging-in-Publication Data

Using time, not doing time: practitioner perspectives on personality disorder and risk / edited by
Allison Tennant and Kevin Howells.
  p. cm.
 Includes bibliographical references and index.
 ISBN 978-0-470-68350-7 (cloth) – ISBN 978-0-470-68349-1 (pbk.)
 1. Violence–Forecasting. 2. Personality disorders. 3. Mentally ill offenders. 4. Violent
offenders–Psychology. 5. Sex offenders–Psychology. I. Tennant, Allison. II. Howells, Kevin.
 RC569.5.V55U85 2010
 616.85′81–dc22

A catalogue record for this book is available from the British Library.

Set in 10/12 pt Galliard by Toppan Best-set Premedia Limited

Printed in Singapore by Markono Print Media Pte Ltd
1 [2010]

Contents

About the Contributors

Kerry Beckley is a chartered clinical psychologist. She currently works part time within the Personality Disorder Service at Rampton Hospital in Nottinghamshire Healthcare Trust and is a senior clinical tutor on the Trent Doctorate in Clinical Psychology. Her main area of clinical interest is in the application and integration of schema therapy to forensic settings. She is also an accredited schema therapist.

Dr Michael Daffern is a clinical psychologist by training. He has worked in prisons and in general and forensic mental health services. Currently, he is a Senior Lecturer with the Centre for Forensic Behavioural Science, Monash University, Consultant Principal Psychologist with Forensicare, and Special Lecturer within the Division of Psychiatry at The University of Nottingham. His research interests include behavioural assessment methods, offender rehabilitation, personality disorder, and aggression and other problem behaviours within institutions.

Dr Neil Gordon is a psychotherapist, organizational consultant and clinical supervisor. He is an honorary teaching fellow at Sheffield Hallam University and on the course team of the Metanoia Institute (London), Doctorate in Psychotherapy programme. Neil has conducted research exploring how psychotherapists in high secure settings adapt their approaches in a context-sensitive way and has a particular interest in the relationship between organizational culture and team behaviours. He co-leads the schema therapy group programme at Rampton Hospital and was formerly responsible for multidisciplinary training and workforce development within the Personality Disorder Directorate. Neil is seconded as a senior fellow to the Personality Disorder Institute at Nottingham University, where he is the project lead for the development of the National Personality Disorder Knowledge and Understanding Framework (KUF) commissioned by the Department of Health and Ministry of Justice.

Laura Hamilton is a forensic psychologist and accredited CAT (cognitive analytic therapy) therapist. Currently Laura is working in a split post where she is programme lead for the MSc in Forensic Psychology at Nottingham Trent University and a clinician on the Peaks Unit at Rampton Hospital. Prior to this Laura worked with a range of offending populations in the Prison Service, and during her time on the Peaks Unit developed a specialist interest in boundary management.

Rick Howard has a long-standing interest in personality disorders, which he started researching in the 1970s while employed at Broadmoor Hospital. He recently co-edited, with Mary McMurran, *Personality, Personality Disorders and Violence*. Before returning to take up his current position as senior research fellow at the Peaks Unit, Rampton Hospital, he held academic positions in Ireland, New Zealand and Singapore. Wearing two hats – as cognitive neuroscientist and forensic psychologist – he looks at forensic issues, and personality disorders in particular, through a neuroscientific lens.

Kevin Howells is a chartered clinical and forensic psychologist who has worked as a practitioner, researcher and academic in the fields of forensic psychology and the treatment of offenders. He is currently Professor of Forensic/Clinical Psychology in the Institute of Mental Health at Nottingham University and Academic Chair at the Peaks Unit (DSPD Service) at Rampton Hospital in Nottinghamshire Healthcare Trust. His interests include anger and its treatment, treatment readiness and engagement, the therapeutic climate of forensic units and cognitive behavioural therapy with offenders.

Perdita Jackson gained a maths degree with qualified teacher status before obtaining advanced skills teacher status. She has mentored student teachers and newly qualified teachers in schools as well as teaching adults in a teacher training college. Since working with adult learners in a secure hospital Perdita has gained postgraduate qualifications in literacy and language. She is a Fellow of the Institute for Learning and is currently studying a doctorate in educational leadership where her research interests are in curriculum and programme developments within secure environments.

Lawrence Jones is consultant clinical and forensic psychologist, lead psychologist working on the Peaks Unit, Rampton Hospital, with offenders with personality disorder diagnoses. Previously he worked in prison and community settings with offenders. He is the former chair of the Division of Forensic Psychology and has published and taught on motivational assessment and intervention, working with personality disordered offenders, offence paralleling behaviour, therapeutic communities for offenders, personality disordered sex offenders, case formulation and iatrogenic interventions with personality disordered individuals.

Dr Gopi Krishnan came to work at Rampton Hospital in June 1998 at a time when there was a shortage of consultant psychiatrists and a recruitment campaign had been undertaken in Canada. He initially took up post as consultant psychiatrist in the Personality Disorder Directorate and in April 1999 became lead clinician for this service. Gopi has extensive clinical experience of working with personality disordered patients in a high secure setting. As clinical director, he was responsible for the strategic development and reconfiguration of the Personality Disorder Service and latterly the Peaks in conjunction with the Rampton Hospital management team. In December 2008 he successfully applied for the post of associate medical director and became the professional lead for medical services within the Forensic Services Division.

Dr John Milton is a consultant forensic psychiatrist in the Peaks Unit at Rampton Hospital. He trained as a general and forensic psychiatrist and in recent years has worked in personality disorder services in secure hospital services. He is a full-time clinician with an interest in forensic research.

Louise Sainsbury is a chartered consultant clinical and forensic psychologist in the personality disorder directorate, Rampton Hospital. She has lead on implementing the violence reduction programme within the treatment pathway. Her predominant areas of interest include: attachment theory; engagement and motivation in therapy; and integrating treatment approaches for personality disorder.

Allison Tennant is a nurse consultant and works at the Peaks Unit at Rampton Hospital, Nottinghamshire Healthcare NHS Trust. She is a cognitive behavioural therapist and leads the dialectical behavioural therapy (DBT) programme in the unit. The Peaks Unit provides specialized treatment interventions for men who are deemed to have a dangerous and severe personality disorder. She has adapted the DBT programme to meet the needs of a male in-patient forensic population. Her other interests include treatment evaluation and developing frameworks to ensure that staff receive clinical supervision to help maintain a healthy workforce.

Glen Thomas has worked in the health service for nearly 30 years and in the specialty of forensic addictions for the last 19 years. He has extensive experience of working with a variety of mentally disordered populations with comorbid substance misuse problems across a range of NHS forensic settings. Along with a colleague he has been responsible for the development of the Rampton Hospital Mental Disorder and Substance Misuse Programme. The programme is designed to help patients address the complex area of mental disorder, substance misuse and offending behaviour. The programme is used in a number of high and medium secure forensic services. Glen has extensive experience in facilitating and delivering training in his specialist field and presently runs a number of accredited substance misuse courses at pre- and postgraduate level. He has presented at numerous conferences both within the United Kingdom and abroad over the last 20 years and is consulted widely on his specialist area. He is presently undertaking his PhD with Leicester University looking at the relationships between mental disorder, substance misuse, violence and post-traumatic stress disorder (PTSD).

Clare Thurlow has worked in a secure hospital since 1997 initially working as a technical instructor where she supported a variety of daycare activities. Clare joined the education department in September 2004 and since then has completed various teaching courses. She recently formalized her teaching by successfully completing a Cert Ed in adult education and also a level 4 specialism in literacy. Clare has a specific interest in special educational needs and in teaching basic skills.

David Underwood comes from a corporate training background where he worked for many years as a project manager and technical instructor in the electronics industry before supporting small businesses and local universities and colleges as a consultant. David has worked in a secure hospital since January 2004 initially working as a part-time lecturer and formalizing his teaching qualifications through the successful completion of a Cert Ed. David's interest in computing and music has led to him being instrumental in introducing electronic music and computer projects to patients in a secure environment.

Dr Jackie Withers is an experienced clinician, trainer, supervisor and researcher. She began her career as a nurse and trained as both a general and psychiatric nurse. She then retrained as a clinical psychologist. She has worked across several special-ties, i.e. adult mental health, HIV/AIDS, addiction and forensic client groups, and across a range of settings, e.g. community, day programmes, in-patient, and medium and high secure facilities. Her interest in personality disorder developed when working with complex cases within addictions and then with mentally dis-ordered offenders. Jackie is dual chartered as both a forensic and clinical psycholo-gist; she is also a registered psychotherapist. Jackie is a DBT and CBT (cognitive behaviour therapy) therapist, and also CAT psychotherapist, supervisor and trainer. She has also completed further training in group analytic, psychoanalytic and systemic approaches. Over recent years she has become increasingly interested in the organizational context in which interventions are provided, and the adverse impact of organizational and team dynamics on the effectiveness of specific therapeutic techniques. Jackie is currently working in the Personality Disorder Service at the Humber Centre, Hull.

Preface

The Wiley Series in Personality Disorders publishes both single-authored and multi-authored books. The aim of the series is not merely to present critical findings and commentaries based in excellent science but also to ensure they are grounded in the realities of day-to-day practice and service delivery. The series seeks to draw together work from across the wide spectrum of professional disciplines that are essential to the development of well-balanced theoretical perspectives and truly holistic service delivery. Books in this series will be useful to clinical practitioners, lawyers, policy makers, ethicists, services users, carers and those who fund and manage the complex systems of health, social care and criminal justice.

Over the past 20 years there has been an increasing interest in the interrelationship of personality and mental health and particularly in personality disorders. A number of diverse theoretical clinical approaches have emerged and internationally very different policy and legislative approaches have been adopted to underpin individual countries' attempts to recognize the social complexities presented by and to people with personality disorders. New perspectives continue to emerge and significant human, scientific and financial resources have been focused on challenging existing traditional ideas and seeking a more coherent theoretical framework for interventions based on well-researched empirical evidence.

For many years personality disorders were, and often still are, regarded as untreatable and wrongly identified as being synonymous with dangerousness. In fact people with a personality disorder who pose a high risk of harm to others are a tiny minority whereas this group often self-harm and take their own lives; recent figures for England from the Department of Health (2009) indicate that a range from 47 to 77% of suicides have a personality disorder. The diagnosis has frequently been used as an informal or formal criterion for exclusion from services which others with mental health issues take for granted as well as from ordinary life opportunities such as decent housing and employment.

Personality disorders are not something we catch or are born with but are 'a way of being', developed as we grow up. To have a personality disorder means to have some aspects of your personality that will cause you repeated problems, particularly with relationships. Personality disorders affect people across their life-span and often across generations. People with a personality disorder will often have experienced abuse, trauma, neglect or disrupted care in childhood. In addition to the exclusion they so frequently experience, people with a personality disorder appear more likely to have diagnosable mental illnesses such as depression, panic attacks and addictions including poly-drug abuse.

New approaches in clinical and social interventions coupled with a more benign policy and legislative environment in some countries are leading to real innovation and enhanced life chances for people diagnosed with personality disorder. At the same time a refreshed understanding of the aetiology and development of personality disorder is coming from behaviour genetics and developmental psychology. The developmental explanations of personality disorder are being enhanced by increased understanding of biological and developmental mechanisms. These new approaches and understandings challenge traditional theories about the origins of the diagnoses and the life outcomes that should be expected.

Set in this exciting context of new research enquiry, ethical, social, policy and legislative challenges this book offers an insight into the practical realities of constructing and delivering treatment to some of the most complex and excluded people anywhere. The national personality disorder programme in England is an integrated initiative between a number of government departments. The aspect of the programme which is central to the issues described in this book is the Dangerous and Severe Personality Disorder (DSPD) Programme established in 1999. The model described in 1999 was designed to test, research and further develop intervention programmes in selected high security prisons and hospitals in England.

The authors of this book work at the leading edge of development and service delivery with this complex group of individuals. Rampton Hospital, where the authors are based, has for many years led the way in the treatment of high risk individuals with personality disorders and was an early pilot site for the new initiative. The book sets the scene clearly before looking at critical issues of risk assessment, willingness to engage in treatment and the complexities of sex offender work. The focus switches to particular interventions and treatment issues and finally examines the often neglected areas of maintaining change and recovery, the opportunities adult learning offers for these individuals and the management of the delicate balance between care and control in the high secure environment.

The authors are nationally and internationally recognized experts in this field with extensive experience across a variety of disciplines. They have constructed a clear, coherent and concise text which fits neatly with the aims of this series; to provide practical help to the frontline staff underpinned by excellent science.

Professor Eddie Kane
Personality Disorder Institute, University of Nottingham

Reference

Department of Health (2009). *Recognising complexity; Why personality disorder is everybody's business.* London: Department of Health.

Introduction

Allison Tennant and Kevin Howells

This book addresses clinical practice issues related to the understanding, assessment and, particularly, treatment of people who have been diagnosed as having personality disorders and who have been deemed to pose a high risk of harm to others. Our plan in putting this book together was not to produce an academic or research text but to focus on the experience, practice and emerging ideas and findings of practitioners in the field, those at the coalface of work with this challenging group. The academic and research background to this field of practice has been extensively and critically reviewed in a recent text by Wiley, edited by Mary McMurran and Richard Howard (2009), and the interested reader should read this book.

As well as having a practice focus, our other intention was to reflect the multidisciplinary nature of practice in this field. We have not been able to include contributions from all the varied types of practitioners involved in such work but we have included nursing staff, psychiatrists, psychologists and educationalists. In forensic mental health settings, nursing staff and psychologists play an increasing and large role in the delivery of core psychological treatments, while psychiatrists often have major responsibilities relating to admission and the medico-legal aspects of such work, in addition to diagnostic and treatment roles. Many in-patient services provide a total living environment for the patient and this environment includes educational and occupational activities. We have included discussion of educational issues.

There are many important aspects of services not covered in this volume – occupational therapies, the management and planning of services, staff training, community provision, biological approaches to treatment and delivery of treatments in criminal justice as opposed to mental health settings. These are potential topics for future publications.

In chapter 1, John Milton and Gopi Krishnan, both consultant forensic psychiatrists involved in personality disorder services, trace the recent history of developments in this field, including the medico-legal framework and recent developments in service provision. The notion of risk, including its definition, assessment and management, is a vital one. In chapter 2, Michael Daffern, a clinical psychologist with experience of this work in Australia and the United Kingdom, outlines the state of our knowledge and the methods likely to be used in practice.

The delivery of effective treatment services is not straightforward. One precondition, for example, is that the potential recipient of the treatment offered is ready to undertake treatment and to become engaged in therapeutic work. Kevin Howells, a forensic clinical psychologist, and Allison Tennant, a nurse consultant, describe an approach to understanding readiness and engagement in chapter 3. A second precondition for effective treatment is that the treatment given clearly follows from an analysis of what has contributed to the problems being addressed. This is the task of *clinical formulation,* which is broader than psychiatric diagnosis. Lawrence Jones, a consultant clinical and forensic psychologist, addresses the nature of formulation and how it might be conducted in chapter 4.

A range of types of treatment intervention are currently being delivered to individuals with personality disorders and high risk. In the following five chapters, practitioners heavily involved in particular treatment programmes describe their practice and the issues that arise from it. In chapter 5, Allison Tennant describes the practicalities of delivering dialectical behaviour therapy with this population – a wide-ranging approach which incorporates many methods from cognitive behavioural theory and from Eastern meditative traditions. Cognitive analytic therapy may be less familiar to practitioners in personality disorder services – the background to this theoretical approach and its clinical methods are described by Jackie Withers (a clinical psychologist) in chapter 6. Schema therapy, arising out of cognitive analyses of mental disorder, is discussed by Kerry Beckley (clinical psychologist) and Neil Gordon (nurse consultant) in chapter 7.

The needs of those with personality disorder and high risk are of both a criminogenic and non-criminogenic type. Whereas the previous treatments have a clear, though not exclusive, focus on personality problems, the following three chapters are clearly concerned with criminogenic need. The behaviour most likely to define harm is violence, so it is to be expected that the treatment of violence is a priority. Louise Sainsbury (a clinical psychologist) describes the currently most influential approach to violence treatment in these settings in chapter 8. The second most frequent type of 'harming' behaviours is sexual aggression. Sexual aggression has been targeted in mainstream prison intervention programmes for some years, but how such treatments might need to be modified for a personality disordered population is poorly understood. Lawrence Jones addresses just this issue in chapter 9. Few professionals (or researchers) need convincing that substance misuse is an important contributor to high risk behaviours and that it overlaps with personality disorder. The rationale and content for programmes in this area is discussed in detail by Glen Thomas, a nurse consultant in substance misuse, and Jackie Withers in chapter 10. Jackie Withers also analyses the importance of recovery in chapter 11.

We are convinced that treatment for the people under consideration in this book needs to be multifaceted and to extend beyond conventional notions of therapy. One example of this need is provided by the observation that learning and educational deficits appear to be common. Ideally, attempts to remedy such deficits through education need to be integrated with psychotherapeutic interventions. The potential role for an educational input of this sort is covered in chapter 12 by Perdita Jackson and colleagues, all educationalists, in a unit for dangerous and severe personality disorder. Formal therapeutic interventions can be subverted by boundary violations and uncertainties. In chapter 13, Laura Hamilton (forensic psychologist) unpacks the issues related to boundaries in these particular settings.

Finally, although this book was not planned to cover theoretical and research issues in any depth (see above), clinical work by practitioners cannot be separated from scientific issues and particularly from the need to evaluate what is effective. Richard Howard and Kevin Howells (forensic and clinical psychologists and academics) try to identify in the final chapter some pertinent scientific questions that will need to be addressed in the future.

Reference

McMurran, M. & Howard, R. (Eds.) (2009). *Personality, personality disorder and violence.* Chichester: Wiley-Blackwell.

Chapter One

Setting the Scene: National Developments in Services

John Milton and Gopi Krishnan

Introduction

Changes to mental health legislation are relatively rare. The new Mental Health Act 2007 (in force from 3 November 2008) in England and Wales updated the 1983 Mental Health Act 'to ensure it keeps pace with the changes in the way mental health services are – and need to be – delivered' (Department of Health, 2008, p. 4). Arguably the most dramatic changes affect the detention and in-patient care of individuals with personality disorder which partly drove the government's initial desire to update the legislation. From 1983 until the new Act was enforced, individuals with personality disorder who were assessed for formal detention in hospital were required to meet the legal criterion of 'psychopathic disorder' and also be deemed 'treatable'. However, from November 2008 no separate legal category for personality disorder exists, merely the presence of 'mental disorder', and treatability has been sublimated into the 'appropriate medical treatment' being available in the hospital.

The legislative change from an individual needing to be 'treatable' to a service having treatment for them is a subtle but important distinction and arose from growing government frustration with the way professional practice had developed under the old Act. Although the original so-called 'treatability clause' was introduced into the 1983 Act partly to ensure that individuals who were admitted were able to benefit from the treatment available, critics (for example Hoggett, 1990) argued that it became a tool for use by psychiatrists to avoid admitting the 'unmanageable' on the grounds of 'untreatability'. Instead the new Act now allows for the detention of individuals with personality disorder even though they may refuse to engage in treatment or the treatment may not initially be effective for them.

Using Time, Not Doing Time: Practitioner Perspectives on Personality Disorder and Risk
Edited by Allison Tennant and Kevin Howells
© 2010 John Wiley & Sons, Ltd.

The purpose of this introductory chapter is to trace how and why these developments have arisen, the influence of other settings (such as offender management) on health services and treatment initiatives, the rise of specific services for higher risk individuals with personality disorder and the likely future agenda for service development.

Precursors to change

A personality disordered individual's treatability was one of several areas which brought the issue of risk and personality disorder into sharp relief in the later 1990s. First, specific government criticism of the use of the 'treatability' criterion by psychiatrists arose in England following the 1996 murder of Lin and Megan Russell by Michael Stone, a man said to have 'untreatable' personality disorder (although this was later found to be erroneous). The then Home Secretary (now Secretary of State for Justice) Jack Straw complained that 'it is completely unacceptable that at present the detention of some very dangerous people depends on the random chance of whether a particular psychiatrist believes their condition is treatable' (Straw, 1998).

Second, in 1998 following concerns about patient mismanagement in the personality disorder service at Ashworth High Secure Hospital near Liverpool, an inquiry chaired by Peter Fallon (Fallon *et al.*, 1999) produced some wide-ranging recommendations, not just for high secure clinicians but for all working with personality disordered offenders. These included scrapping hospital order sentences for those with legal psychopathic disorder but maintaining transfers for sentenced prisoners and the creation of small, specialized units in prisons and hospitals. The recommendations were never fully accepted or implemented in a statutory way although they have been anecdotally acknowledged as helpful by clinicians working in the area of personality disorder.

Third, a large survey carried out for the Office for National Statistics in 1997 (Singleton *et al.*, 1998) found that, among those interviewed, over three quarters of men on remand and nearly half of those who were sentenced were considered to have a personality disorder. Problematically, however, only a minority of specialist places for managing offenders with personality disorder (PD) existed and these were mainly located in high security hospitals or in specialist prisons (such as Grendon Underwood prison). Due to some limited – and probably erroneous (D'Silva *et al.*, 2004) – research suggesting that some PD individuals with high psychopathy are 'made worse' (with negative reoffending outcomes) by traditional group approaches to treatment, many such individuals were excluded from interventions in prison to address violence or sexual reoffending.

Hence, spurred on by the Stone case in particular, a joint paper by the Department of Health and the Home Office in England and Wales was issued in 1999 on *Managing Dangerous People with Severe Personality Disorder* (Department of Health, Home Office, 1999). In the executive summary accompanying the paper the stated intention was described as 'a co-ordinated package of arrangements that offer better protection to the public in a way which strikes the right balance between the interests of the individual and society'. Embedded within this was the development of a specialist service, partly in prison and partly in hospitals, to manage offenders who came to be labelled as having dangerous and severe personality disorder (DSPD).

The genesis of newer secure services for personality disorder

Although the initiation of the DSPD project in 1999 appeared to be a somewhat sudden reaction to the Michael Stone case, its origins can arguably be traced through concerns about the unstructured approach to health-based PD services but also the coincidental convergence of a number of criminal justice developments through the 1990s including research about assessment tools, such as the influence of Hare's Psychopathy Checklist (Hare, 1991), and greater understanding of cognitive-behavioural risk-reducing interventions which became known as the 'what works' movement (Andrews & Bonta, 2003; McGuire, 1995). This is worthy of greater elaboration.

Developments in health-based PD services

So what was the position regarding NHS-based secure PD services in the early 1990s and where were the problems that could have culminated in the Fallon Inquiry? The first issue is that, until recently, PD services in forensic settings were essentially clinical and academic backwaters. There was little focus on health-based PD services which have traditionally been the poor relation of services managing individuals with psychosis. This lack of focus was not novel to health settings however. Even within the criminal justice system, risk-reduction initiatives rarely singled out offenders on the basis of their specific mental disorder, more on account of their offence type such as sexual or violent offenders.

Despite legal psychopathic disorder (then defined in the 1983 Mental Health Act as 'a persistent disorder or disability of mind ... which results in abnormally aggressive or seriously irresponsible conduct' generally equating to clinical personality disorder) being maintained as a separate clinical category, only a minority of patients with PD were (and still are) admitted under the Mental Health Act to non-forensic settings such as acute psychiatric wards – even within forensic settings following the 1983 Act, from almost 15% of all admissions in 1983 to 0.04% by 1993 (Home Office Statistical Bulletin, 1995). However high secure hospitals (such as Broadmoor, Ashworth and Rampton hospitals) have tended to maintain a greater proportion of such patients, with almost 26% labelled with PD uncomplicated by comorbid psychosis or learning disability in a three-hospital survey of the hospital population conducted in 1993 (Taylor *et al.*, 1998). Hence, high security hospitals became areas of relative experience and expertise in the management of disordered offenders with PD.

By the mid-1990s approximately 400 beds were occupied within high secure hospitals by patients with primary personality disorder while units in lower security, such as regional secure units, usually only had a handful of patients with PD as their primary problem. However, there were a number of unanswered questions such as (a) how did such patients come to be selected to be admitted to high security, (b) what treatment did they require or receive and (c) what was their outcome? As one author put it, 'What is special about those classified and accepted for admission by a special hospital psychiatrist? Tens of thousands of men are convicted of violent crimes every year; a handful find their way into Special Hospitals – how do they get selected?' (Chiswick, 1992).

The first question of how offenders were selected for admission to high security also intrigued Collins (1991) at Rampton Hospital who compared those referrals with psychopathic disorder who were accepted for admission with those who were rejected. He was unable to find any discriminating factors across a range of demographic, offence or clinical domains and concluded that the admission process was 'arbitrary'. Even today clinicians assessing offenders with PD for admission, for example to a medium secure PD unit, find little to differentiate those accepted for admission from those rejected (Milton *et al.*, 2007).

Regarding the second question of what treatment patients with PD actually receive, for several years it seems that no systematic treatment approach was described for the in-patient treatment of PD in high security. However, the so-called therapeutic 'milieu' effect was regarded as a significant factor. Although ill defined in high secure hospitals, similar approaches within hospital, such as the Henderson Hospital, and prison-based therapeutic communities (with, for example, community meetings and structured activities in addition to group and individual therapies) were given weight by follow-up studies, albeit in a slightly different format (Chiesa & Fonagy, 2003; Lee *et al.*, 1999), with positive clinical outcomes.

However, the difficulty in determining a suitable and methodologically valid treatment approach was not unique to high secure PD settings and perhaps not surprising as a review of treatments for PD found no conclusive evidence of benefit from any specific approach (Dolan & Coid, 1994). Again, a recent systematic review of treatment for borderline personality disorder found few methodologically robust studies to give guidance to clinicians in determining any evidence-based psychological approach (Binks *et al.*, 2006) although guidance about suitable treatment approaches has recently been issued to clinicians regarding both anti-social (NICE, 2009a) and borderline PD (NICE, 2009b).

Regarding the third question of outcome, this has generally been regarded as criminological outcome, that of reoffending by patients after discharge into the community. Although no specific studies were commissioned to follow PD patients in particular after discharge from hospitals in England and Wales, research data have confirmed that patients categorized with legal psychopathic disorder tend to have a poorer criminological outcome (for example Buchanan, 1998) although this may be tempered by a more favourable psychosocial outcome compared with patients suffering from mental illness (Steels *et al.*, 1998). A lack of outcome data remains a significant concern within the research community although may eventually be addressed, albeit with quasi-clinical outcomes, as those who commission services will require financial answers about their cost-effectiveness.

Despite these problems, and concerns about the 'elastic' nature of the psychopathic disorder concept which it was argued could allow almost any violent offender to be classified for admission (Chiswick, 1992), a majority of forensic psychiatrists at that time continued to support the inclusion of personality disorder within mental health legislation and that there should be specific treatment facilities within prisons and high security to support this (Cope, 1993). However, there was confusion about assessment, including how treatability (required for legal psychopathic disorder) might be determined.

This area was helpfully addressed by an important report produced by a Working Group on Psychopathic Disorder (Reed, 1994). It argued for much greater clarity and structure to assessment for personality disorder to 'promote the adoption of multi-method criteria for categorizing severe personality disorders'. It recommended the use of standard diagnostic instruments for Axis II categorization (from structured interview), a measure of psychopathy, a dimensional assessment of personality and a psychodynamic formulation.

Reed's findings regarding assessment were endorsed by the Royal College of Psychiatrists in 1999 although another report on diagnostic and assessment criteria in PD (Meux & McDonald, 1998) also acknowledged that assessment methods remained inadequate and recommended establishing research projects to develop customized assessment tools, neurocognitive instruments and outcome measures. Adopting assessment protocols with congruence between individual healthcare units and specialist prison services would have been an important starting point. Such information would also 'promote a greater consistency among future clinical and research studies' (Reed, 1994). However, a subsequent survey of all secure forensic units in England and Wales (Milton, 2000) found that there was still a degree of idiosyncratic use of assessment tools in practice.

Developments in criminal justice settings

Within the criminal justice services, both in prison and probation, the 1990s saw a number of important developments which would lead to them stealing a march on health services in the area of risk assessment and intervention. Although this initially began in relation to psychopathy, there were general implications for personality disorder and related services and later for the structure of DSPD assessment and interventions.

The development of the Psychopathy Checklist – Revised (PCL-R) by Hare (1991), as an empirical descriptor for the characteristics of psychopathy noted by Cleckley (1976), was an important addition to the assessment armamentarium. The discovery that a higher PCL-R score (equating to the presence of more psychopathic traits) was correlated with recidivism was highly notable (Hart *et al.*, 1988). This was followed by the development of further tools, such as the HCR-20 (Historical, Clinical, Risk Management-20; Webster *et al.*, 1997), for the assessment of risk.

Around this time psychologists working in criminal justice settings began to tease out the components of effective offender rehabilitation, leading to the 'risk–need–responsivity' principles (Andrews & Bonta, 2003). This essentially described how treatment would be most effective when services are matched with the offender's risk of reoffending; that services should be targeted towards higher risk offenders; that criminogenic needs are generally 'dynamic' factors which may be altered as opposed to static risk factors which are unchangeable; and that interventions should be responsive by providing treatment that addresses an offender's individual characteristics, such as learning style and personality. Overturning the 'nothing works' nihilism of 1970s offender rehabilitation, this became summated as the 'What Works' approach (McGuire, 1995).

Using the above principles, many of the subsequently developed treatment approaches adopted a cognitive-behavioural emphasis, with group-based manual-oriented interventions with high adherence to the treatment model. Thus several risk-reducing group approaches were developed for criminal justice settings. One such example is the Sex Offender Treatment Programme (SOTP) which was developed and initiated nationally in the early 1990s. Ongoing evaluations have yielded positive results indicating reductions in recidivism for some groups (Friendship et al., 2003). More recently there has been recognition within offender management services that there is greater scope still for enhancing rehabilitative approaches. The emergence of a 'Good Lives' strategy (for example Ward et al., 2006), where risk avoidance is added to by development of active rehabilitation and skills-based approaches, is predicted to produce encouraging results.

Despite the positive aspects to offender management in prison and probation settings, there have still been some notable problems. For example, there is a (perhaps understandable in view of a manualized approach) rigidity to some programme-based interventions which can lead to treatment 'drop-out' by a significant proportion of higher risk individuals. Analysis of the characteristics of 'drop-out' offenders has revealed a significant number have unaddressed mental health needs, often in the domain of personality disorder (Jones, 2002). In addition, based on the early and potentially erroneous research that individuals with high psychopathy cannot benefit from treatment as usual (or that their risk could be made greater), such individuals have been excluded from many risk-reducing interventions. This has led to either 'drop-outs' serving determinate sentences coming to the attention of supervising services just prior to their community release which have little to offer as positive interventions or being considered too psychopathic to be offered treatment.

Developments in interventions for personality disorder

Following on from Dolan and Coid's (1994) exposure of the dearth of evidence of effective treatments for personality disorder, a number of psychological treatment approaches developed during the 1990s which were to become equally relevant to forensic settings. Although interventions such as 'Reasoning and Rehabilitation' (Ross & Fabiano, 1991) had been used in offender settings and often addressed traits associated with common personality disorders such as impulsivity or paranoid thinking styles, several interventions emerged which specifically targeted personality disorder symptom or trait areas such as dialectical behaviour therapy (DBT; Linehan et al., 1991), cognitive analytic therapy (CAT; Ryle & Kerr, 2002) and schema therapy (Young et al., 2003). For example, DBT's use of techniques to address the emotional dysregulation of borderline personality disorder could allow an indirect influence on impulsive violence. In the case of schema therapy, allowing individuals to understand their 'mistrust/abuse' schema may assist in reducing the hypersensitivity associated with paranoid personality disorder and hence reduce some forms of instrumental violence. What these therapy modalities shared was a tendency to be structured, systematically delivered by trained staff, time-limited and with relative treatment fidelity, in many ways mimicking the developments in the criminal justice arena.

On the heels of the adoption of specific treatment approaches into forensic settings was a national, governmental recognition that individuals with PD were effectively being excluded from generic as well as forensic services. The imaginatively titled *Personality Disorder: No Longer a Diagnosis of Exclusion* from the National Institute for Mental Health in England (NIMHE, 2003) provided guidelines for all health services providing management of individuals with PD and made funding available over a three-year period. Although this raised the profile of the treatment needs for those with personality disorder, not just in forensic settings, it remains unclear how much influence the 'Exclusion' document has had on service strategy and development.

At this point it is important to mention that there have historically been pockets of expertise within health settings for individuals with personality disorder. Specifically a major evidence base which helped to inform the early drive towards developing the therapeutic milieu for DSPD services and the 'Exclusion' initiative came from the therapeutic community movement (for example Lee *et al.*, 1999) and led to an expansion of a network of therapeutic community services.

Therefore, a number of the newer initiatives for personality disorder have been employed in forensic areas with mentally disordered offenders. What is now needed is evidence of their efficacy in these transferred settings and how they might be integrated as a treatment package or strategy with, for example, other interventions with different end goals such as violence reduction. Although many of the treatment principles, such as being of cognitive-behavioural orientation, may be related to those used in offender management, evidence needs to be gathered demonstrating that they can be married together successfully.

High-risk PD services: A service waiting to happen or a driven political agenda?

At face value, it would appear that a minister's 'riposte' to psychiatry in the wake of some high profile murders led to a top-down, new agenda to develop a cutting-edge, novel service to meet the public protection demands posed by dangerous offenders with a difficult-to-manage personality disorder. While that might have been partly true, we believe in retrospect that there may well have been a ground-swell leading to similar developments, either within health or criminal justice settings, even without the Stone case. For example, the new thinking arising from Fallon, the need to demonstrate effective treatments and to develop a systematic approach within health services for PD, the success of the 'what works' approach in offender management and the potential to transfer it to health settings, the recognition of the size of the problem within prisons but also that a significant minority of offenders, potentially with PD, were being excluded or dropping out of offence programmes, might have led to the development of specific initiatives for such a subgroup. We believe that the Stone case acted as the 'tipping point' (to borrow from Grodzins, 1958, and recently Gladwell, 2000) which galvanized somewhat unusually two government departments and allowed the development of a broad range of pilot initiatives with a high level of clinical and research funding for a group of offenders who might otherwise not get a service.

Following the launch of the DSPD proposals in 1999, critics (for example Mullen, 1999) argued that there are considerable concerns attached to developing a service specifically to detain individuals with PD who are deemed to be high risk but potentially of equivocal treatability. Some of these are philosophical although some are born out of research interests. For example, fundamentally there has been unease amongst many clinicians regarding the prominence of the public protection agenda at the apparent expense of a treatment component, potentially using a medical approach to circumvent any breach of human rights legislation. Some have argued that the medicalization of risk management for this group of offenders resulted from the government's dissatisfaction at the perceived inadequate response of the criminal justice system to sentence such individuals, where an offence has been committed, to sentences offering greater post-release supervision such as discretionary life sentences for qualifying offences (Eastman, 1999).

In addition, although the vision of Philip K. Dick's (1956) *Minority Report* short story (recently a film) where mutant 'Precogs' preventatively identify 'Precrimes' is compelling, the reality of the sensitivity and specificity of DSPD's chosen instruments is far from science-fact. Based on research such as a systematic review by Buchanan and Leese (2001) of the proposed DSPD assessment measures, they reported that six DSPD individuals would need to be detained in order to prevent one violent act over a one-year period. They noted that the number needing detaining, for example in a community setting, would probably be even greater if more conservative base rates for violence, such as 5%, are used.

On the other hand, some have argued that the DSPD initiative is an opportunity to provide a service for some high-risk individuals with mental disorder who were clearly not having their needs met. Others such as Coid and Maden (2003) have suggested that such work clearly falls within the risk management role of mental health clinicians who should be more influential in assisting a multiagency approach to risk management, particularly in community settings.

DSPD services: A challenging outlook

As for any new initiative, there are inevitably challenges which can be seen either as necessary detours or as insurmountable obstacles. Perhaps in response to previous criticism of the loose or overly flexible concept of legal psychopathic disorder, admission to a new bespoke (DSPD) service has been subjected to greater 'gatekeeping' by its clinicians. In order to ensure that only the most dangerous are admitted (what has been termed the 'critical few'), and coincidentally to assist in research endeavours (a quasi-experimental design with defined parameters), individuals thought to be worthy of admission have to undergo a detailed observational and psychometric evaluation to determine the presence of so-called dangerous (relating to risk) and severe (relating to highly pathological) personality disorder. This perhaps brave attempt at operationalizing criteria for admission to a mental health service is unusual although it will be interesting to assess how determined the clinicians and administrators are at maintaining such a threshold in the face of potential clinical expediency or public ('the greater good') protection. A further proposal, which formed part of the original Department of Health Mental Health Bill (Department of Health, 1999), of mental health tribunals to sanction lengthier admissions would have added a layer of quasi-judicial legitimacy to the assessment process.

There are additional risks for developing a service with the DSPD parameters as described above. First, most obviously, and yet unproven, is the need for the interventions to work, either to reduce severity or frequency of the facets of personality disorder which cause subjective distress or 'damage' to others. Maden (2007) has cautioned against any over-optimistic claims about CBT-based initiatives with this population. Importantly, there is a significant research component to the DSPD project to answer questions about outcome although the real question, that of 'is offending reduced?', will inevitably take time to become clear. At the very least, investigators will have some idea about 'what doesn't work' or what initiatives cannot be transported into this population. Some may see the need for such evaluation as unfair for DSPD as, unlike the built-in evaluation of offender programmes in prison, few psychiatric services so far have been required to evaluate, even broadly, their treatment or programme management arrangements.

Second, the assembled patient population, deemed by some as the 'unmanageable', is difficult to work with. In addition to the deliberate collection of individuals with likely lower motivation, such patients are likely to exhibit greater subversion to hospital systems and the planned treatment approaches for psychopathy are experimental. Thus, although there are the lessons learned from the Fallon Inquiry (1999) which have undoubtedly influenced the environmental and operational design, clinicians in this service can expect substantial challenges in a range of clinical and security-related domains and an efficient public relations strategy may be required to manage any media fall-out.

Third, there are likely to be 'attacks', either legal challenges by patients or sniping by colleagues from the establishment. Legal challenges by patients about what constitutes appropriate medical treatment in relation to their own clinical treatability may follow for some cases with lower motivation or for those transferred to hospital towards the end of determinate sentences. Challenges to the Scottish Assembly's equivalent of such detention was held to be compatible with the European Court of Human Rights (*Hutchinson Reid* v. *UK* 50272/99 [2003] ECHR 94).

In addition, there may well be those within 'traditional' services, certainly within the Prison Service, who may see the novelty of DSPD (apparently deemed by some prison officers as the 'Darts Snooker Pool Department') as a 'too-soft' response to offenders who are felt to require a greater punitive approach to their broader rehabilitation. A more passive but insidious problem may be a labelling effect of being a DSPD individual which more generic PD and other forensic services may shy away from, encouraging a parallel PD service framework to develop rather than an integrated one.

Lastly, there is the need for the authorities to consider the likelihood of these pilot services creating a DSPD legacy of individuals on 'notional' mental health orders, detained in a health system essentially by default after their determinate sentences have expired following transfer from prison. Although a number of such transfers are effected deliberately at the end of a sentence where multiple community agencies are alarmed about unmanageable community risk (often referred to as 'directions' to hospital regardless of the receiving clinicians' views), such individuals and many of the DSPD cases are likely to require long-term placements due to their undiminished risk. This 'legacy' could well prove problematic if the DSPD pilot is deemed to be ineffective or not cost effective and such patients require assimilation into the wider hospital population. Recently a case challenging the transfer of a prisoner with personality disorder at the end of their sentence has led to the view from the Ministry of Justice that it will no longer consider such late transfers without clear grounds for mental disorder and the likely benefits of treatment (*R [TF]* v. *SSJ* [2008] EWCA Civ 1457).

DSPD and 'higher risk' community PD services: Future horizons

Despite acknowledgement that the management of individuals with PD was previously under-resourced (NIMHE, 2003), recent investment has been unprecedented. As well as the DSPD programme for hospital places (such as the Peaks Unit at Rampton Hospital and the Paddocks Unit at Broadmoor Hospital), in December 2007 the Department of Health and Ministry of Justice commissioned the development of the National Knowledge and Understanding Frameworks on Personality Disorder (www.pdinstitute.org.uk/downloads/upload_7504.pdf) to support people to work more effectively with personality disorder.

Although an economic evaluation has been built into the research portfolio mainly addressing the costs of setting up and running the new prison and hospital services, searching longer-term questions are likely to be asked about outcome in the face of a service that is two or three times more expensive than a generic prison place.

Community-based clinicians, while welcoming a repository for the secure management of higher risk individuals with PD at critical times, may well look on jealously at the concentration of financial resources for the 'critical few' when arguably such resources could be maximized by offering briefer interventions to a greater number of similar individuals with PD who are, say, about to be released under probation supervision. Initial DSPD plans had provision for 'step-down' and community-based services although whether there will be a cross-flow of DSPD-labelled individuals and other forensic patients to established or new services remains to be seen. However, this is likely to become more important as some patients make sufficient progress to warrant placements in the distal part of the DSPD service arrangements such as medium security or supported hostels. There will need to be an urgent expansion of community and low secure provision, and linking with other agencies, to ensure the opportunity for patients to progress and particularly to offer hope to some sceptical patients that discharge from hospital remains feasible.

As long as a project as expensive as the DSPD initiative (particularly the hospital-based service) remains a pilot with only limited 'proof' of efficacy, within a changing geopolitical landscape it is likely to be at risk of funding cuts or diversion of resources to the 'next big thing' unless preliminary criminological or other psychosocial data can demonstrate success. There is also a lesson to be considered for big projects such as DSPD, which are initially based on 'best-guess' evidence of what works to reduce offending, from SOTEP (Sex Offender Treatment Evaluation Project) in the US (Marques *et al.*, 1994) which had some interesting parallels with the DSPD project. The SOTEP in-patient programme at Atascadero State Hospital in California, through its design, was probably the most ambitious research programme for treatment and evaluation of sex offenders ever undertaken. It was highly resourced, research and evaluation focused and even involved changes in the state law to allow participants to be mandated there for treatment. Despite employing a 10-year prospective, randomized controlled trial approach to interventions, the programme showed minimal treatment efficacy. Therefore the DSPD data are likely to be awaited with interest.

In the meantime systematic reviews of the limited evidence for both psychological and pharmacological interventions for a variety of subtypes of personality disorders (analogous to that of Binks *et al.*, 2006), including schizoid, dependent and narcissistic PD, continue and are likely to report to the Cochrane database in the coming months. This will be of assistance to the bulk of clinicians working with lower risk individuals with primary or comorbid PD in community or non-secure settings as well as those in forensic services.

Ultimately the future for community management of higher risk individuals with PD may lie in the public protection agenda, perhaps focused upon by Multi-Agency Public Protection Panels (MAPPPs). The involvement of mental health professions as already described by Coid and Maden (2003) could, with sufficient vision and political will, take an even broader step forward by considering the primary prevention arm of higher risk PD services, i.e. the use of the public health agenda for managing or even the prevention of psychopathy or risk-related personality disorder. As Coid (2003a, 2003b) has previously described, this is a logical step within the public protection agenda in addition to other social policy measures. For example, adopting strategies identifying high risk individuals at an earlier stage, particularly in adolescence or even childhood, may be fruitful and economically viable (Scott *et al.*, 2001) and several potential research initiatives already have been identified (Harrington & Bailey, 2003) which may have important implications for public health approaches. Evaluation of high risk patients with PD, such as the DSPD service, will hopefully provide useful pointers to prevent the high risk PD cases of tomorrow.

References

Andrews, D. & Bonta, J. (2003). *The psychology of criminal conduct*, 3rd edition. Cincinnati, OH: Anderson Publishing.

Binks, C., Fenton, M., McCarthy, L., Lee, T., Adams, C. & Duggan, C. (2006). Psychological therapies for people with borderline personality disorder. *Cochrane Database of Systematic Reviews*, Issue 1. Art. No.: CD005652. DOI: 10.1002/14651858. CD005652.

Buchanan, A. (1998). Criminal conviction after discharge from special (high security) hospital. Incidence in the first 10 years. *British Journal of Psychiatry*, *172*, 472–476.

Buchanan, A. & Leese, M. (2001). Detention of people with dangerous severe personality disorders: A systematic review. *The Lancet*, *358*, 1955–1959.

Chiesa, M. & Fonagy, P. (2003). Psychosocial treatment for severe personality disorder: 36-month follow-up. *British Journal of Psychiatry*, *183*, 356–362.

Chiswick, D. (1992). Compulsory treatment of patients with psychopathic disorder: An abnormally aggressive or seriously irresponsible exercise? *Criminal Behaviour and Mental Health, 2*, 106–113.

Cleckley, H. (1976). *The mask of sanity*, 5th edition. St. Louis, MO: Mosby.

Coid, J. (2003a). Formulating strategies for the primary prevention of adult antisocial behaviour: 'High risk' or 'population' strategies? In D. Farrington & J. Coid (Eds.) *Early prevention of adult antisocial behaviour* (pp. 32–78). Cambridge: Cambridge University Press.

Coid, J. (2003b). Epidemiology, public health and the problem of personality disorder. *British Journal of Psychiatry, 182*, s3–s10.

Coid, J. & Maden, A. (2003). Editorial: Should psychiatrists protect the public? *British Medical Journal, 326*, 406–407.

Collins, P. (1991). The treatability of psychopaths. *Journal of Forensic Psychiatry, 2*, 103–110.

Cope, R. (1993). A survey of forensic psychiatrists' views on psychopathic disorder. *Journal of Forensic Psychiatry, 4*, 215–236.

Department of Health (1999). *Reform of the Mental Health Act: Proposals for consultation.* Retrieved 19 October 2009 from www.dh.gov.uk/en/Publicationsandstatistics/ Publications/PublicationsPolicyAndGuidance/DH_4007127

Department of Health, Home Office (1999). *Managing dangerous people with severe personality disorder.* Retrieved 19 October 2009 from www.dh.gov.uk/en/ Publicationsandstatistics/Publications/PublicationsLegislation/DH_4009414

Department of Health (2008). *Code of Practice: Mental Health Act 1983.* Retrieved 19 October 2009 from www.dh.gov.uk/en/Publicationsandstatistics/Publications/ PublicationsPolicyAndGuidance/DH_084597

Dick, P. (1956). The minority report. *The collected stories of Philip K. Dick*, Volume 4. 1st Carol Pub.

D'Silva, K., Duggan, C. & McCarthy, L. (2004). Does treatment really make psychopaths worse? A review of the evidence. *Journal of Personality Disorders, 18*, 163–177.

Dolan, B. & Coid, J. (1994). *Psychopathic and antisocial personality disorders: Treatment and research issues.* London: Gaskell.

Eastman, N. (1999). Public health psychiatry or crime prevention? Editorial. *British Medical Journal, 318*, 549–551.

Fallon, P., Bluglass, R., Edwards, B. & Daniels, G. (1999). *Report of the Committee of Inquiry into the Personality Disorder Unit, Ashworth Special Hospital.* London: HMSO.

Friendship, C., Mann, R. & Beech, A. (2003). The prison-based Sex Offender Treatment Programme: an evaluation. *Findings 205.* London. Home Office. Retrieved 19 October 2009 from www.homeoffice.gov.uk/rds/pdfs2/r205.pdf

Gladwell, M. (2000). *The tipping point: How little things can make a big difference.* New York: Little, Brown and Co.

Grodzins, M. (1958). *The metropolitan area as a racial problem.* Pittsburgh, PA: University of Pittsburgh Press.

Hare, R. (1991). *Revised Psychopathy Checklist.* Toronto, Ontario: Multi-Health Systems Inc.

Harrington, R. & Bailey, S. (2003). *The scope for preventing antisocial personality disorder by intervening in adolescence.* NHS National Programme on Forensic Mental Health Research and Development. Retrieved 19 October 2009 from www.dspdprogramme. gov.uk/media/pdfs/ASPD_Adolescence.pdf

Hart, S., Kropp, P. & Hare, R. (1988). Performance of psychopaths following conditional release from prison. *Journal of Consulting and Clinical Psychology, 56*, 227–232.

Hoggett, B. (1990). *Mental health law*, 3rd edition. London: Sweet and Maxwell.

Home Office Statistical Bulletin (1995). *Statistics of mentally disordered offenders, England and Wales 1993.* Issue 01/95. Retrieved 19 October 2009 from www.homeoffice.gov. uk/rds/pdfs2/hosb195.pdf

Jones, L. (2002). *Iatrogenic interventions with personality disordered offenders.* Paper presented at the Division of Forensic Psychology conference, Manchester.

Lee, J., Manning, N. & Rawlings, B. (1999). *Therapeutic effectiveness. A systematic international review of therapeutic community treatment for people with personality disorders and mentally disordered offenders.* York: University of York/NHS Centre for Reviews and Dissemination.

Linehan, M., Armstrong, H., Suarez, A., Allmon, D. & Heard, H. (1991). Cognitive behavioural treatment of chronically parasuicidal borderline patients. *Archives of General Psychiatry, 48,* 1060–1064.

Maden, A. (2007). Dangerous and severe personality disorder: antecedents and origins. *British Journal of Psychiatry, 190* (suppl), s8–s11.

Marques, J., Day, D., Nelson, C. & West, M. (1994). Effects of cognitive/behavioural treatment on sex offenders' recidivism: preliminary results of a longitudinal study. *Criminal Justice and Behaviour, 21,* 28–54.

McGuire, J. (Ed.) (1995). *What works: Reducing re-offending.* Chichester: John Wiley & Sons.

Meux, C. & McDonald, R. (1998). *Assessment and diagnostic criteria.* London: High Security Psychiatric Services Commissioning Board.

Milton, J. (2000). A postal survey of the assessment procedure for personality disorder in forensic settings. *Psychiatric Bulletin, 24,* 254–257.

Milton, J., Duggan, C., McCarthy, L., Costley-White, A. & Mason, L. (2007). Characteristics of offenders referred to a medium secure NHS personality disorder service: The first five years. *Criminal Behaviour and Mental Health, 17,* 57–67.

Mullen, P. (1999). Editorial: Dangerous people with severe personality disorder. British proposals for managing them are glaringly wrong – and unethical. *British Medical Journal, 319,* 1146–1147.

National Institute for Clinical Excellence, NICE (2009a). *Antisocial personality disorder: Treatment, management and prevention.* Retrieved 19 October 2009 from www.nice.org.uk/Guidance/CG77

National Institute for Clinical Excellence, NICE (2009b). *Borderline personality disorder: Treatment and management.* Retrieved 19 October 2009 from www.nice.org.uk/Guidance/CG78#summary

National Institute for Mental Health in England, NIMHE (2003). *Personality disorder: No longer a diagnosis of exclusion – policy implementation guidance for the development of services for people with personality disorder.* Retrieved 19 October 2009 from www.dh.gov.uk/en/Publicationsandstatistics/Publications/PublicationsPolicyAndGuidance/DH_4009546

Reed, J. (1994). *Report of the Department of Health and Home Office Working Group on Psychopathic Disorder.* London: Home Office.

Ross, R. & Fabiano, E. (1991). *Reasoning and rehabilitation: A handbook for teaching cognitive skills.* Ottawa, Ontario: T3 Associates.

Ryle, A. & Kerr, I. (2002). *Introducing cognitive analytic therapy: Principles and practice.* Chichester: John Wiley & Sons.

Scott, S., Knapp, M., Henderson, J. & Maughan, B. (2001). Financial cost of social exclusion: Follow up study of antisocial children into adulthood. *British Medical Journal, 323,* 191.

Singleton, N., Meltzer, H. & Gatward, R. (1998). *Psychiatric morbidity among prisoners in England and Wales.* London: Stationery Office.

Steels, M., Roney, G., Larkin, E. *et al.* (1998). Discharged from hospital: A comparison of the fates of psychopaths and the mentally ill. *Criminal Behaviour and Mental Health, 8,* 37–53.

Straw, J. (1998, 31 October). Straw's riposte on mental treatment. *The Times,* p. 21.

Taylor, P., Leese, M., Williams, D., Butwell, M., Daly, R. & Larkin, E. (1998). Mental disorder and violence. A special (high security) hospital study. *British Journal of Psychiatry, 172,* 218–226.
Ward, T., Gannon, T. A. & Mann, R. E. (2006). The Good Lives Model of offender rehabilitation: Clinical implications. *Aggression and Violent Behaviour, 11,* 77–94.
Webster, C. D., Douglas, K. S., Eaves, D. *et al.* (1997). *HCR-20: Assessing risk of violence (version 2).* Vancouver: Mental Health Law & Policy Institute, Simon Fraser University.
Young, J., Klosko, J. & Weishaar, M. (2003). *Schema therapy: A practitioner's guide.* New York: Guilford Publications.

Legal cases

Hutchinson Reid Hutchinson Reid v. UK *50272/99* (2003) ECHR 94. Retrieved 19 October 2009 from www.bailii.org/eu/cases/ECHR/2003/94.html
R (TF) v. *SSJ* (2008) EWCA Civ 1457. Retrieved 19 October 2009 from www.bailii.org/ew/cases/EWCA/Civ/2008/1457.html

Chapter Two

Risk Assessment for Aggressive Behaviour in Personality Disorder

Michael Daffern

Background

Aggression and violence pose significant problems for mental health services, the criminal justice system and for society in general; their social and economic costs are immense (Howells *et al.*, 2008). Compared with patients with other mental disorders, those with personality disorder (PD) are at a significantly greater risk of aggressive and violent behaviour (Wallace *et al.*, 1998). Associations between aggression and violence and PD are strongest with the Cluster B PDs, particularly borderline (BPD) and antisocial (APD). BPD and APD are reported as common comorbid diagnoses in studies of male and female violent offenders (Coid, 1992), female inmates of a high secure prison (Warren *et al.*, 2002) and patients of a high secure DSPD service (Howard *et al.*, submitted). Psychopathy, a particular form of PD commonly associated with aggressive and other criminal behaviour, is associated with all of the Cluster B disorders, particularly APD (Blackburn, 2007). Given the obvious risk of aggression and violence, the National Institute for Health and Clinical Excellence (2009) has recommended that healthcare professionals in forensic or specialist personality disorder services should consider, as part of a structured clinical assessment, formal violence risk assessment. Specific instruments are recommended including the 'Historical, Clinical, Risk Management-20 (HCR-20) to develop a risk management strategy' (p. 8). The aim of this chapter is to examine approaches to violence risk assessment and to consider risk assessment in the dangerous and severe personality disorder (DSPD) context specifically.

Using Time, Not Doing Time: Practitioner Perspectives on Personality Disorder and Risk
Edited by Allison Tennant and Kevin Howells
© 2010 John Wiley & Sons, Ltd.

Predicting aggression using personality disorder diagnosis

Though certain PDs are associated with an increased risk for aggression, the available research has thus far not been able to establish an unequivocal functional relationship (i.e. a causal link). According to Howard (2007), the identified associations are confounded by the fact that diagnostic criteria for some PDs include measures of aggressive behaviour. For example, the diagnostic criteria for APD includes: 'irritability and aggressiveness, as indicated by repeated physical fights or assaults' (DSM-IV-TR; American Psychiatric Association, 2000, p. 706); criteria for BPD includes: 'inappropriate, intense anger or difficulty controlling anger (e.g. frequent displays of temper, constant anger, recurrent physical fights)' (DSM-IV-TR; American Psychiatric Association, 2000, p. 710). This issue of tautology is particularly problematic, in that much of the research examining associations between PD and aggression has been conducted in offenders with convictions and therefore an established history of aggression; their aggressive behaviour is used as the dependent variable (i.e. aggression), but it is also used to confirm diagnosis. The use of PD to predict aggressive behaviour is therefore clearly compromised.

An additional problem with the use of PD to assess risk for aggression is that the PD diagnosis is categorical and does not easily lend itself to measures of intra-individual variation in risk state (i.e. why this person is at risk of being aggressive now rather than last month), though dimensional scores can be calculated with the aid of some structured measures of PD (see for example the International Personality Disorder Examination, IPDE; Loranger *et al.*, 1994). It is, however, unclear whether severity of DSM-IV PD fluctuates and whether these fluctuations correlate with the frequency, severity or density of aggressive behaviour (the so-called functional link). Further, even if an association between PD and aggression is accepted, the diagnosis in itself does not facilitate the creation of a psychological formulation of the aggressive behaviour from which particular interventions may be applied. Given the limitations associated with the use of PD diagnosis to predict aggressive behaviour it is important to examine alternate and more comprehensive risk assessment methods.

The risk assessment task: Approaches and technologies

Questions surrounding the capacity of mental health clinicians to accurately assess risk for aggression are long-standing; a multitude of scholars have entered the risk assessment field, resulting in a burgeoning literature and an impressive number of risk assessment tools, checklists, instruments and measures (i.e. technologies). Early risk assessment studies, which predominantly relied on review and follow-up of clinicians' unaided clinical appraisals of risk, revealed extremely poor predictive validity. In the now classic monograph, Monahan (1981) reached the conclusion that violence could not be predicted with any satisfactory level of accuracy and that any attempt to do so violates the civil liberties of the person being assessed.

Reasons for the limited predictive validity of unaided risk appraisals

There are many reasons for the inaccuracies observed in early research into clinical appraisals of risk for aggression. One of the most important (see Monahan, 1981) is that clinicians fail to consider base rates for aggression. Base rate refers to the probability that an event will occur in a particular sample. Contrary to popular opinion, aggression is uncommon. It is increasingly difficult to accurately predict something if it is rare. Ignorance of base rate results in an overestimation of risk; this results in high rates of *false positives* (i.e. predicting somebody will be aggressive when in fact they would not). The most impressive and probably famous demonstration of this base-rate problem is with the case of Johnny Baxtrom (Steadman & Cocozza, 1974). Johnny Baxtrom was detained in the Dannemora State Hospital in New York state when in 1966 the US High Court ruled that his institutionalization, and that of almost 1000 other patients detained under equivalent legislation, was illegal. Subsequently, these patients were released and Steadman and Cocozza (1974) were able to follow them up to determine whether they reoffended aggressively (as was predicted). They found that fewer than 3% of those able to be followed up were actually violent in the subsequent two to three years.

In addition to issues of base rate, limited accuracy in unaided clinical appraisals of risk is also due to errors in assessing clinicians' appraisal and decision making. Tversky and Kahneman (1974) have described three cognitive heuristics that are used when people make judgements under uncertainty: (a) *representativeness*, (b) *availability*, and (c) *adjustment from an anchor*. These and other cognitive biases and errors in attribution and appraisal are documented in Box 2.1. These errors in appraisal contribute to inaccurate probability estimates.

Improving on the poor performance of unaided clinical appraisals: Structured methods

Demands on mental health professionals to improve predictive accuracy beyond that revealed through scrutiny of research reliant on unaided clinical appraisals have resulted in substantial efforts to develop and enhance risk assessment methods and technologies. As attribution and other errors in appraisal seem to contribute to compromised risk-related decision making, researchers have created structured technologies. These are based on the empirical literature and the common views of experienced mental health professionals. Two particular approaches have developed: one relying on *actuarial models*, the other focusing on *structured clinical appraisals*. It is generally accepted that these methods are superior (in terms of their predictive accuracy) to unaided clinical appraisals and that this is because objective decision making is unobstructed by observer biases. The relative predictive performance of actuarial and structured clinical appraisal methods is, however, the subject of considerable controversy (see below). Before turning to this controversy, it is important to discuss in more detail the nature of each approach and prototypical examples of each method.

1. *Actuarial models.* Actuarial methods utilize formal decision algorithms developed on the basis of empirical research findings. In actuarial models the assessment

---

BOX 2.1   Cognitive heuristics and other biases in appraisal and
decision making

(a)   The *representativeness heuristic* is where commonality between people or
      objects of similar appearance is assumed. In risk assessment, a patient with
      certain features (characteristics, historical events) that are commonly seen
      in aggressive offenders may therefore be assumed to be at risk for
      aggression.

(b)   The *availability heuristic* is where assessors base their decision on how
      easily an example can be brought to mind. In these instances the ease
      (mentally *available*), vividness or emotional impact of an example is relied
      upon to determine the frequency, proportion or likelihood of an event
      rather than using the actual statistical probability. For example, a person
      could be deemed to be at high risk for aggression because the assessor
      can recall an occasion when the person was actually aggressive.

(c)   *Adjustment from an anchor* refers to the common human tendency to rely
      too heavily (i.e. anchor) a judgement based on one piece of information.
      For example, assessors may focus their risk assessment exclusively on a
      patient's single severe act of aggression to make their risk prediction
      (worse still, they may judge a person's likelihood or risk on some irrelevant
      characteristic).

(d)   The *fundamental attribution error* (Ross, 1977). This is the tendency for
      people to over-emphasize stable dispositional factors while under-empha-
      sizing situational factors. That is, observers tend to ascribe the causes of
      a person's aggressive behaviour to characteristics of the person (e.g. they
      lack empathy, are cruel and impulsive) rather than consider transient
      (state-based) factors within the individual or characteristics of the social
      environment (e.g. the person was under stress and confronted by others).

(e)   *Type II errors*: A Type II error is a *false negative*. In risk assessment this
      is when a person is assessed as posing a low risk for aggression when, after
      release or risk assessment, they end up behaving aggressively. Risk asses-
      sors are particularly wary of Type II errors because the error means an
      aggressive act has occurred and there is a new victim, and the assessor's
      integrity and that of the service they work within may be threatened. To
      avoid these concerns assessors typically make conservative assessments of
      risk, overestimating its likelihood (thereby increasing the likelihood of a
      Type I error, resulting in false positives – when people are considered high
      risk when in fact they might not have behaved aggressively; see previous
      discussion re: Johnny Baxtrom).

---

of risk is calculated mathematically by including only those variables considered
by the model. The Violence Risk Appraisal Guide (VRAG; Webster *et al.*, 1994)
is perhaps the most widely used and known of these actuarial methods; its development and use is typical of the actuarial approach. The VRAG was developed
using data from a cohort of patients detained in the Penetanguishene Mental
Health Center between 1965 and 1980. Follow-up data pertaining to aggressive

behaviour were collected from Royal Canadian Mounted Police files. Hospital records were reviewed and potentially relevant variables were coded; the relationships between these variables and aggressive outcome were determined statistically. Twelve variables that demonstrated stable relationships across samples were retained on the basis of statistical criteria. These variables included the Hare Psychopathy Checklist (PCL) score, age at index offence, degree of victim injury and history of alcohol abuse. In practice, an algorithm is applied to weight an individual's scores on the 12 variables. The overall score is used to assign individuals to one of nine risk categories, each of which is associated with a probability of reoffending. There is a considerable research literature supporting the use of the VRAG. In a medium secure unit within the United Kingdom, Doyle *et al.* (2002) compared the predictive validity of the VRAG with that of the PCL-SV (Psychopathy Checklist: Screening Version) and the historical scale of the HCR-20. Results showed all risk assessment measures were correlated significantly with each other and with aggression.

Although the VRAG shows good predictive validity, like other actuarial schemes, it is based upon static risk factors that do not change according to fluctuations in mental state and psychosocial functioning. It does not support dynamic appraisal of risk and because it is based on static factors it does not assist in the identification of treatment targets that might remediate risk level. Nor, like many other actuarial schemes, does it assist in the identification of important dimensions of risk including the nature, severity, frequency and imminence of future aggression. For this reason, some scholars have argued that actuarial methods need to be supplemented by clinical appraisals. However, controversy remains about the degree to which clinical appraisal should also be considered.

2. *Structured clinical judgement.* Structured clinical appraisal methods (also known as structured professional judgement or structured clinical judgement) act as an *aide-mémoire* or guide for clinicians (although, unfortunately, some clinicians treat these structured methods as quasi-actuarial tools and restrict the focus of assessment to a consideration and scoring of those items contained in the instrument). Structured clinical appraisal methods demand structure and comprehensiveness (inclusive but not necessarily limited to the items and characteristics included in the guide). These methods do not dictate how the variables are to be considered or measured against each other, though the two most commonly used instruments, the HCR-20 (Webster *et al.*, 1997) and the VRS (Violence Risk Scale; Wong & Gordon, 2006), do emphasize the difference between so-called historical or static factors, which may be considered as long-standing but probably persistent problems with interpersonal functioning (Wong & Gordon, 2006), and clinical factors. These clinical factors are state-based measures of functioning which are related to violent behaviour. They may have their origin in historical events. The HCR-20 also demands that assessors attempt to project into the future and assess, for example, the person's likelihood of being supported, exposed to destabilizers (e.g. drugs), stressed and non-compliant. The HCR-20 and VRS differ in terms of their final indicated risk levels. The HCR-20 does not provide risk levels that are associated with a certain number of risk factors whereas the VRS does.

The HCR-20 is the most frequently used and well-researched structured clinical appraisal instrument. It was developed to assist assessors in structuring their

assessment and to ensure comprehensiveness by enforcing consideration of empirically supported and operationalized risk factors (Douglas *et al.*, 2003). It comprises
20 items: ten historical items (reflecting the person's psychosocial adjustment and
history of violence), five clinical items (observations of the person's current or
recent functioning) and five risk management items (risk factors that reflect the
evaluator's opinions regarding the adequacy of the person's plans for, and capacity
to cope with, institutional and community integration). In practice, evaluators
determine the presence of the standard 20 risk factors and rate the extent of their
presence on a three-point scale. Administration of the HCR-20 by trained raters
results in high levels of agreement. It has been validated in various countries in
personality disordered offenders and both forensic and civil psychiatric patients.
Its predictive accuracy is comparable to other risk assessment measures. It assesses
dynamic and static variables and includes the construct of psychopathy within the
historical scale.

Although it is possible to simply sum the items so that a total score can be calculated (and the greater the number of risk factors present is arguably related to
risk level), the HCR-20 was not designed to be used in this way; there are no fixed
guidelines about how risk factors are combined to reach an overall judgement (low,
medium or high level of risk). The various studies describing its predictive accuracy
have typically compared low and high scorers, used the total as a continuous score
to determine survivability (how long it would take before somebody was aggressive)
or compared those above a median with those below a group's median score.
Permission to deviate from a linear relationship is made available to assessors.

Another contemporary structured risk assessment method is the VRS (Wong
& Gordon, 2006). The VRS was designed to integrate the assessment of risk,
need, responsivity and treatment change into a single instrument. It comprises six
static and 20 dynamic items that are either empirically or theoretically linked to
violent recidivism. It assesses the client's level of aggression risk, identifies treatment targets linked to aggression, assesses the client's readiness for change and
their post-treatment improvements on the treatment targets. The VRS static variables can predict general and violent recidivism, but remain unchanged with treatment; the dynamic variables are changeable risk predictors; they can be used as
treatment targets and can measure changes in risk. Each dynamic variable identified
as a treatment target is assessed to determine the client's stage of change, according to a modified version of the Transtheoretical Model of Change (TM; Prochaska
et al., 1992). Progression in treatment from a less advanced to a more advanced
stage of change for each treatment target is an indication of improvement, which
should correspond with risk reduction in that treatment target. Progress through
the stages during the treatment programme are reflected as risk reduction. Although
there is less research on the predictive accuracy of the VRS, research tends to show
that the VRS also results in high levels of agreement between raters.

Actuarial versus structured methods: Key issues

There exists ongoing concern about the relative merits and predictive superiority
of actuarial and structured clinical appraisal methods. Many studies have shown
the two approaches have comparable predictive accuracy. Proponents of actuarial
methods assert the predictive superiority of their approach and warn against struc-

tured methods primarily because these methods introduce 'allegedly flawed' clinical judgements, spoiling the empirically derived calculation of risk probability (Quinsey *et al.*, 1998). Conversely, actuarial risk assessment methods have been criticized because:

1. their predictive superiority is overstated;
2. the actuarial approaches neglect idiosyncratic but important characteristics of the individual that pertain to risk; and
3. they may lack generalizability and applicability beyond the development sample (Douglas *et al.*, 2003; Monahan *et al.*, 2001).

Further, and critically for clinicians engaged in the management and treatment of patients, these actuarial methods incorporate static (unchangeable) predictors of risk (e.g. criminal history and early behavioural problems); these cannot be used to assess criminogenic need or responsivity. As such, they cannot guide treatment, nor do they lend themselves to the reappraisal of risk.

Resistance to actuarial (and structured) methods is not new. Grove and Meehl (1996) identified a range of reasons why mental health professionals resist mechanical methods. These reasons range from practitioners' attachments to particular theories, a perception that these mechanical methods are dehumanizing, a preference for clinical intuition, limited education about the enhanced predictive validity of mechanical approaches, and a belief in the superiority of their own methods. A further objection to the use of mechanistic approaches is that these approaches generate predictions based upon aggregate or group data, whereas mental health clinicians focus on predictions that are relevant to the individual. This argument has recently been fortified following Hart *et al.*'s (2007) reanalysis of data used in the development samples of various actuarial risk assessment instruments. Hart *et al.* (2007) concluded that these instruments' margins of error were too high to allow specific predictions to be applied to individuals. Essentially, the issue here is whether it is appropriate to extrapolate an individual's risk level from that of a group. According to Hart and colleagues (2007), the variation in outcome for individuals within the groups (as determined by the actuarial risk assessment) is too large; in each group there are individuals who do not reoffend violently and some who do. In other words, while the majority in a high risk group will reoffend violently, there will be some who will not.

If group data shows strong predictive accuracy but there is individual variation, then the task for assessors is to identify those individual characteristics which should be taken into account, to separate low and high risk patients within each risk category. Again, this is not a novel idea; many risk assessment technologies accept clinicians' need and willingness to modify actuarially derived risk estimates. Even staunch advocates of actuarial methods, such as Grove and Meehl (1996, p. 14), accept the possibility of adjusting mechanistic predictions based on the presence of an important fact about an individual. Frequent adjustment of actuarially derived scores is, however, discouraged. Grove and Meehl (1996) argue that assessors should realize that 'in general, they do not do as well as the equation and then to realize how they can improve upon the equation once in a while by clear cut "broken leg" countervailings but that they should set a high threshold for countervailing the equation' (p. 16).

Although it is unclear what these important countervailing factors are, evidence exists which supports the notion that clinical appraisals may improve, rather than tarnish, purely mechanistic predictions. For example, recent research with the HCR-20 shows that the predictive validity of the HCR-20 is enhanced when formal algorithmic models are supplemented by informed, structured clinical judgement (Douglas *et al.*, 2003). In a pseudo-prospective design, 100 forensic psychiatric patients, who had been found not guilty by reason of a mental disorder and were subsequently released to the community, were assessed with the HCR-20 (retrospectively through review of case notes including social, psychological, psychiatric, medical, criminal and legal information). Each of the 20 items was scored and the raters then made a judgement as to whether the patient presented a low, medium or high level of risk, emulating the summary judgements made by mental health professionals in actual clinical practice. The HCR-20 showed moderate to strong predictive accuracy and was more accurate than the actuarial model created by simply summing the 20 items, as one would in a true actuarial model. Identifying the factors that improve rather than detract from accurate assessments derived from mechanistic models, and assigning appropriate weight to clinicians' appraisals of risk, is complex and far from certain; it is clearly an area worthy of future research. Nevertheless, many scholars support the use of the structured clinical judgement approach and argue that actuarial instruments should support, rather than replace, clinical judgement (Monahan *et al.*, 2001).

Finally, the accuracy of risk assessment methods may vary according to context and length of follow-up. In hospital, short-term unaided clinical appraisals of risk seem to be adequate – though some structured methods such as the Dynamic Appraisal of Situational Aggression: Inpatient Version (DASA; Ogloff & Daffern, 2006) do outperform unaided clinical appraisals. Short-term predictions may be reasonably accurate because observers are able to account for the patient's current mental state in addition to fluctuating environmental variables (Nijman *et al.*, 2002), as well as the patient's typical reactions to the common antecedent interactions (Daffern & Howells, 2002) that precipitate acts of in-patient aggression. Furthermore, others (Doyle & Dolan, 2006) have shown that the inclusion of dynamic clinical and risk factors (including social functioning, mental state and contextual factors) improves upon the predictive accuracy of static historical factors, particularly in risk assessment for the short term.

Integrating structured and clinical risk assessment methods: Structured Multiple Sequential Functional Analysis (sMSFA)

Understanding the factors contributing to the development, expression and maintenance of aggression is often accomplished in clinical practice through functional analysis. Function analytic assessment approaches to understanding aggression (Daffern & Howells, 2002) are typically achieved through consideration of the behaviour of interest, the individual's predisposing characteristics (including the individual's personality), and assessment of the antecedent events, which are important for the initiation of the behaviour, and the consequences of the behaviour, which maintain and direct its developmental course. The clinical tradition has emphasized the uniqueness of the individual and asserted that individualized assessment contributes to a more comprehensive clinical formulation, which has the potential to promote effective treatment and risk management. Nevertheless, given the clear superiority of structured risk assessment methods, the task for mental health professionals is how to understand the acquisition, development and maintenance of the aggressive behaviour through functional analysis whilst drawing upon the benefits of structured risk assessment methods.

According to Gresswell and Hollin (1992), historical information can be broken down into a series of sequential functional analyses, a process known as Multiple Sequential Functional Analysis (MSFA; Gresswell & Hollin, 1992). This is a comprehensive behavioural method for parsing case history to identify the determinants, development and functions of behaviour over time. MSFA examines the learning from each Antecedent (A): Behaviour (B): Consequence (C) sequence, and assumes each A: B: C sequence becomes part of the individual's learning history and hence antecedent to the next A: B: C stage. Key events in each stage of the person's development are examined, to determine the context and dispositional factors that contribute to the acquisition of an aggressive repertoire, the impact of the person's acquired aggressive behaviour on their development, and the events and personological limitations of the person which maintain and expand their aggressive behaviour from childhood, through adolescence into adulthood.

MSFA was initially described without any superimposed structure. This allowed for the analysis of an individual's problem behaviour to be conducted ideographically and guided by the mental health professional's skills and familiarity with the presenting problem behaviour. This is consistent with the principle of aetiological heterogeneity (that an individual's problem behaviour has unique origins) that is a cornerstone of behavioural assessment methods. However, the well-known attribution and appraisal errors affecting conventional unaided clinical appraisals of risk have the potential to misguide a clinical assessment paradigm such as MSFA. MSFA may not take into account those characteristics of the person, their history and current functioning, which are known risk factors for aggressive behaviour. To ensure the MSFA approach to understanding aggression (from which risk assessment followed by risk management interventions and treatment can occur) is comprehensive and systematically inclusive of empirically valid indicators of risk, a structured MSFA (sMSFA) method is required. Inclusion of items drawn from the HCR-20, particularly the historical items, or another reliable and valid risk assessment method, is recommended. Using a structured risk assessment method hones the review of an individual's developmental history; the risk factors contained within the risk assessment instrument become anchor points for an assessor's review.

In the sMSFA assessment, as with any assessment of aggression or risk for violence assessment, it would also be important to reflect upon theoretical models of aggression such as the General Aggression Model (GAM; Bushman & Anderson, 2001) to ensure that the assessment and description of the person's aggressive behaviour is valid. According to the GAM, aggression occurs because individuals acquire and apply aggression-related knowledge structures (scripts and schemas). It is argued that these structures develop through observation and interactions with others and that with repeated exposure, hostile knowledge structures become more complex, differentiated, and difficult to change. In this way, repeated exposure to aggression can make hostile knowledge structures chronically accessible, essentially creating an established repertoire of aggressive behaviour. A focus on the acquisition of aggressive scripts and violence-related schema hones the assessment of childhood and assists assessors in considering the relevance of events occurring during the person's childhood and adolescence and how they impact on the person throughout their life.

What follows is a brief hypothetical summary, punctuated by interpretative comments, of a young man with personality disorder. Key aspects of his background are presented to highlight the sMSFA risk assessment process.

Case example: Mr Smith

Mr Smith is a solidly built, heavily tattooed 23-year-old. He is the only child of unstable parents whose relationship was permeated by drug abuse, criminal behaviour, violence and separation consequent to Mr Smith's father's imprisonment. Mr Smith suffered early childhood maladjustment; he was removed from the family home at the age of two after parental neglect and his father's violence towards him and his mother. He spent his childhood living with his grandmother and, after she died, in foster care. In foster care he was sexually abused. Mr Smith was returned to his mother's care at the age of 12. Mr Smith left his mother's home at 15 years of age because, according to his mother, he was 'difficult to manage'. Mr Smith describes an ambivalent relationship with his mother; he idealizes her but occasionally describes resentment, saying she did not support him, was unreliable, and 'kicked him out' of the family home.

Mr Smith attended numerous primary schools and one secondary school before he terminated his formal education, refusing to attend from the age of 14. His early schooling was marked by social isolation and bullying. Mr Smith was an overweight and socially anxious child who felt alienated and tormented by other children. He described feeling unprotected by teachers; he resented their unwillingness to protect him. Prior to terminating his education, Mr Smith often truanted, was violent towards other students and on one occasion threatened a teacher with the knife he carried for protection. He is illiterate and innumerate. He acknowledges childhood defiance but considers this necessary to protect himself.

In the introduction to this case, we can see how childhood maltreatment contributes to the acquisition of aggressive scripts and maladaptive schemas. Certain inherited influences may also have made aggression more likely. Children with a temperament predisposing them to antagonism (opposition) may cause punitive or even aggressive reactions from parents. An additional complication was that Mr Smith's parents did not model appropriate problem solving or emotional control; thus, when maladaptive schemas were activated, Mr Smith ruminated over violent fantasies and occasionally acted violently.

The impact of an emerging repertoire of aggressive behaviour and an aggressive-prone social information processing style on the accomplishment of social and psychological developmental tasks is required in any risk assessment. As a child becomes progressively more aggressive, the quality and types of their social interactions also change (Huesmann, 1994). Aggressive children will be drawn to peer groups who reinforce and model antisocial behaviour through a process of selective affiliation, and because they will be excluded from non-aggressive peer groups who denounce their aggressive tendencies. Association with aggressive and antisocial peers may weaken resistance to conventional behaviour and expose the child to other forms of aggression, to attitudes supportive of aggression and possibly to substance use. In addition, the child/adolescent's academic performance may suffer, which may also, in turn, affect employment prospects.

For Mr Smith, many of these problems are evident. Early exposure to violence resulted in the acquisition of aggressive scripts. These were activated when he felt fearful. He was sensitive to abuse and when he felt other people were mistreating him he began rehearsing aggressive scripts. He learned to use violence as a way of controlling others. In adolescence, he associated with other antisocial youth, and relationships with prosocial peers contracted.

From early adolescence, Mr Smith used an assortment of drugs, including cannabis and inhalants, typically in the company of his peers. He experimented with amphetamines and then opiates during middle adolescence. He was dependent on amphetamines at the time of his index offence. His drug use exposed him to antisocial peers, inhibited his academic and scholarly pursuits and, subsequently, limited employment opportunities, both because he was preoccupied with seeking drugs, and because he was often sacked due to being intoxicated at work or unwilling to attend work due to withdrawal following intoxication.

In Mr Smith's case, drug use satisfied social and emotional needs. He lacked resources to develop and maintain prosocial relationships and probably enjoyed associating with reckless and antagonistic individuals. His poor emotional control also rendered him vulnerable to drug abuse; when he felt anxious or distressed, he used drugs to improve his mood. Combined with his limited academic accomplishments and conventional interests, drug use also interfered with employment. In general, unemployment creates financial stress, and limits exposure to prosocial peers and conventional activity. In Mr Smith's case, employment difficulties also contributed to conflict with his girlfriend and her family.

Mr Smith regularly assaulted others when intoxicated; this included his girlfriend, the mother of his five-year-old child. Mr Smith despaired when he assaulted his girlfriend; he has cut himself in this state after hitting her. Mr Smith could not recall how long he had been in a relationship with his ex-girlfriend, but cited the use of alcohol and drugs by both he and his former girlfriend as the main reason for the breakdown of their relationship.

Regarding his criminal history, Mr Smith started stealing from shops in childhood, often accompanying friends when they stole from houses. He has an established history of violence, and has charges for assault, assault occasioning grievous bodily harm and attempted murder. The index offence is murder. Mr Smith, in the company of friends, killed a man during a fight in a hotel. Mr Smith had been drinking with friends when the victim allegedly bumped into Mr Smith's friend. A fight between the two men ensued, during which Mr Smith's friend was knocked to the ground. Mr Smith stabbed the victim with the knife he typically carried for 'self-protection'.

On the unit, Mr Smith impresses as self-assured and superficial; he displays a need to impress others and he is quick to anger. He is sensitive to perceived abuse and has a strong desire to protect himself and his friends. He ruminates (often for hours on end) about others he believes have mistreated him. He holds beliefs supportive of violence, for instance believing that it is appropriate to stand up for his friends and to assault anybody who insults him or his friends. He has ambivalent interpersonal relationships, particularly with his family, but also in romantic/ intimate relationships and friendships. He describes a need to stand by his friends but at the same time speaks dismissively about them, calling them 'no-hopers'. He is at risk of being influenced by negative peers due to his impaired psychosocial functioning and inadequately consolidated identity. Presently, though he attends various psychological programmes targeting his violent behaviour, he does not appreciate his own vulnerabilities and he has continued to behave violently within the unit.

As can be seen from the aforementioned summary, Mr Smith has many of the HCR-20 risk factors. Although advocates of actuarial approaches may argue that a valid assessment of risk could be conducted by simply summing risk factors, the sMSFA facilitates a more clinically meaningful and theoretically valid description of violent behaviour, and perhaps a more accurate prediction of violence. Treatment planning is also aided. Limits on space do not allow for an extensive description or analysis of Mr Smith's acquisition of violent behaviour or to document his risk assessment and treatment planning. Nevertheless, the brief description of his background suggests that several key behaviours (overt and covert) were learned at different developmental phases and demonstrates how the GAM and a structured instrument such as the HCR-20 may be woven into a clinical risk appraisal.

Risk and dangerous and severe personality disorder

A critical task for mental health professionals working within the new DSPD initiative is the assessment, management and reduction of risk for violence. Only patients with PD who are considered to be at risk of serious criminal behaviour can be detained and only for the period in which they are deemed to be at risk. Once those factors that contribute to risk have resolved, the patient is supposed to be discharged to the community or returned to prison to serve their sentence. As such, risk contributes substantially to assessment of suitability for admission, the level of security and supervision, opportunities during incarceration, the intensity of treatment required and, importantly, when the person will be discharged. Indeed, discharging patients with PD from high security psychiatric institutions to less secure settings, and ultimately to the community, depends substantially on reductions in risk, often more than on demonstrated change in the severity of the PD per se (Duggan, 2007). Familiarity with risk assessment approaches, their associated technologies, and the limits of these methods and technologies is, consequently, inescapable.

The validity of several aspects of the DSPD assessment process has been challenged since the Home Office and the Department of Health published its White Paper on mental health law reform in 2000; the risk criterion has been the subject of particular controversy (Buchanan & Leese, 2001; Farnham & James, 2001). The reason why this criterion should receive particular critique is unclear when (a) diagnosis of PD and methods to establish severity of PD are invariably unreliable, and (b) it is unclear whether a functional link between PD and aggression can be established. According to Buchanan and Leese (2001), the available tools which are used to support the risk assessment process are not sufficiently accurate and are therefore likely to generate an excessive number of false positives (decisions that result in a person being assessed as high risk when in fact they were not, if given the opportunity, aggressive). Such errors in assessment are particularly problematic when prisoners are detained at the expiration of a prison sentence.

According to Buchanan and Leese (2001):

> The decision as to what rate of error should be deemed acceptable from the point of view of preventive detention is ultimately a moral one which will be affected, not only by the likely number of mistakes, but by the conditions under which people are to be detained. (p. 1955)

This quote alerts readers to several important practical, statistical and ethical issues pertaining to the DSPD risk assessment process; these are the focus of the remainder of this chapter. Firstly, Buchanan and Leese (2001) introduce to the discussion the issue of error. This has recently been the focus of considerable controversy (see the discussion relevant to Hart *et al.*, 2007 above). The second prominent matter is related to legitimacy of preventative detention and the role of risk assessment in this process. Risk assessment in this context intensifies concerns which mental health professionals often have about the validity of risk assessment approaches and technologies. Contemporary aggression risk assessment technologies have primarily been developed to determine whether prisoners are likely to offend during release on parole. Mental health professionals engaging in this risk assessment task may not be as concerned about the reliability of their chosen risk assessment method/technology if they see parole as a privilege. For some mental health professionals the possibility of inaccurate appraisals during assessments for preventative and indefinite detention weighs more heavily, causing reappraisal of the appropriateness and accuracy of their preferred approach to risk assessment. Finally, Buchanan and Leese (2001) suggest mental health professionals may be more willing to engage in risk assessment if the outcome of risk assessment is improved treatment opportunity with the possibility of enhanced outcomes for the person and society, rather than incarceration, established exclusively for the benefit of others.

Whether labelling a patient as DSPD creates increased therapeutic opportunity is presently unclear. Prisoners detained at the expiration of their sentence and admitted to one of the high secure hospital sites would undoubtedly argue that such identification has profoundly negative consequences. However, for those patients who have been excluded from mental health services and denied treatment in prisons because they are deemed to be untreatable and potentially disruptive to rehabilitation programmes, admission to DSPD services may well provide an opportunity for change and increased well-being. If one accepts that the DSPD programme creates treatment opportunities and if one is also mindful of the fact that patients with DSPD cannot be detained beyond the point at which they no longer pose a risk, then Buchanan and Leese's (2001) quote alerts us to a further demand on risk assessors – to use risk assessment methods that are sensitive to change, so that risk reassessment can assist determination of readiness for release. Accordingly, it is imperative that the risk assessment methods used to determine admissibility are linked to risk reduction strategies and that the risk assessment methods are the same measures used periodically to determine whether patients are (a) responding to treatment and (b) ready for discharge.

This demand on risk assessment methods reflects a general trend in the risk assessment literature. Rather than focus exclusively on the appraisal of dangerousness, contemporary risk assessments are probabilistic, incorporate dynamic (changeable) risk factors which are sensitive to change, and are, as a result, linked to risk management interventions. Risk assessment should be considered a prelude to risk management, the task with which mental health professionals are largely involved. When risk assessment methods that are insensitive to change are used to determine admissibility, then a two-stage assessment process is required. Firstly, there would be a need to determine risk level. A second assessment would then be generated to formulate the patient's aggressive behaviour. Treatment planning would presumably be derived from this second, more clinically focused assessment. Although this is a feasible approach, the clinical formulation and treatment planning may be unrelated to those factors considered in the risk assessment and reassessment. If a person's admission is to be determined by a particular risk assessment instrument then it is only logical and fair that their progress be determined through reassessment with the same instrument.

Conclusions

Violence risk assessment is a core component of the DSPD initiative and for the treatment and management of patients with APD and BPD generally. Familiarity with the limitations and benefits of unaided clinical appraisal and a facility with the most reliable, valid and useful risk assessment technologies are prerequisites for decision makers involved in the care and treatment of patients with PD. Structured methods are more reliable and valid than many claim and they are almost certainly superior, in terms of predictive accuracy, to unstructured methods. Structured methods demand systematic and transparent assessment that undoubtedly assists communication of risk and identification of areas of agreement and disagreement. Nevertheless, these structured technologies are not immune from criticism. Mental health clinicians are encouraged to explore this evolving literature and to undertake additional training in: (1) decision making, (2) risk assessment and (3) risk assessment technologies. The risk assessment literature is evolving; clinicians and scholars continue to develop and modify technologies, apply them to novel environments and to different populations. The only certainty with risk assessment is that it will continue to expand; inevitably, new technologies will be offered. Though some may resent the focus on risk assessment within forensic psychology and psychiatry, violence risk assessment is a necessary consideration for practitioners responsible for the care and management of patients with APD but also for patients with other PDs who have aggressive tendencies.

A necessary precondition for acceptable risk-related decision making is that the technology chosen to assess risk should be capable of guiding treatment. Adequate predictive accuracy is insufficient. The risk assessment method should highlight characteristics of the individual and their situation that can be remediated (thereby reducing risk). Further, the measure must also be sensitive to change so that treatment progress, and hence readiness for discharge, whether it be from hospital or from management conditions within the community, can be considered fairly. The HCR-20 and VRS both satisfy these requirements; the HCR-20 has the advantage of a considerable evidence base, and the VRS is promising because it has the capacity to assess the patient's motivation to change relevant dynamic risk factors, thereby providing guidance for mental health professionals as to the most appropriate method for approaching treatment. The VRS also allows for reappraisal of motivation and links this directly to changes in risk state. As such, the VRS is in sympathy with the principles of risk, need and responsivity (Andrews & Bonta, 2003), the guiding principles of offender rehabilitation.

The methods and technologies used for assessing risk are likely to vary depending upon the population being assessed, the duration of follow-up and the environment in which the person is being assessed (or considered for transfer). In the psychiatric hospital, the three points at which risk is assessed (on admission, intermittently throughout hospitalization, and for consideration of release) are most probably assisted by different types of risk assessment schemes. Instruments such as the HCR-20 or VRS are well suited to assessments on admission and to determine suitability for discharge; their use may not be practical and they may not be sufficiently sensitive to day-to-day fluctuations in risk state. Though limited research into the application of these measures with high risk and severely personality disordered patients exist (see, for exception, Daffern & Howells, 2007), structured methods such as the Broset Violence Checklist or the Dynamic Appraisal of Situational Aggression: Inpatient Version (DASA; Ogloff & Daffern, 2006) may be more effective in the prediction of imminent aggression during institutional care. These instruments may also have utility in the daily monitoring of patients at risk for aggression who are living in the community; however, this proposition is yet to be scrutinized. In the interests of parsimony, the HCR-20 appears most capable of assisting all assessment tasks; several clinical and risk items are strongly predictive of imminent aggression (Ogloff & Daffern, 2006). Dynamic items from the VRS may similarly be predictive of imminent aggression, though this has not been subjected to empirical scrutiny.

Finally, the risk assessment literature has proceeded with a primary focus on male offenders. The criminogenic needs of women may differ and sex differences may exist in personality and PD, in particular psychopathic PD (Dolan & Völlm, 2009; Salekin *et al.*, 1997). The prevalence of psychopathy, its symptom presentation and diagnostic comorbidity, as well as its ability to predict criminal recidivism, differ for females as compared with males. Some have disputed the relevance and validity of traditional risk assessment measures for women (Odgers *et al.*, 2005). As such, an exclusive reliance on equivalent risk-related criteria and methods for assessing risk as used in men would appear contra-indicated for women. Importantly, before ardent supporters of unaided clinical risk appraisal promote this approach for women, it should be borne in mind that the unaided risk assessment approach seems to be even less valid in the assessment of risk for aggression in women (Lidz *et al.*, 1993). Extreme caution should be applied during the assessment of risk and therefore suitability for admission of women to DSPD.

References

American Psychiatric Association (2000). *Diagnostic and statistical manual of mental disorders, fourth edition, text revision (DSM-IV-TR)*. Washington, DC: American Psychiatric Association.

Andrews, D. A. & Bonta, J. (2003). *The psychology of criminal conduct*. Cincinatti, OH: Anderson.

Blackburn, R. (2007). Personality disorder and psychopathy: Conceptual and empirical integration. *Psychology, Crime and Law, 13,* 7–18.

Buchanan, A. & Leese, M. (2001). Detention of people with dangerous severe personality disorders: a systematic review. *The Lancet, 358,* 1955–1959.

Bushman, B. J. & Anderson, C. A. (2001). Is it time to pull the plug on the hostile versus instrumental aggression dichotomy? *Psychological Review, 108,* 273–279.

Coid, J. W. (1992). DSM-III diagnosis in criminal psychopaths: a way forward. *Criminal Behaviour and Mental Health, 2,* 78–94.

Daffern, M. & Howells, K. (2002). Psychiatric inpatient aggression: A review of structural and functional assessment approaches. *Aggression and Violent Behavior, 7,* 477–497.

Daffern, M. & Howells, K. (2007). The prediction of imminent aggression and self-harm in personality disordered patients of a high security hospital using the HCR-20 clinical scale and the Dynamic Appraisal of Situational Aggression. *International Journal of Forensic Mental Health, 6,* 137–143.

Dolan, M. & Völlm, B. (2009). Antisocial personality disorder and psychopathy in women: A literature review on the reliability and validity of assessment instruments. *International Journal of Law and Psychiatry, 32,* 2–9.

Douglas, K. S., Ogloff, J. R. P. & Hart, S. D. (2003). Evaluation of the structured professional judgment model of violence risk assessment among forensic psychiatric patients. *Psychiatric Services, 54,* 1372–1379.

Doyle, M. & Dolan, M. (2006). Predicting community violence from patients discharged into mental health services. *British Journal of Psychiatry, 189,* 520–526.

Doyle, M., Dolan, M. & McGovern, J. (2002). The validity of North American risk assessment tools in predicting inpatient violent behaviour in England. *Legal and Criminological Psychology, 7,* 141–154.

Duggan, C. (2007). To move or not to move – that is the question! Some reflections on the transfer of DSPD patients. *Psychology, Crime and Law, 13,* 113–121.

Farnham, F. R. & James, D. (2001). 'Dangerousness' and dangerous law. *The Lancet, 358,* 1926.

Gresswell, D. M. & Hollin, C. R. (1992). Towards a new methodology for making sense of case material: An illustrative case involving attempted multiple murder. *Criminal Behaviour and Mental Health, 2,* 329–341.

Grove, W. M. & Meehl, P. E. (1996). Comparative efficiency of informal (subjective, impressionistic) and formal (mechanical, algorithmic) prediction procedures: The clinical-statistical controversy. *Psychology, Public Policy, and Law, 2*, 293–323.

Hart, S. D., Michie, C. & Cooke, D. J. (2007). Precision of actuarial risk assessment instruments: Evaluating the 'margins of error' of group *v.* individual predictions of violence. *British Journal of Psychiatry, 190*, s60–s65.

Howard, R. C. (2007). What is the link between personality disorder and dangerousness? A critique of 'dangerous and severe personality disorder'. *British Journal of Forensic Practice, 8*, 19–23.

Howard, R. C., Daffern, M., Mannion, A. & Howells, K. (submitted). Admission to the Peaks DSPD unit: Truly dangerous and severe?

Howells, K., Daffern, M. & Day, A. (2008). Aggression and violence. In K. Soothill, M. Dolan & P. Rogers (Eds.), *Handbook of forensic mental health* (pp. 351–374). Cullompton: Willan.

Huesmann, L. R. (Ed.). (1994). *Aggressive behavior: Current perspectives.* New York: Plenum Press.

Lidz, C. W., Mulvey, E. P. & Gardner, W. (1993). The accuracy of predictions of violence to others. *Journal of the American Medical Association, 20*, 231–235.

Loranger, A. W., Sartorius, N., Andreoli, A., Berger, P., Buchheim, P., Channabasavanna, S. M. *et al.* (1994). The International Personality Disorder Examination. The World Health Organization/Alcohol, Drug Abuse, and Mental Health Administration international pilot study of personality disorders. *Archives of General Psychiatry, 51*, 215–224.

Monahan, J. (1981). *The clinical prediction of violent behavior.* Rockville, IN: National Institute of Mental Health.

Monahan, J., Steadman, H. J., Silver, E., Applebaum, P. S., Robbins, P. C., Mulvey, E. P. *et al.* (2001). *Rethinking risk assessment: The MacArthur study of mental disorder and violence.* Oxford: Oxford University Press.

National Institute for Health and Clinical Excellence (2009). *Antisocial personality disorder: Treatment, management and prevention.* Retrieved 19 October 2009 from www.nice. org.uk/Guidance/CG77/NiceGuidance/pdf

Nijman, H. L. I., Merckelbach, H. L. G. J., Evers, C., Palmstierna, T. & Á Campo, J. M. L. J. (2002). Prediction of aggression on a locked psychiatric admissions ward. *Acta Psychiatrica Scandinavica, 105*, 390–395.

Odgers, C. L., Moretti, M. M. & Reppucci, N. D. (2005) Examining the science and practice of violence risk assessment with female adolescents. *Law and Human Behavior, 29*, 7–27.

Ogloff, J. R. P. & Daffern, M. (2006). The Dynamic Appraisal of Situational Aggression: An instrument to assess risk for imminent aggression in psychiatric inpatients. *Behavioral Sciences and the Law, 24*, 799–813.

Prochaska, J. O., DiClemente, C. & Norcross, J. C. (1992). In search of how people change: Applications to addictive behaviours. *American Psychologist, 47*, 1102–1114.

Quinsey, V., Harris, G., Rice, M. & Cormier, C. (1998). *Violent offenders: Appraising and managing risk.* Washington, DC: American Psychological Association.

Ross, L. (1977). The intuitive psychologist and his shortcomings: Distortions in the attribution process. In L. Berkowitz (Ed.), *Advances in experimental social psychology,* Volume *10* (pp. 173–220). New York: Academic Press.

Salekin, R. T., Rogers, R. & Sewel, K. W. (1997). Construct validity of psychopathy in a female offender sample: A multitrait-multimethod evaluation. *Journal of Abnormal Psychology, 106*, 576–585.

Steadman, H. J. & Cocozza, J. J. (1974). *Careers of the criminally insane: Excessive social control of deviance.* New York: Lexington Books.

Tversky, D. & Kahneman, A. (1974). Judgement under uncertainty: Heuristics and biases. *Science, 185,* 1124–1131.

Wallace, C., Mullen, P., Burgess, P., Palmer, S., Ruschena, D. & Browne, C. (1998). Serious criminal offending and mental disorder. Case linkage study. *British Journal of Psychiatry, 172,* 477–484.

Warren, J. I., Burnette, M., South, S. C., Chauhan, P., Bale, R. & Friend, R. (2002). Personality disorder and violence among female prison inmates. *Journal of the American Academy of Psychiatry and the Law, 30,* 502–509.

Webster, C. D., Douglas, K. S., Eaves, D. & Hart, S. D. (1997). *HCR-20: Assessing risk of violence (version 2).* Vancouver: Mental Health Law & Policy Institute, Simon Fraser University.

Webster, C. D., Harris, G., Rice, M., Cormier, C. & Quinsey, V. (1994). *Violence prediction scheme: Assessing dangerousness in high risk men.* Toronto: Centre of Criminology, University of Toronto.

Wong, S. C. P. & Gordon, A. (2006). The validity and reliability of the violence risk scale: A treatment-friendly violence risk assessment tool. *Psychology, Public Policy and Law, 12,* 279–309.

Chapter Three

Ready or Not, They Are Coming: Dangerous and Severe Personality Disorder and Treatment Engagement[1]

Kevin Howells and Allison Tennant

Previous work on readiness for treatment has largely focused on general offenders or on specific problem areas, such as substance abuse and anger regulation. It is proposed in this chapter that offenders with accompanying mental disorders are a group for whom treatment engagement is likely to be particularly challenging. Readiness issues arising in treating patients admitted to services for dangerous and severe personality disorders will be discussed and analysed. The Multifactor Offender Readiness Model (MORM) can usefully be applied to this particular population and the model suggests strategies both for assessment of readiness and for planning interventions to enhance engagement in treatment. Readiness needs to be addressed at the level of internal patient characteristics, the therapeutic programme delivered and the overall institutional and organizational setting.

The concept of readiness in offender treatment was developed initially by researchers interested in rehabilitation outcomes in Canada (Serin, 1998) and in Australasia (Howells & Day, 2003; Ward *et al.*, 2004). Low readiness and engagement have been seen as an endemic problem in offender groups, but there has been relatively little consideration of their applicability to mental disorders or to individuals who are offenders but also have a co-occurring mental disorder. We propose in this chapter that the combination of offending and mental disorder poses particularly severe problems in relation to readiness for and engagement in treatment. We will illustrate these problems by considering patients/offenders admitted to treatment services under the Dangerous and Severe Personality Disorder (DSPD) programme in England and Wales. For purposes of brevity, we

Using Time, Not Doing Time: Practitioner Perspectives on Personality Disorder and Risk
Edited by Allison Tennant and Kevin Howells
© 2010 John Wiley & Sons, Ltd.

will refer to these offenders as 'patients', whilst acknowledging they also have histories of offending and that some are treated within the prison system.

It was acknowledged from the outset of the DSPD programme that these patients would pose particular challenges to services. The targeted group were individuals with severe personality disorders in combination with high levels of risk, in terms of their previous histories and probable future behaviour. Risk in this context typically refers to violent, including sexually violent, offences.

DSPD patients have a range of severe problems that, in aggregate, suggest they might reasonably be described as providing an extreme example of low treatment readiness – 'low readiness writ large'. They fall at the extreme end of the distribution of traits relating both to criminality and to personality disorder, including a significant group who meet the criteria for psychopathy on the PCL-R (Psychopathy Checklist – Revised). In addition, their previous histories within prison settings suggest that they have *either* not been offered mainstream offender programmes on the basis of staff perceptions that they were unsuitable and unable to benefit (for example because of psychopathic or borderline personality disorder characteristics) *or* they were given treatment but failed to demonstrate sufficient change to reduce concerns about future risk *or* they failed to complete treatment or fully comply with treatment requirements.

Some distinctions: Resistant, unready, unmotivated or unresponsive?

All of these terms, and others, have been used to describe patients and offenders who have been difficult to engage in treatment. It has been argued elsewhere (Howells & Day, 2003) that the term *resistant* is unhelpful, unless as a shorthand summary of the wide range of variables shown to be related to treatment engagement (see below).

The term *unmotivated* fares somewhat better but motivation is a relatively narrow-band construct and is concerned with what we shall refer to (below) as volitional processes, that is those involved in the pursuit of personal goals. Motivational variables, therefore, are only one segment of the broader phenomenon of readiness.

Unresponsiveness (or low responsivity) refers, at least in the offender rehabilitation literature, to the therapeutic programme itself, rather than to the treatment participant, and is an apt description when the programme has not been adapted to fit the characteristics and styles of learning of the particular group being offered treatment. Responsivity forms part of the risk/needs/responsivity framework proposed by Andrews and Bonta (2003). In the MORM model (below), responsivity can be reconstrued as the readiness of the programme for the individuals being treated.

The preferred term here (following Howells & Day, 2003 and Ward *et al.*, 2004) is *readiness* for treatment. Low readiness is defined by Howells and Day (2003) as 'the presence of characteristics (states or dispositions) within either the client or the therapeutic situation which are likely to impede engagement in therapy and which, thereby, are likely to diminish therapeutic change'. As the definition suggests, a low readiness factor may be a long-term and enduring aspect of the person (for example, intellectual disability) or it may be temporary (for example, a state of depression). The same would hold for the readiness of the therapeutic situation: relevant factors may be long term (for example, a climate antipathetic to therapy) or temporary (staff shortages undermining therapeutic activity).

Beyond stages of change

Most forensic practitioners would quickly acknowledge the importance of readiness and motivational factors for offender populations (McMurran, 2002) and it is likely that many clinical and forensic services address low motivation and engagement to some degree, though efforts are likely to be impeded by the absence of a satisfactory theoretical, empirical and methodological (measurement) base. The Transtheoretical Model of Change (TMC; Prochaska & DiClemente, 1984) has been one of the most popular and influential models in considering readiness and motivational factors in forensic settings and is integral to some programmes currently delivered in DSPD sites. Amongst the many contributions of the TMC has been the delineation of *stages of change*, allowing specification of where the individual patient is in the change sequence and suggesting the content and processes that might be important in stage-matched interventions.

There have been critiques of the concept of stages of change in general (Bandura, 1997) and with particular reference to offending behaviour (Casey *et al.*, 2005). Bandura (1997), for example, has argued that 'human functioning is simply too multifaceted and multidetermined to be categorized into a few discrete stages' (p. 8). The construct validity of some stages of change measures has also been the focus for criticism (Littell & Girvin, 2002). Conceptual and measurement aspects of stages of change in relation to violent behaviour have been addressed by Williamson *et al.* (2003), with a particular focus on the treatment of anger problems. Similarly Tierney and McCabe (2001) have evaluated the utility of the model in relation to sexual offending against children. As violent and sexual offending are the two forms of offending behaviour that constitute the index offences for patients admitted to DSPD units (Peaks Academic and Research Unit, 2006) such analyses are clearly relevant in devising and implementing treatment interventions for DSPD patients.

Figure 3.1 shows stages of change for a sample of patients admitted to the Peaks Unit between 2004 and 2006 on the VRS measure (Violence Risk Scale; Wong & Gordon, 2000). These results confirm that many DSPD patients are at an early stage in the change process and that therapeutic interventions would need to be adapted to accommodate this fact, as suggested by the responsivity principle in offender rehabilitation (Andrews & Bonta, 2003; Howells *et al.*, 2005).

The MORM approach to low readiness

The absence of integrated theoretical models for looking at readiness and engagement in forensic populations led Ward *et al.* (2004) to review the general literature on these topics and to construct a model of readiness for treatment.

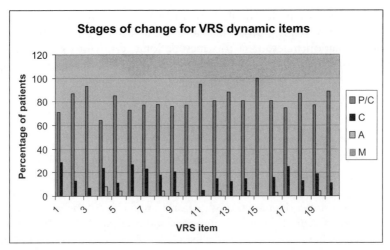

Figure 3.1   Stages of change for DSPD admissions to Peaks on VRS (Wong & Gordon, 2000) (P/C = precontemplation; C = contemplation; A = action; M = maintenance)

The MORM attempts to specify both internal (within the patient) and external (within the treatment setting) factors influencing programme engagement. *Cognitive factors* include appraisals and beliefs about the treatment on offer, for example its relevance and likely effectiveness, about the therapists, about the criminal justice or health system and about self-efficacy (perceived ability to meet the requirements of the programme).

Affective factors include the level of general distress of the patient but also specific emotional reactions (for example, guilt and shame) to previous offending. In addition, it has been proposed that the capacity of the patient to access, experience and express emotions is a necessary condition for engagement in therapy (for a fuller account of affective factors and readiness, see Howells & Day, 2006).

Volitional factors comprise the personal goals being pursued by the patient, the location of offending behaviour within the goal system of the patient, that is, the functions it serves for them (see Daffern *et al.*, 2007), the effectiveness of strategies for achieving personal goals and the congruence of personal goals with the explicit or implicit goals of the therapeutic programme being offered. It has been suggested that a goal systems perspective (Karoly, 1999) provides a useful framework for understanding personal goals and how goal-seeking processes may affect readiness to engage (Howells & Day, 2003; Ward *et al.*, 2004).

Behavioural factors include evaluations of their problem behaviours (for example, previous offending, as actually being a problem), help-seeking behaviours and, importantly, the diverse behavioural and cognitive skills required to become engaged in the treatment programme on offer.

Identity factors include core values and beliefs that constitute the person's identity. Identity is closely related to how personal goals are prioritized and indicates the kind of life sought, and, relatedly, the kind of person he or she would like to be. The important issue for readiness is that an individual's personal identity must allow for the possibility of an offence-free lifestyle (and includes the possibility of change) and is not based too strongly on being an offender.

The *external readiness conditions* will not be reviewed in detail in this paper, though there is some consideration below of the effects of the social and therapeutic climate of the treatment setting. This factor can clearly be located within the category of external readiness conditions (Ward *et al.*, 2004).

The clinical reality and theory-based formulation of low readiness

The fact that severe problems of low readiness exist in the DSPD population is widely recognized by clinicians. A common difficulty, however, is how to formulate the readiness problems observed in a systematic, theory-informed way that can give coherence, direction and structure to therapeutic endeavours to improve readiness and engagement. For the purposes of the present paper, the following exercise was undertaken. One of the authors (AT – a nurse consultant on a DSPD unit, involved substantially and on a daily basis in patient assessments and in therapy) was asked to describe her experience and observations of readiness, motivation and engagement problems in patients since the inception of the unit. At this time AT was unfamiliar with the MORM approach. The other author (KH) undertook the task of attempting to map the observations made onto the MORM – a model derived from work on general offenders rather than a DSPD population and summarized above. The italicized comments in brackets after each observation suggest how the observation fits the MORM framework.

Observed problems of low readiness and engagement (AT)

a. 'During his time in prison he was accepted onto various treatment programmes, but never completed any' (said of a particular patient). *{Confirms previous engagement problems and negative expectancies.}*

b. 'On admission to hospital some patients/inmates do not perceive themselves to have mental health problems (they are not mad) and therefore (believe that they) should not be in a healthcare setting. To be labelled a patient and be "nutted off" is a profound experience, as is being cared for by nurses rather than prison officers.' *{Identity impairing readiness.}*

c. 'Some individuals have determinate sentences, and therefore have a release date fixed firmly in their minds. So how do individuals make sense of these significant changes in their lives? Admission to a high secure hospital can radically change their future plans, hopes and dreams. Their status under the Mental Health Act means there is no fixed term date of release. The rage and perceived injustice of this is acutely felt, and often projected onto the nurses that receive these men.' *{Coercive context and incompatible goals impairing readiness.}*

d. 'Their outrage at being confined, unfairly in their opinion, is for all to see, as their energy and basic survival strategies come to the fore. Patients often state that they have been "stitched up" by the system. This is where the journey begins when their motivation is at an all time low and resistance is high. This is not the case for every individual as some appear eager to accept help in the hope that this will improve their quality of life.' *{Affective state and hostile beliefs about the inappropriateness of treatment impair readiness.}*

e. 'The patient may believe that if they can demonstrate that they are not treatable and do not engage in therapy, then the hospital should release them, on the grounds of untreatability. If patients invest in this belief and hope that this may help them to be released, then attempts by clinicians to engage individuals are often met with hostility as they believe their solicitors will get them out.' *{Goal is release rather than to obtain treatment.}*

f. 'Building positive and trusting relationships takes time and consistent effort. Some individuals will only converse with senior members of staff and directly challenge junior members by discounting what they say and do. The patient will question the staff's personal authority and dismiss them, when they can't get their needs met. On a daily basis junior staff are taunted and called names as they go about their work.' *{Cognitive appraisals of low trustworthiness.}*

g. 'Certain individuals can have a profound effect on others and on their motivation to engage in the treatment process. What is valued by some patients is this masculine mystique of being tough, strong, not losing face and not complying with those in authority. An uncritical, narrow and rigid concept of masculinity.' *{Identity, in this case, exaggerated masculinity, impairs readiness.}*

h. 'Patients bring with them a culture of violence (which) defines what is valued and provides role models to others living in the same environment. To be different from others can be difficult when you don't choose who you want to live with.' *{Criminal goals and social identities impair readiness.}*

i. 'Individuals can find it retraumatizing to listen to others' narratives of both abuse and offending behaviour. Resentment, fear, and shame are just some of the emotions that are experienced during some group therapy sessions. Afterwards individuals are sometimes fearful of their own disclosures and are frightened for their own physical safety.' *{Affective reactions impair readiness.}*

j. 'Individuals with high IQs quickly get bored and become problematic or mischievous towards others if they are not being stimulated educationally. Likewise those who have learning difficulties may drop out, to not lose face.' *{Low programme readiness and responsivity to patient characteristics.}*

k. 'Some individuals cannot read or write and feel embarrassed and ashamed to admit this in front of others; this can lead to drop-out.' *{Deficient behavioural and cognitive skills; low programme readiness or responsivity.}*

l. '(Some) patients just resign themselves to life in hospital. These individuals are often lethargic, spend their time sleeping, indulge their therapists and say they want to change, hook them in and then resist. This approach avoidance type behaviour is often a symptom of institutionalized living.' *{Impairments of goal-seeking or motivated state.}*

m. 'Patients are assessed and their treatment needs are identified and their treatment plan is neatly presented. Their part in this process is to agree that they require this particular intervention and turn up. Clinicians explain how this treatment may help them in their future. The process begins; the individual attends the session, doesn't like particular group members, finds some of the content boring and quits. His case is reviewed by his clinical team and a discussion takes place about his drop-out. Individuals naturally try and persuade him to continue, without success. Six months later a referral takes place for either the same treatment or to try something else and the process begins again, with half hearted agreement.' *{A nice summary of the sometimes dispiriting realities of dealing with low engagement in this setting.}*

Observations on methods and strategies used in the unit to improve readiness and engagement (AT)

1. 'Patients disengage from treatment for a variety of reasons and it is therefore of clinical significance that reasons for disengagement are identified on an individual basis. It is paramount that the response to patient disengagement behaviours is individually determined but that the principles are consistent across patients and that the clinical team provide guidance with regard to a structured response to the identification, formulation and management of disengagement behaviours.' *{Wide-ranging assessment, formulation, intervention strategy to address low readiness.}*

2. 'Precommitment and motivational work is a prerequisite before any type of formal group work. Clinicians can then individually assess what factors will hinder and help progress. Individual learning styles should be considered as some respond better to different styles and methods of delivery.' *{Ensure readiness and responsivity of the treatment programme itself.}*

3. 'Previous experience of therapy should also be explored; for some this may have been aversive. It is important to have these discussions, to explore anxieties and fears, to ensure the same thing does not happen again.' *{Address negative cognitive expectancies which impair engagement.}*

4. 'On completion of a treatment intervention, individuals would naturally expect to see visible progression in terms of moving on; this is often not the case. Some are asked to repeat particular programmes again, and are given ambiguous explanations for this decision. There is no wonder that patients feel hopeless and powerless to make change when clinicians themselves are not clear about what is the specific outcome of a treatment intervention. Clinicians need to get much better at specifying clearly what will be the expected outcomes of a particular intervention and give the individual regular feedback on their progress. The progress should include a range of measures including psychometric feedback, daily structured clinical observation and clear treatment targets that are articulated by clinicians and the patient himself. If the clinical team can articulate a "sense of purpose" and "sell" this to the individual through a structured therapeutic regime of care, then patients are more likely to respond.' *{Instil optimism re: goal pursuit and achievement.}*

5. 'Feeling physically and emotionally safe is important. Providing an effective structure to the day is important for both staff and patients. External controls provided by the ward regime and rules provide a psychological internal locus of control. Although patients often complain bitterly about adhering to rules and regulations, on further exploration they say they feel safe. If patients are secure in their knowledge that staff will deal with inappropriate behaviour then

this may enhance their willingness to engage.' *[Ensure a treatment-supportive climate in the setting.]*

6. 'Previous perceived failure should be analysed in detail to discover what factors impeded progress. Many individuals are ill-prepared to go into any type of group setting without preparation.' *[Deal with negative cognitive expectancies and behavioural deficits.]*

In addition to these clinical observations, we would also like to draw attention to other aspects of low readiness likely to be important for a high risk and personality disordered patient population.

Particular characteristics of personality disorder

Those admitted to DSPD services are characterized by high levels of psychopathic, antisocial and borderline traits (Peaks Academic and Research Unit, 2006), with most exceeding thresholds for a clinical diagnosis of personality disorders of these types. Psychopathic disorder, as defined by the PCL-R (Hare, 2006), has been widely observed to be associated with poor treatment engagement and with high levels of disruptive behaviour in the treatment itself (Hemphill & Hart, 2002; Wong & Hare, 2005). Impulsivity, 'conning' and lying in such patients all fall within the *behavioural* component of MORM. We know little, in terms of empirical studies, about the *cognitive* factors that might apply to this group, in particular about how individuals high in psychopathy might perceive treatment and therapists, their expectancies and their perceived self-efficacy in the treatment setting.

Psychopathy is largely defined by *affective* deficits (Hare, 2006); thus it is to be expected that many such individuals will fail to meet the readiness requirement of sufficient distress in relation to their predicament, to their criminal identity and to their previous offending. Guilt and shame reactions are, by definition, low in such patients. Normal, affective reactions are a necessary condition for establishing normal relationships and the capacity for relating to others is, in turn, a requirement for developing an effective therapeutic alliance, which is hence likely to be difficult to achieve (Seto & Quinsey, 2006).

Volitional (goal) deficits in psychopaths are suggested by observations that treatment is often disrupted by attempts to seek status and dominance and to exert control over others (Attrill, personal communication, 2004; Hemphill & Hart, 2002). Whereas readiness deficits in psychopathic individuals may be characterized by diminished affective reactions, borderline disorder and borderline features are associated with very high emotional reactivity and poor emotional regulation, traits which may need modulating if the person is to become engaged in other therapeutic tasks.

Very little is known about personal *identities* in individuals with these disorders, nor about the extent to which they might identify themselves with criminal or mentally disordered identities. Whether identities change in the direction of 'mentally disordered patient' or 'someone with personality problems', as opposed to 'an offender' when the transition is made from a prison to a hospital setting is a very important issue and one, we would argue, that is central to improved readiness. Research to test this hypothesis would be straightforward to undertake, using methods such as repertory grid techniques (Houston, 1998), and such work is overdue.

There are preliminary indications that some DSPD patients have significant cognitive deficits which may diminish their capacity to engage fully in therapeutic programmes. At the Peaks Unit, virtually all patients admitted undertake neuro-psychological assessments. St Ledger *et al.* (2007) have reported the presence of a range of memory, linguistic and attentional problems in this population, though it remains to be established whether this profile is typical of DSPD admissions as a whole and to what degree it differs from that found in other high risk offender groups.

Readiness of the setting for treatment

It is possible that features of institutional life, particularly in prisons, work against the effectiveness of therapeutic programmes. Such institutions may, therefore, in the terminology of this chapter, be unready for delivering effective treatment, or, at least, face considerable obstacles and difficulties in achieving this goal. In general, the provision of therapy is not a primary goal for prison systems. Even where therapeutic goals are acknowledged as important, for example in specialist therapeutic prisons, they are sometimes secondary to the custodial and deterrence functions of imprisonment.

In the context of DSPD high security settings, considerable attention appears to have been paid at the planning stage to ensuring that that the institutional milieus are therapeutic and supportive of the goals being pursued within specific therapies (for example, violence programmes, sex offending programmes, sub-stance misuse, Chromis). For the two sites located within prisons the challenge of maintaining a therapeutic rather than a custodial regime is necessarily greater than it is within high security mental health services, where enabling patients to improve their well-being and social adjustment have, historically, been core, high priority goals, though in the past, mental health services have also struggled to prevent institutional environments from becoming 'toxic' (Davies, 2004).

Monitoring therapeutic climate

It is important to assess the readiness of the institutional climate within which treatment is delivered. The measurement of institutional climate is particularly important in forensic settings such as DSPD units because of the challenges posed by developing a new clinical service for a patient group which is not well under-stood and which is widely perceived as challenging to deal with. How patients and staff perceive the units is largely unknown. Formal clinical measurement of social climate would allow for ongoing feedback to staff, patients and managers and provide an opportunity for reflection and for initiatives to improve climate, should the latter become necessary. Formal, quantitative measurement also makes it pos-sible to monitor changes in social climate over time.

Schalast (2007) has developed scales for measuring climate specifically in forensic units which appear to be psychometrically sound and are now available in English translation. Over the past year we have conducted some pilot work at

Rampton using Schalast's EssenCES measure (Howells & Stacey, 2006). This produces three factor-analytically derived scales, measuring (a) the perceived therapeutic climate ('therapeutic hold'), (b) support (of patients for each other), and (c) safety. This last scale provides a useful reminder that 'custodial' or 'security' aspects ensuring a sense of safety, for patients and staff, may be a precondition for therapeutic endeavours and should not be seen as antipathetic to therapy.

As for intrapersonal readiness factors, milieu variables may also be dynamic rather than static, changing in response to events and circumstances. For illustration, Figure 3.2 shows changes in the climate profile over a six-month period on the Peaks DSPD Unit, changes being in the direction of improved climate, as particular stresses in the environment reduced.

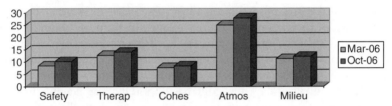

Figure 3.2 Perceptions of climate (combined staff and patients): safety, therapeutic, cohesiveness, positive atmosphere and good milieu (high scores = positive)

BOX 3.1   Assessment and therapeutic questions related to readiness

How does the patient perceive the therapeutic programme?
Does the patient believe he or she is capable of change?
How does the patient perceive the therapeutic staff and the system?
What expectations has the patient acquired, e.g. from previous exposure to therapy?
What is the patient's affective state?
What emotional reactions does s/he have to their offending and other related problems?
What are the personal goals of the patient?
Are personal goals congruent with the goals of the programme?
What is the self-identity of the patient and is it compatible with treatment?
Does the patient have the behavioural and cognitive skills required by the programme?
Does the patient have the capacity to form a therapeutic alliance?
What support is given by staff and other patients for therapeutic engagement?
What support is given by relatives and friends for therapeutic engagement?
How does the patient perceive coercion into treatment?
Has the programme been adapted for the (DSPD) population?
Is the climate of the service supportive of engagement, therapy and of change?

In summary, the MORM approach (Howells & Day, 2007; Ward *et al.*, 2004) and other conceptualizations of treatment readiness (Serin, 1998) might be viewed as usefully alerting clinicians to some basic questions that need to be asked in relation to the treatment of high risk offenders (see Box 3.1).

As is apparent from the above discussion, such questions, basic though they may be, are far more finely discriminating than the conventional questions of the sort 'Is s/he motivated?'. Good practice in addressing readiness deficits in personality disordered offenders will require (a) a systematic methodology for assessing all of these variables, (b) the creation of a 'readiness profile' for each individual which maps precisely where their readiness problems lie, (c) a critique of the programme and the setting in order to identify readiness-impairing features, and (d) a comprehensive, multilevel intervention strategy to enhance intrapersonal and programme readiness.

Acknowledgements

We would like to thank Aisling Mannion, Jacqueline Stacey and Dr Norbert Schalast for their assistance with stages of change and climate data.

Notes

1. Reproduced with permission from 'Readiness for treatment', *Issues in Forensic Psychology*, 7, 11–20. © The British Psychological Society.

References

Andrews, D. A. & Bonta, J. (2003). *The psychology of criminal conduct*, 3rd edition. Cincinnati OH: Anderson.

Attrill, G. (2004). *Personal communication*.

Bandura, A. (1997). The anatomy of stages of change. *American Journal of Health Promotion*, 12, 8–10.

Casey, S., Day, A. & Howells, K. (2005). The application of the transtheoretical model to offender populations: Some critical issues. *Legal and Criminological Psychology*, 10, 1–15.

Daffern, M., Howells, K. & Ogloff, J. R. P. (2007). What's the point?: Towards a methodology for assessing the function of psychiatric inpatient aggression. *Behavior Research and Therapy*, 45, 101–111.

Davies, S. (2004). Toxic institutions. In P. Campling, S. Davies & G. Farquharson (Eds.), *From toxic institutions to therapeutic environments: Residential settings in mental health services*. London: Gaskell.

Hare, R. D. (2006). Psychopathy: A clinical and forensic overview. *Psychiatric Clinics of North America*, 29, 709–724.

Hemphill, J. F. & Hart, S. D. (2002). Motivating the unmotivated: Psychopathy, treatment and change. In M. McMurran (Ed.), *Motivating offenders to change: A guide to enhancing engagement in therapy* (pp. 193–219). Chichester: Wiley.

Houston, J. (1998). *Making sense with offenders: Personal constructs, therapy and change*. Chichester: Wiley.

Howells, K. & Day, A. (2003). Readiness for anger management: Clinical and theoretical issues. *Clinical Psychology Review, 23*, 319–337.

Howells, K. & Day, A. (2006). Affective determinants of treatment engagement in violent offenders. *International Journal of Offender Therapy and Comparative Criminology, 50*, 174–186.

Howells, K. & Day, A. (2007). Readiness for treatment in high risk personality disordered offenders. *Psychology, Crime and Law, 13*, 47–56.

Howells, K., Day, A. & Davey, L. (2005). The future of offender rehabilitation. In D. Chappell & P. Wilson (Eds), *Issues in Australian crime and criminal justice* (pp. 419–434). Chatswood: LexisNexis Butterworths.

Howells, K. & Stacey, J. (2006, December). *Monitoring the social climate of the Peaks Unit.* DSPD National Research Conference, York.

Karoly, P. (1999). A goal systems–self-regulatory perspective on personality, psychopathology and change. *Review of General Psychology, 3*, 264–291.

Littell, J. H. & Girvin, H. (2002). Stages of change: A critique. *Behavior Modification, 26*, 223–272.

McMurran, M. (Ed.) (2002). *Motivating offenders to change: A guide to enhancing engagement in therapy.* Chichester: John Wiley & Sons.

Peaks Academic and Research Unit (2006). *Evaluation of clinical database.*

Prochaska, J. O. & DiClemente, C. C. (1984). *The transtheoretical approach: Crossing traditional boundaries of therapy.* Homewood, IL: Dow Jones-Irwin.

Schalast, N. (2007). *Ward climate questionnaire.* Retrieved 30 October 2009 from www.forensik-essen.de

Serin, R. (1998). Treatment responsivity, intervention and reintegration: A conceptual model. *Forum on Corrections Research, 10*, 29–32.

Seto, M. C. & Quinsey, V. L. (2006). Towards the future: Translating basic research into prevention and treatment strategies. In C. J. Patrick (Ed.), *Handbook of psychopathy.* New York: The Guilford Press.

St Ledger, R., Mooney, P. & Cooper, A. (2007, March). *Neuropsychological assessment in a dangerous and severe personality disorder (DSPD) service: Description of an initial cohort.* Annual conference of British and Irish Group for the Study of Personality Disorder, Cambridge.

Tierney, D. W. & McCabe, M. P. (2001). The validity of the transtheoretical model of behaviour change to investigate motivation to change among child molesters. *Clinical Psychology and Psychotherapy, 8*, 176–190.

Williamson, P., Day, A., Howells, K., Bubner, S. & Jauncey, S. (2003). Assessing offender motivation to address problems with anger. *Psychology, Crime and Law, 9*, 295–307.

Ward, T., Day, A., Howells, K. & Birgden, A. (2004). The Multifactor Offender Readiness Model. *Aggression and Violent Behavior, 9*, 645–673.

Wong, S. & Gordon, A. (2000). *Violence risk scale.* Unpublished report.

Wong, S. & Hare, R. D. (2005). *Guidelines for a psychopathy treatment program.* Toronto: Multi-Health Systems.

Chapter Four

Case Formulation with Personality Disordered Offenders

Lawrence Jones

Case formulation has been significantly neglected in the forensic literature until fairly recently when some practitioners (e.g. Drake & Ward, 2003; Ward, 2000) have begun to advocate its use, particularly with complex individuals. Working with people, with both problems relating to personality disorder and risk of offending, requires the practitioner to be familiar with the literature in both of these areas so as to enable them to develop an holistic and integrated account. With a small number of exceptions (e.g. Hogue *et al.*, 2007; Howells *et al.*, 2007; Livesley, 2007) there have been few attempts to integrate these disparate fields. This chapter will attempt to introduce some of the issues facing the practitioner attempting to develop a collaborative case formulation for problems in these two areas.

Little work has been done on the validity and reliability of case formulation approaches and the work that has been done (see Kuyken, 2006 for a review) suggests that, as a methodology, it is not without its problems. Most of this work has been done in standard clinical settings and none has been done with practitioners in forensic settings working with personality disordered individuals. In this chapter a model for developing case formulations of different kinds, attempting to address issues of reliability and validity, will be suggested.

Types of formulation

Blackburn *et al.* (2006) describe three different kinds of formulation: 'generic', 'case level' and 'situation level', each level with an increasing degree of specificity (see Figure 4.1).

Using Time, Not Doing Time: Practitioner Perspectives on Personality Disorder and Risk
Edited by Allison Tennant and Kevin Howells
© 2010 John Wiley & Sons, Ltd.

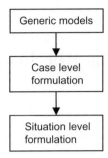

Figure 4.1   Levels of formulation

Generic models

These are models or theoretical accounts of a disorder, often defined within a diagnostic framework – which assumes homogeneity – in the literature. Persons (2008) describes these as 'nomothetic' formulations which need to be 'individual-ized' to account for the individual case. Any case formulation is an application of these 'models' to individual cases. Ward and Beech (2006) describe case formulation as a 'micro theory' and recommend using a theoretical model such as their Integrated Theory of Sex Offending (ITSO), which is an example of a generic theory, as a 'cognitive tool' or 'conceptual resource' to build an account of an offence (with the ITSO it would be a sexual offence) that can inform treatment.

The integrative model of personality disorder, developed by Livesley (e.g. 2003, 2007), is another example of a generic model. Persons (2008) differentiates between this type of model which attempts to explain a specific kind of behaviour, and more general evidence-based theories (such as operant conditioning), arguing that they are both useful in developing a formulation. A truly idiographic account, however, involves identifying themes for an individual case and developing a theory to account for that. Often these themes map neatly onto pre-established generic models; however, there are occasions when the behaviour is unique to the individual case, and cannot be shoe-horned into a generic framework. It is this kind of idiographic work that then contributes to further investigation at a nomothetic level.

Some interventions advocate one generic model as the model to use for all offenders of a particular kind. When there is little heterogeneity in the population there is an argument for using these, but the more complex the case, the more there is a requirement to adapt the intervention to the individual case using a range of different generic models; when working with personality disordered individuals this involves drawing on personality disorder models and offending behaviour models (such as those of Egan, 2008, Livesley, 2007, and Persons, 2008 for personality disorder, and Ward & Beech, 2006 for offending behaviour noted above).

It can not be assumed that interventions based on tailored formulations are going to be more effective than those based on 'one size fits all'. Kuyken (2006) describes a number of studies that found that manualized or multimodal interventions were more effective than tailored interventions and cites one study (Nelson-Gray *et al.*, 1989) where one group of patients received a tailored intervention matched to their specific problem and another group received an intervention not matched to their problem, which found no difference between the two groups in the outcome. The learning point from this research is probably that more inclusive formulations, whether one size fits all or individualized, are more likely to address outcome-relevant targets than interventions with an overly narrow focus. However, one of the advantages of a tailored intervention should be that it reduces the costly strategy of targeting everything when you do not know enough about an individual. A choice needs to be made between a costly 'blunderbuss' approach and a less costly, clearly targeted approach that is an educated gamble and could miss the point.

Case level formulation

This involves making a comprehensive account of all the patient's relevant presenting problems (not one specific problem), identifying hypotheses about what triggers problems for that individual and drawing links between different kinds of problems with common underlying causes. It also attempts to make sense of the problems, in terms of their onset, in the context of that individual's history. Case level formulations are particularly useful for accounting for the range of different behaviours linked with different states amongst individuals with personality disorders. The sometimes rapid switches in state and behaviour, characteristic of borderline personality disorder and some other personality disorders, need to be understood to make sense of an individual's propensity to behave in different ways at different times and in different situations. Cognitive analytic therapy formulations (e.g. Ryle, 1997), developed for people with personality disorders, attempt to map out an individual's range of problems at this level of description. This helps the clinician recognize that different kinds of problems can be experienced in different states – for example, in the context of a secure relationship, somebody might be relatively violence free but, in the context of a state of distress associated with the ending of a relationship, become very violent. The way in which an individual shifts between self-states can also be useful to map out; Golynkina and Ryle (1999) have developed a model for assessing this.

Kuyken *et al.* (2009) similarly offer two kinds of case level conceptualizations: the 'descriptive' conceptualization, which simply describes the problems the individual has, and the 'longitudinal' conceptualization, which describes how the problem developed in terms of predisposing factors and protective factors. This developmental perspective can be useful in thinking through what kinds of intervention could be effective for this individual.

Situation level formulation

These are also described by Blackburn *et al.* (2006) as 'mini formulations' (see also the concept of cross-situational conceptualization in Kuyken *et al.*, 2009). Following Persons and Tomkins (1997), these are construed as hypotheses about establishing and maintaining factors of a 'particular problematic situation' that needs to be understood collaboratively in order to bring about change. Blackburn *et al.* (2006) argue that they should be deducible from the case level formulation and therefore can be used to test the validity of that formulation. Sometimes it can be useful to develop a 'mini-formulation' (see also Charlesworth & Reichelt,

2004) that is aimed at care planning a particular problem (and does not require a detailed understanding of the whole range of factors for an individual).

Perhaps the most commonly used model for formulation in the forensic field is functional analysis (e.g. Sturmey, 1996). This approach involves identifying setting conditions, antecedents (things that lead up to the event) and consequences (was the behaviour reinforced or punished when it occurred) for a particular target behaviour, with a view to identifying what contingencies are establishing and maintaining it. The psychological mechanisms used to account for the target behaviour are behavioural (reinforcement, removal of reinforcement, punishment and removal of punishment) and are fundamentally 'transdiagnostic' (see Harvey *et al.*, 2004), which means that they can be used to explain presentations within a range of different diagnoses. Functional analysis is the 'bread and butter' of forensic formulation but is rarely written about or explored in the literature. More recently clinicians have also included constructs such as 'schema activation', 'schema modes' and 'affect' analysis of the function of offending; in behavioural terms these are internal behaviours that serve as setting events (or 'establishing operations') changing what is reinforcing for an individual when they are in different states (see discussion above on 'self-states').

Functional analysis as a model has been extended by Gresswell and Hollin (1992) with the introduction of Multiple Sequential Functional Analysis (MSFA) which uses the results of one functional analysis as the antecedents for another functional analysis in order to describe a developmental sequence of behaviours.

Causal modelling framework

In this section, a framework that was specifically developed in order to capture and clarify different causal models of the same problem will be introduced. This framework can be used for describing generic, case level and situational models. It was developed by Morton and Frith (1995) and Morton (2004) to describe the diverse ways of accounting for the development of problems such as dyslexia and conduct disorder; the model claims to be theory neutral and consequently has the potential to facilitate the integration of formulations developed within different psychological frameworks (e.g. behavioural and neuropsychological). The model is very similar to the diagrammatic formulation models developed by Haynes (e.g. Haynes *et al.*, 1997), Petermann and Muller (2001) and Padesky and Mooney's (1990) 'five part' model. They identify four 'levels of discourse' or ways of talking about causal factors: environment, brain, cognition (which includes emotion) and behaviour. They then use diagrams to identify causal pathways using these (see Figure 4.2).

Hypothesized causes of behaviour are shown as arrows between boxes within each of the areas of the diagram. So, for example, environmental causal pathways are shown as in Figure 4.3.

Figure 4.3 illustrates a hypothesis involving an environmental influence on a cognitive factor which is also influenced by a biological factor. In this example, it is a hypothesis that peer pressure to believe that bullying is a good thing, along with a trait of being interested in dominating others, which also strengthens the belief that bullying is a good thing, together lead to actual bullying behaviour.

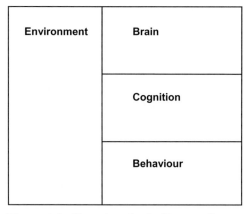

Figure 4.2   Four domains in Morton diagram

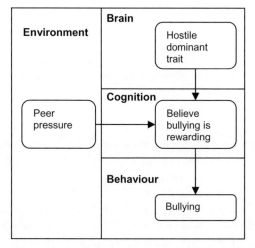

Figure 4.3   Morton diagram illustrating simple causal model

This form of notation has the additional advantage of making the formulation accessible to the individual it is constructed with and to clinical teams. It also allows clinicians to look at the interactions between these four levels of explanation, thereby avoiding a too narrow approach to conceptualizing complex problems.

Validity and reliability of case formulation

Validity (does it actually account for what it says it is accounting for?) and reliability (would two well-trained clinicians reliably come up with the same ideas about what causes an individual's offending if presented with the same information?) are real problems for case formulation. Kuyken (2006) reviews this problem and has developed a set of criteria for *evidence-based* formulation. He discusses two types of criteria: top-down and bottom-up.

Top-down criteria

Is the theory on which the formulation is founded (i.e. the generic model) evidence-based?
If the formulation is based on a theory where there is little evidence, for example that offending is caused by the lack of some mysterious energy, then it is not likely to be as useful as one based on a theory where there is some evidence, for example that offending is caused by the reinforcement history associated with it.

Bottom-up criteria

Is the formulation reliable?
Is the formulation based on reliable inferences?
Can clinicians agree on the formulation? Or is it the result of one clinician's idio-syncratic take on things?

Is the formulation valid?
Does it match up with the client's experience, the therapist's clinical impressions and the clinical supervisor's impressions? Are there any standardized measures being used to assess it? These can then allow the practitioner to compare outcomes with other similar interventions in the literature.

Does the formulation improve the intervention and the therapy outcomes?
If the formulation has no impact on the intervention or the outcomes of the therapy then it is not useful; the only reason for developing a formulation is to derive a set of treatment needs that can be effectively targeted in order to bring about change. Is the formulation acceptable and useful? Do the client and the clinical team understand it and take it as something that they are willing to work with or does it just sit in a report, generally ignored by the clinical team and the client?

Testing formulations and addressing bias

There are a number of reasons for testing the integrity of a case formulation in a forensic setting. It can be to improve the quality of the formulation by, for example, avoiding biases and omissions. Alternatively it can be in order to examine the legal defensibility of the formulation (how might it be challenged in a legal context). Finally, evaluation can be done in order to ensure that the formulation is communicable.

There are three primary strategies for testing formulations.

Practitioner's personal checking routine   Most clinicians go through a kind of error-checking routine in order to test out their clinical judgements. It is some-times useful to attempt to spell out what this routine is and establish a practice algorithm (a guideline for doing a clinical task), for example:

- Identify key assumptions and causal arguments.
- Identify counterarguments for each of these and address them.
- Create alternative explanations for the behaviour.
- Either: indicate why not using these alternatives or integrate aspects of alternatives that are attractive into revised account.

One strategy for doing this is to imagine the formulation being critically reviewed in a legal context such as a court or tribunal, and developing the arguments for the formulation in response to imagined challenges.

Peer review   This is a process whereby an individual practitioner presents their formulation to their peer group and seeks feedback about the formulation and the way in which the formulation is used to support particular interventions with the particular case. Peers then comment on factors such as the evidence base for targeted causal factor(s) (when this exists), omissions of significant causal factors and prioritization of resources in terms of intervention. In addition the logic, coherence and biases evidenced by the formulation can be commented on. Peer review should prevent some of the biases reviewed by Kuyken (2006) and Kuyken *et al.* (2009).

Single case methodology   This is often seen as a central component of the scientist practitioner model. Essentially this approach involves systematic evaluation of operationalized hypotheses deriving from the formulation. These can be used to test out both specific causal links hypothesized within a formulation and the overall impact of an intervention deriving from the formulation (Davies *et al.*, 2007). Typically this approach involves graphing changes in variables over time and analysing the extent to which change has been evidenced. Without this kind of evaluation, it is difficult to know if the target areas suggested by the formulation have actually changed at all.

Who are case formulations for?

There are a range of different needs, amongst different practitioners within a particular individual's milieu, for kinds of knowledge about that individual's functioning. It may be a mistake to assume that one way of thinking about formulation is going to be effective and useful in all contexts. Different contexts often require different ways of talking about formulation.

Ideally, a case formulation should be a collaborative endeavour and should result in an agreed way of describing and understanding the problems which an individual has. The specifically forensic (possibly also encountered in some other areas of practice such as working with psychosis) problem – of there being a part of the formulation and possibly even the set of presenting problems that are not agreed, recognized or understood by the client – raises some significant issues for the practitioner in this field. Disagreements about formulations can result in individuals not engaging in interventions that could result in them being moved on into conditions of lesser security. As a practitioner, there are significant pressures from the client and sometimes their legal representatives to see things in a less risky way. Other systemic factors, such as perceptions of the consequences of getting a judgement wrong – personal, institutional and national – can put pressure on the practitioner to see more risk.

However, it is not just the clinician and the patient who need to have an understanding of the patient's problems. Families and significant others need to make sense of what has become of their loved one. A formulation can give some shape to the way in which their understanding of why an offence took place is framed. There is a sense in which having an 'explanation' or 'reason' for somebody committing an offence can be used by the individual as a way of avoiding responsibility for it: 'It wasn't me, it was my abandonment schema being activated'; 'It was because I was abused and nobody listened to me'; 'I was dropped off the sofa when I was five'. The need for some family members to develop a potentially collusive exculpatory account for the offence is balanced against their genuine need to understand 'why' the offence was committed.

Similarly, staff teams need an account to make their work with the individual tolerable and meaningful. In the absence of a formulation, folk formulations inevitably proliferate. The question of 'why' the offence happened is answered with everyday (as opposed to psychological) constructs such as 'fate', 'evil' and 'luck' (good and bad). Whilst these constructs may not be at the forefront of the way in which people talk about the clients, they often tacitly or implicitly underpin the kinds of thinking that people have about the client.

Formulation of what problems?

For a formulation to be useful it needs to focus on a specific problem and not on vague or general ones. Typically, in forensic settings, the target behaviours being formulated are index or other similar offences. In a personality disorder service within a forensic setting, case formulation can prove useful for a number of purposes.

1.   The link between personality disorder and offending

The link between personality and offending is important in that it is one of the criteria that brings an individual into treatment. If it was considered that the offending behaviour was unrelated to a personality disorder, there would be no justification for intervening outside a prison context. Case formulation can be used to try and make sense of the possible ways in which personality, conceived as traits and associated state repertoires, can impact on risk. Nomothetic frameworks for doing this include Livesley (2003) and Egan (2008).

2.   Clinically relevant behaviour (e.g. specific instances of offending or actively avoiding offending)

Making sense of offending behaviour or offence-paralleling behaviour (e.g. Jones, 2004; see also Kohlenberg & Tsai's 1994 discussion of 'clinically relevant behaviour') with a view to identifying clinically relevant treatment targets is a critical task for forensic practitioners. From a strengths-focused perspective, it is also important to understand both why an individual has managed to successfully avoid offending and why they have been able to have insight into their problem behaviour. It is also important to attend to underlying problems or problem themes.

Historically there are events where an individual has been effective or evidenced strengths have been ignored by clinicians who have been preoccupied with what has gone wrong and with 'pathology'. Kuyken *et al.* (2009) describe a model for incorporating strengths and resilience into case formulation. A strengths-based approach needs also to look at and assess an individual's strengths and develop formulations for when an individual has effectively managed their behaviour as well as looking at when self-regulation has failed.

3. Responsivity or motivational issues

Understanding why a particular individual is not engaging is also an area where case formulation can be useful. Disengagement and non-engagement is a critical issue for personality disordered offenders. Jones (2002) proposes a framework for developing case formulations looking at why an individual has not engaged; this is a critical task for personality disordered offenders who have often failed to engage or respond to previous interventions. A useful generic assessment model for this is Ward *et al.*'s (2004) Multifactor Offender Readiness Model (MORM).

Who makes formulations?

A number of different individuals attempt to develop explanations for the offence and the problems related to it. Attending to these simultaneous formulations is critical to the task of intervention (see Figure 4.4).

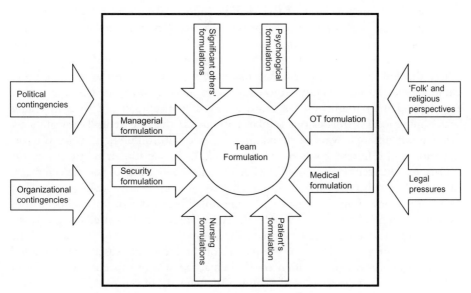

Figure 4.4 Types of formulation in forensic setting

There is inevitably a plethora of different ways of conceptualizing an individual case in any multidisciplinary setting. It is also inevitable that fracture lines can develop in the team because differences of language and beliefs about what is going on for a particular individual can end up being 'played' by the individual, or indeed by the group, and there can be systemic dynamics which characterize the organization and political contexts in which the interventions are taking place. It is a critical skill of practitioners working in this field to be able to conceptualize and analyse both of these kinds of processes; the patients' and the systemic context (see Tarrier & Calam, 2002).

The patient's own pretreatment formulation

Each individual entering a treatment process has their own way of conceptualizing what their problems are and what kinds of change process would be necessary to bring about change. Along with non-treatment staff formulations they often rest upon a folk or common language way of thinking about problems. One of the aims of a formulation, ultimately, is to give the patient some idea of how people see their problems and the causal factors that underpin it. Without the patient being persuaded of this formulation, any hope of a collaborative intervention is unlikely to be effective. Constructs such as 'evil' and 'willpower' are common causal elements of such formulations. A critical aspect of this is cultural sensitivity (Lo & Fung, 2003); being dismissive or insensitive to cultural issues in clients and indeed amongst colleagues can result in formulations getting lost or derailed through reactance or lack of understanding.

Security formulations

Most security judgements involve some form of more or less explicit formulation. Judgements about the kind of risk that an individual patient presents, and the kinds of strategy necessary to manage this risk, are very much at the heart of the work of staff involved in thinking about security issues – which should be all staff – in a forensic setting. It is often the case, however, that parts of the organization where this kind of thinking is taking place are separated from those where other clinical issues are also being explored. Practitioners involved in working with a particular patient might also slip into a way of conceptualizing their problems which minimizes or misses out thinking about risk management. Team splits are often about different ways of thinking, associated with different aims for the formulation and different kinds of evidence-seeking to support or refute those formulations. Different biases enter in when clinicians only think of risk management, or only think about bringing about change. A conservative risk management framework, for example, might see any emotional behaviour or unusual behaviour as being potentially offence-related. All data is interpreted as predicting relapse, even in the absence of a link between the data and relapse – in the nomothetic literature (generic model) or in the history of the individual case. Anecdotal and uncorroborated evidence is often considered acceptable in this context. Different criteria might, however, be used to judge the veracity of claims of change; anecdotal and uncorroborated evidence become unacceptable and other kinds of evidence are challenged as biased or superficial. Change is seen as unprovable whereas risk is seen as proven and irrefutable. This difference in evidence and ways of thinking about causal factors is driven by the different weightings given by individual practitioners to the undesirability of false-positive (the mistake of saying somebody is something when they are not) and false-negative (the mistake of saying somebody is not something when they are) judgements of both risk and change.

Medical formulation

Typically, medical models are based on diagnoses as opposed to 'transdiagnostic' (Harvey *et al.*, 2004) constructs used by psychologists. Sometimes, but not always, diagnoses are based on a theoretical model indicating why a particular constellation of symptoms are found to cluster together. Offering medication, even in the absence of an explicit diagnosis, comes with an implicit causal model based on the psychopharmacological model underpinning the use of the drug. Use of serotonin reuptake inhibitors, for example, implies that a hypothesis that an individual has a deficit involving unusually low levels of serotonin has been proposed. Scott (1998) describes the importance of encouraging the patient to develop an understanding of how the biological account of their presentation fits with other (e.g. more psychological) formulations, in order to protect against the patient only accepting one or other intervention as valid, as a consequence of not understanding that they are both plausible and interacting accounts.

Morton diagrams are a good way of showing how a number of different causes can contribute to one problem, thereby explaining why it would be useful to intervene in a number of different ways at the same time. The integration of a biological and cognitive causal pathway can be illustrated in the same diagram (see Figure 4.5).

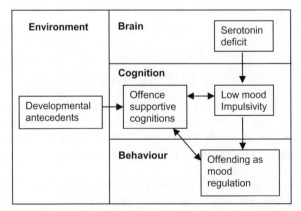

Figure 4.5   Integrating biological formulation with cognitive formulation

Fictional case: 'Peter'

The generic models used for this case were drawn from Livesley (2007), who developed a framework for working with personality disorder, the trait personality literature summarized by Egan (2008), Ward and Beech's (2006) Integrated Theory of Sexual Offending (ITSO) and the neuropsychological literature (see Figure 4.6).

Peter was born into a difficult family. His mother had a history of major depression and his father, when he was at home, had a history of being very violent both inside and outside the family. Peter himself had experienced numerous assaults at the hands of his father and there was corroborating evidence from the social services indicating that he had to be removed from the family home for his own protection. Whilst he was in care, he experienced a number of episodes of sexual abuse and had been bullied badly by his peers. He reported also being 'forced' to sexually assault other children whilst in care. His offending history started young; he set light to a school building whilst he was in primary school and was expelled from two secondary schools. Social work reports suggest that he would often deny any involvement in offending even when he had been caught in the process of commit-ting an offence. This pattern of behaviour persisted into his later years. He had a long-standing involvement with drink and drugs starting from the age of 12 when he was reported to have stolen alcohol from his parents and was frequently caught drinking. He reported using cannabis heavily. In later life he developed significant problems with drink. He reported some use of heroin and cocaine but this was not at a level to cause obvious problems in his lifestyle.

Peter's index offence was a sexual assault on his ex-partner. He offended against her after he had experienced her rejecting him and had become enraged. He had a history of versatile offending ranging from acquisitive, violent, sexual (including one USI [unlawful sexual intercourse] and a previous assault on an ex-partner) and traffic offences. He was assessed as meeting criteria for DSM-IV antisocial PD and borderline PD on the International Personality Disorder Examination (IPDE).

Case level formulation

The self-states shown in Table 4.1 were identified as being part of Peter's state repertoire. Each of Peter's self-states are associated with patterns of behaviour and relating to others (Livesley, 2003; Ryle, 1997). The first two states are states linked with strengths that Peter has identified himself as having.

A self-state formulation identified that at the time of the offence Peter shifted from feeling despairing to feeling numb and taking drugs to becoming enraged, entitled and feeling powerful and controlling. This sequence of states was monitored on the ward to see if he was entering into an offence-paralleling behaviour.

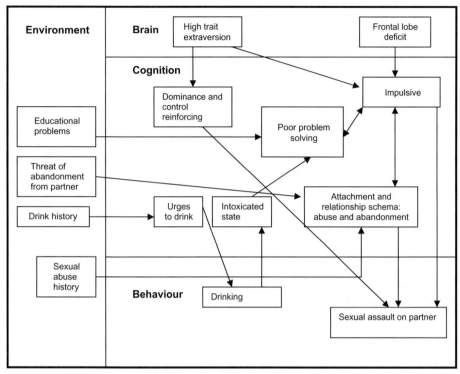

Figure 4.6 Example formulation

Table 4.1 Self-state formulation

Self-state	Schema	Reciprocal role	Typical behaviour
Sober sensible adult	Self and other valuing	Respecting valuing to Respected valued	Problem solving
Being brave	Belief in the tolerability of difficult emotions	Looking after to Looked after	Emotional tolerance
Bored and wanting excitement	Belief in intolerability of boredom	Neglecting to Neglected	Seeking sensations and risk taking
Numb through drugs or emotionally cutting off	Belief in emotional avoidance as legitimate coping	Emotionally avoiding to Emotionally cut-off	Insensitive to consequences of behaviour on self and others
Despairing and vulnerable (when he felt rejected)	Belief in self as victim, undesirable, unloved	Rejecting to Rejected	Withdrawal and become cut-off or becoming enraged
Enraged and dangerous	Victim stance	Victimizing to Victimized	Self or other harm
Powerful and controlling	Entitled	Controlling to Controlled	Exploiting self and others

Neuropsychological assessment suggested executive functioning deficits indicating that he finds it difficult to change a course of action once he has started on it and he may struggle to generate options when he is problem solving. These deficits may have got in the way of Peter thinking about the long-term consequences of what he was doing at the time of the offence (Hypothesis 1). These difficulties were probably exacerbated by stress (Hypothesis 2), particularly in the context of relationships, as he had significant issues around attachment (Hypothesis 3).

His characteristic style of relating to others was to be overbearing and domineering but often he would experience himself as a victim of others' controlling behaviour. This was driven by a combination of:

a. his problem-solving difficulties resulting in others controlling him, often in a coercive manner; and
b. experience of controlling abuse from parents and carers in the past.

He sought to control and dominate because he found it gave him a sense of power which he enjoyed and sought to offset feelings of weakness and vulnerability linked with rejection through these behaviours (Hypothesis 4). Power was also intrinsically reinforcing for him. The avoidance of vulnerability was also reinforcing (see Table 4.2).

The hypotheses identified above can be monitored using the following observations and psychometrics.

Hypothesis 1
Monitoring and rating evidence of quality of problem solving in day-to-day problems.

Hypothesis 2
Monitoring and ratings of adverse changes in problem solving associated with stress.

Table 4.2 Behavioural analysis

Antecedents/setting events	*Behaviour*	*Consequences*
Rejected by partner	Sexual assault on	**Immediate**
Feeling despairing and	partner	Felt powerful and in control
rejected		Stopped feelings of
Entitlement schema activated		vulnerability and rejection
Enraged state linked with		Satisfied need for revenge
thoughts of revenge		**Longer term**
		Felt anxious about getting
		caught
		When caught felt despairing
		and rejection again

Hypothesis 3
Monitoring and ratings of adverse impact of relationship breakdowns or ruptures on ward behaviour and problem solving.

Monitoring and ratings of beliefs about and responses to relationship ruptures and endings as a trigger for potential offence-paralleling behaviour, or evidence of having developed alternative ways of coping.

Hypothesis 4
Monitoring and rating of power-oriented behaviour on the ward becoming more intense and frequent when he is exposed to situations where he could feel vulnerable.

Conclusions

Multiple episodes of formulation are evident in any forensic setting and the consequences, for the patient and the team, of allowing these different attempts to make sense of the patient to remain fragmented could be serious. Integrating diverse formulations is desirable. It is possible, and indeed desirable, to capture the clinical diversity within a single descriptive framework. Morton's diagrammatic model can be useful for this. Other kinds of formulation, such as case level formulations identifying self-state repertoires, functional analysis of offending behaviour and offence-paralleling behaviour, are also useful.

Blackburn *et al.* (2006) have, as their last step in a practice guideline, a consideration of 'what would be the most suitable … formulation framework to employ with the patient' (p. 124). They later describe a choice to not use a schema model and opt for a traditional cognitive behaviour therapy model because they felt that this would allow the individual to focus more on their strengths and not get caught up in seeing their caring for others as an attempt to gain affection as opposed to a personal strength of which they could feel proud. This process of selecting the formulation most useful for the individual case is very much part of the clinical task in clinical team meetings. Kuyken *et al.* (2009) also describe different uses for different kinds of formulation, at different stages of the therapeutic process. Some individuals, for example, have a very medical model approach and seek medication for most problems; at times staff go along with this, if it appears to be effective and helps them to engage in other kinds of intervention; at other times they argue for a more psychological intervention if, for example, it is felt to be an avoidance strategy. Case formulation is critical to the development of interventions that are likely to be effective for complex cases. Perhaps the most critical factor in working with a formulation is the ownership and comprehension of that formulation in the clinical team and with the client. These factors are strongly influenced by the intelligibility of the formulation. There is a real tension between the need for simplicity and the complex clinical reality that we need to address; Sim *et al.* (2005) write: 'if the conceptualization is too simple, salient aspects of the case may be missed, and, conversely, if the conceptualization is too complex, it may become too unwieldy and time consuming for practical use'; this is particularly true when working with complex cases.

References

Blackburn, I. M., James, I. A. & Flitcroft, A. (2006). Case formulation in depression. In N. Tarrier (Ed.), *Case formulation in cognitive behaviour therapy: The treatment of challenging and complex cases*. London: Routledge.

Charlesworth, G. M. & Reichelt, F. K. (2004). Keeping conceptualizations simple: Examples with family carers of people with dementia. *Behavioural and Cognitive Psychotherapy, 32*, 401–409.

Davies, J., Howells, K. & Jones, L. (2007). Evaluating innovative treatments in forensic mental health: A role for single case methodology. *Journal of Forensic Psychiatry and Psychology, 18*(3), 353–367.

Drake, D. R. & Ward, T. (2003). Practical and theoretical roles for the formulation based treatment of sexual offenders. *International Journal of Forensic Psychology, 1*(1), 71–84.

Egan, V. (2008). The 'Big Five': Neuroticism, extraversion, openness, agreeableness and conscientiousness as an organizational scheme for thinking about aggression and violence. In M. McMurran & R. Howard (Eds.), *Personality, personality disorder, and risk of violence: An evidence-based approach*. Chichester: John Wiley & Sons.

Golynkina, K. & Ryle, A. (1999). The identification and characteristics of the partially dissociated states of patients with borderline personality disorder. *British Journal of Medical Psychology, 72*, 429–445.

Gresswell, D. M. & Hollin, C. (1992). Towards a new methodology for making sense of case material: An illustrative case involving attempted multiple murder. *Criminal Behaviour and Mental Health, 2*, 239–341.

Harvey, A. G., Watkins, E., Mansell, W. & Shafran, R. (2004). *Cognitive behavioural processes across psychological disorders: A transdiagnostic approach to research and treatment*. Oxford: Oxford University Press.

Haynes, S. N., Leisen, M. B. & Blaine, D. D. (1997). Design of individualized behavioral treatment programs using functional analytic clinical case models. *Psychological Assessment, 9*, 334–348.

Hogue, T. E., Jones, L., Talkes, K. & Tennant, A. (2007). The Peaks: A clinical service for those with dangerous and severe personality disorder. *Psychology, Crime and Law, 13*(1), 57–68.

Howells, K., Krishnan, G. & Daffern, M. (2007). Approaches to the treatment of DSPD. *Advances in Psychiatric Treatment, 13*, 325–332.

Jones, L. F. (2002). An individual case formulation approach to the assessment of motivation. In M. McMurran (Ed.), *Motivating offenders to change*. Chichester: Wiley.

Jones, L. F. (2004). Offence paralleling behaviour (OPB) as a framework for assessment and interventions with offenders. In A. Needs & G. Towl (Eds.), *Applying psychology to forensic practice*. Blackwell: British Psychological Society.

Kohlenberg, R. J. & Tsai, M. (1994). Functional analytic psychotherapy: A radical behavioral approach to treatment and integration. *Journal of Psychotherapy Integration, 4*, 175–201.

Kuyken, W. (2006). Evidence-based case formulation: Is the emperor clothed? In N. Tarrier (Ed.), *Case formulation in cognitive behaviour therapy: The treatment of challenging and complex cases*. London: Routledge.

Kuyken, W. A., Padesky, C. A. & Dudley, R. (2009). *Collaborative case conceptualization: Working effectively with clients in cognitive-behavioural therapy*. New York: Guilford Press.

Livesley, W. J. (2003) *Practical management of personality disorder*. New York: Guilford Press.

Livesley, W. J. (2007). The relevance of an integrated approach to the treatment of personality disordered offenders. *Psychology, Crime & Law, 13*(1), 27–46.

Lo, H. T. & Fung, K. P. (2003). Culturally competent psychotherapy. *Canadian Journal of Psychiatry, 48*, 161–170.

Morton, J. (2004). *Understanding developmental disorders: A causal modelling approach.* Oxford: Blackwell Publishing.

Morton, J. & Frith, U. (1995). Causal modelling: A structural approach to developmental psychopathology. In D. Cicchetti & D. J. Cohen (Eds.), *Manual of developmental psychopathology*, Volume 1 (pp. 357–390). New York: Wiley.

Nelson-Gray, R. O., Herbert, J. D., Herbert, D. L., Sigmon, S.T. & Brannon, S. E. (1989). Effectiveness of matched, mismatched, and package treatments of depression. *Journal of Behavior Therapy and Experimental Psychiatry, 20*, 281–294.

Padesky, C. A. & Mooney, K. A. (1990). Clinical tip: presenting the cognitive model to clients. *International Cognitive Therapy Newsletter, 6*, 13–14.

Persons, J. B. (2008). *The case formulation approach to cognitive behaviour therapy.* New York: Guilford Press.

Persons, J. & Tomkins, M. (1997). Cognitive behavioural case formulation. In T. Eells (Ed.), *Handbook of psychotherapy case formulation.* New York: Guilford Press.

Petermann, F. & Muller, J. M. (2001). *Clinical psychology and single-case evidence: A practical approach to treatment planning and evaluation.* Chichester: Wiley.

Ryle, A. (1997). *Cognitive analytic therapy and borderline personality disorder: The model and the method.* Chichester: Wiley.

Scott, J. (1998). Where there's a will ... cognitive therapy for people with chronic depressive disorders. In N. Tarrier, A. Wells & G. Haddock (Eds.), *Treating complex cases: The cognitive behavioural therapy approach.* Wiley: Chichester.

Sim, K., Gwee, K. P. & Bateman, A. (2005). Case formulation in psychotherapy: Revitalizing its usefulness as a clinical tool. *Academic Psychiatry, 29*, 289–292.

Sturmey, P. (1996). *Functional analysis in clinical psychology.* Chichester: Wiley UK.

Tarrier, N. & Calam, R. (2002). New developments in cognitive behavioural therapy case formulation: Epidemiological, systemic and social context: An integrative approach. *Behavioural and Cognitive Psychotherapy, 30*, 311–328.

Ward, T. (2000). The role of formulation-based treatment for sexual offenders. *Behaviour Change, 17*(4), 251–264.

Ward, T. & Beech, A. (2006). An integrated theory of sexual offending. *Aggression and Violent Behaviour, 11*, 44–63.

Ward, T., Day, A., Howells, K. & Birgden, A. (2004). The Multifactor Offender Readiness Model. *Aggression and Violent Behavior, 9*, 645–673.

Chapter Five

Dialectical Behaviour Therapy Targeting Violent Behaviour in a Male Forensic In-Patient Setting

Allison Tennant

This chapter explores the complexities faced by clinicians in treating men who have seriously offended against others and who also have multiple personality problems. This chapter describes what dialectical behaviour therapy (DBT) is, the empirical support and the DBT stages of treatment. The case vignette describes how the therapist organized the treatment and suggests how a (DBT) informed approach can be built into an overall care pathway. The chapter concludes with a section that describes the patient's view of receiving DBT therapy and what we can learn as therapists.

What is dialectical behaviour therapy (DBT)?

The literature suggests that the treatment of personality disorder is inherently complex, therefore a range of treatment approaches are selected by clinicians to meet a particular treatment need. Thus particular interventions may focus on biological factors, cognitive style, interpersonal difficulties, attachment issues, motivational aspects, behavioural problems or past traumatic experiences, for example. As Livesley (2003a) recognizes, personality disorder comprises all of these, therefore a single approach is not effective. DBT integrates a range of treatment approaches that are supported by a substantial empirical and theoretical literature and offers the clinician a framework that helps them to structure their treatment in a systematic and consistent way.

DBT was developed by Marsha Linehan (1993) and is underpinned by biosocial theory which suggests that some individuals are predisposed to be emotionally

Using Time, Not Doing Time: Practitioner Perspectives on Personality Disorder and Risk
Edited by Allison Tennant and Kevin Howells

sensitive in nature, and are exposed to living in an environment that is invalidating or punishing in some way. These cumulative factors create difficulties for some individuals in relation to regulating their emotions and their interpersonal day-to-day functioning. Such people often present to mental health services with diverse problems such as para-suicidal and suicidal behaviours, anxiety-based disorders and substance misuse problems. DBT treatment aims to help individuals to stabilize their emotions in order to reduce life-threatening and impulsive behaviour. DBT integrates cognitive-behavioural interventions with Eastern meditational practices (Zen) and dialectical philosophy (Heard & Linehan, 1994). The idea is to integrate a depth and breadth of treatment strategies such as problem solving, exposure techniques, skills training, contingency management and cognitive modification.

The dialectical approach aims to help the patient and therapist examine both sides of the perspective; a dialectic is viewed as a line or continuum that connects any two opposing poles. For example, the overriding dialectic in the therapeutic relationship is the notion of accepting the patient in the moment without blaming or making judgements about their behaviour, while holding onto the reality that their behaviour needs to change. Dialectical processes pervade every aspect of DBT and are woven into the therapeutic process. In practice this involves the therapist making the effort to 'reframe' dysfunctional behaviours that are part of the patient's learned problem-solving repertoire, and to focus the therapy on active problem solving, which is balanced with validation of how difficult it is to change. An emphasis only on change strategies may push the patient into defensive practices and may invalidate their attempts to make change. Many individuals with personality disorder problems have rigid thinking styles and report that they are judgemental about themselves and others. This can lead into extreme styles of thinking and behaving; therefore it can be helpful to analyse what the internal and external factors are that obstruct change. Institutionalized living can often exaggerate extreme types of behaviour, and the strength of a dialectical approach can liberate individuals to find a more balanced position, rather than an entrenched and contradictory reaction to the situation. The example below describes the author's experience of some dialectical positions that individuals with antisocial characteristics often experience in their lives; the challenge is to find a way to synthesize these extreme positions and find a different path. Table 5.1 identifies some of the

Table 5.1 Dialectical tensions

Trust	*versus*	Suspicion
Emotional insensitivity	*versus*	Emotional sensitivity
Emotional impulsivity	*versus*	Emotional tolerance
Tough	*versus*	Weak
Public	*versus*	Private face
Excitement	*versus*	Unstimulating
Prosocial	*versus*	Antisocial
Genuine	*versus*	Insincere
Judgemental thinking	*versus*	Non-judgemental thinking
Bad	*versus*	Good
Right	*versus*	Wrong
Fair	*versus*	Unfair

extreme behaviours that individuals demonstrate. Some individuals will tell you their life history on a first encounter and trust you implicitly with this information whilst others behave in opposite ways and are suspicious and hostile in their daily interactions. During DBT these dialectical tensions will be highlighted and alternative styles are explored.

The empirical basis of dialectical behaviour therapy

DBT was originally developed as a specific treatment for women diagnosed with borderline personality disorder (BPD) who had chronic problems with para-suicide and suicidal behaviours (Linehan, 1993). One of the first evaluative studies to measure efficacy of DBT (Linehan *et al.*, 1991) randomized women with severe BPD and a recent history of para-suicidal behaviour; this was compared to treatment as usual. The findings noted a reduction in the severity and frequency in the first four months, and a reduction in in-patient hospital days. In addition therapy-interfering behaviours such as sporadic attendance at therapy sessions were reduced. Another major randomized study included 58 women with BPD to either DBT or treatment as usual (TAU) (Verheul *et al.*, 2003). The authors found that there was a significant reduction in para-suicidal behaviour and other impulsive behaviours. Interestingly, a higher percentage of patients in the DBT programme stayed with their individual therapist for the whole programme compared to the treatment as usual. Linehan (2006) studied women who met the criteria for borderline personality disorder and had severe chronic suicidal ideation. She found that the proportion of individuals with a suicide attempt during the first year of treatment and one-year follow-up was half that of individuals randomly assigned to non-behavioural community psychotherapy. Further studies into standard DBT indicated decreased anger and improved interpersonal functioning (Linehan *et al.*, 1994) at one-year follow-up, significantly less para-suicidal behaviour, less anger and improved reported social adjustment (Linehan *et al.*, 1993). Koons *et al.* (2001) further supported these findings, indicating a greater reduction in suicidal ideation, hopelessness, depression and anger expression. There was also a reported reduction in para-suicidal acts, anger experience, dissociation and the number of hospitalizations.

Since then the therapy has been adapted to meet treatment needs of different populations including those in in-patient settings (Kroger *et al.*, 2006), those with eating disorders (Telch *et al.*, 2001), elderly depressed individuals (Lynch *et al.*, 2003), and those with attention deficit disorder (Hesslinger *et al.*, 2002).

An evidence base is materializing in the use of DBT in forensic settings, in particular with male personality disordered offenders. McCann *et al.* (2000) reported reductions in depressed and hostile mood, paranoia and psychotic behaviours. Interestingly a reduction in staff burn-out was also reported. Further studies in this area indicated the potential for DBT to significantly impact upon violent behaviour and anger (Evershed & Tennant, 2003). Applying DBT within in-patient forensic settings does produce challenges as constraints are apparent. One of these is whether skills acquired in treatment can be generalized effectively in other settings. Also in-patient units can bring patients into contact with a number of stressors that are unconnected with their care and multiple examples of dysfunctional coping behaviours that they may model. Other potential adaptations to DBT have been suggested in the sex offender literature and how DBT can be applied to this client group (Shingler, 2004).

Treatment pathway

Figure 5.1 illustrates the stages of DBT therapy and describes a typical care pathway from the referral stage into the DBT programme through to discharge. The first part of the process involves the assessment and pretreatment phase. This process can take from six weeks to six months; this may be dependent on the complex needs of the patient and their motivation to engage in the treatment process. The therapist must get commitment from the individual to reduce either self-harm or violent behaviour. Commitment also requires the person to attend both individual and group skills therapy weekly, to complete homework assignments and to record daily incidents of self-harm and violent behaviours. If the individual at this stage is non-committed then they are not ready for DBT therapy and will not start the treatment. It is better to start therapy at a later date than to accept them on to the programme from which they then drop out. The individual may need further time to reflect on their future or may need further motivational work. If individuals miss four consecutive DBT sessions with no valid reason they may be given a brief break or will be out of therapy; paradoxically these rules help to keep people in the therapy.

Stage 1: Assessment and pretreatment phase

In a high secure (dangerous and severe personality disorder [DSPD]) hospital setting, in the early stages of therapy, it is important to gather information about the patient and conduct the relevant assessment measures, as part of case formulation (Koerner & Linehan, 1997). In the pretreatment phase, interventions cannot begin until agreement has been reached on the primary treatment targets and the patient is willing, to some extent, to work towards change. The practical nature of the relationship takes precedence and the therapist has to work hard to convince the person that it is worth a try. The therapist cannot make a person change, but can influence change through the therapeutic relationship. Ambivalence about change is a common experience and individuals oscillate between 'I want to' and 'don't want to'. Such behaviours are characteristic of addictive behaviours and for many reasons individuals become attached to their addictive behaviour. Exploring ambivalence is always at the centre of the therapy and yet can be overlooked by therapists. It is suggested by Howells and Tennant (2007) that individual readiness for treatment should be analysed in detail using, for example, the Multifactor Offender Readiness Model (MORM).

In forensic settings particularly, an overemphasis on safety and risk issues can take precedence. If therapy centres on criminogenic needs and does not pay attention to individual strengths that help to motivate individuals (McMurran & Ward,

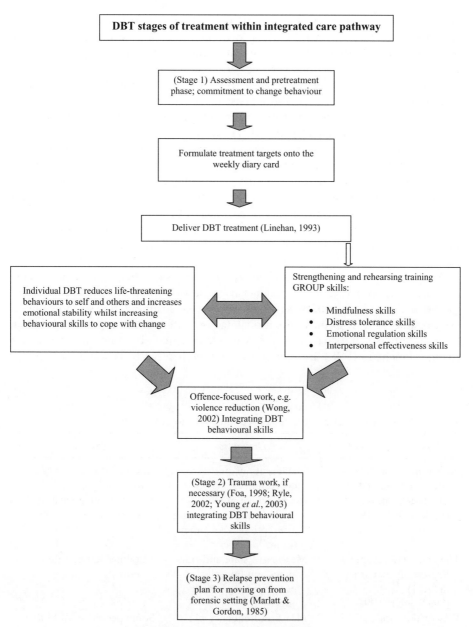

Figure 5.1 Treatment pathway

2004), this can lead to resistance and disengagement. Similarly, if the environment is too risk and safety focused, then this has a detrimental impact on the therapeutic milieu; this is a dialectical tension. Linehan (1993) recognized early on in her work that gaining commitment from individuals to change one day does not mean that it stays that way. Motivation has to be nurtured; the therapist has to search for those wishes, desires or needs that resonate in the person's current context. Gathering information about the impact of working with other therapists and how they have experienced that therapy helps the therapist to build connections and helps patients to identify their own concerns and expectations. Seeing situations through their eyes can illustrate how power dynamics permeate and structure all their interactions with us. Formulating these issues early on in the treatment process can alert us quickly to problems that our therapy-interfering behaviour may be producing. Also it is useful to explore previous learning experiences and identify how the individual likes to learn and what hampers their learning. This exploration enables the therapist to plan the content and style of interactions together with the hope of stimulating interest in the therapist and the therapy. This experimental approach to learning helps to revisit and relearn skills the person may already have. Utilizing a skills strength based model helps to empower individuals and may promote new learning. Ward and Stewart (2003) point out how valuable it is for clinicians to embrace a holistic approach that brings meaning and purpose to individuals. This helps to foster engagement early on and creates some positive energy in those first encounters with the patient.

A detailed assessment is useful, firstly, to establish a diagnosis of personality disorder and, secondly, to help clinicians tease out what the treatment targets should be. Livesley (2003b) suggests assessment spanning the six domains of psychopathology symptoms, situational factors, affect and impulse regulation, traits, interpersonal behaviours and self-system; these become the targets for change. Linehan (1993) also conducts a comprehensive behavioural analysis for

Table 5.2 Typical psychometric tests used in (DBT) forensic setting

Psychometric assessment	Description	Example item
Beck Depression Inventory (Beck & Steer, 1987)	Manifestations of depression	I do not expect things to work out for me
Beck Hopelessness Scale (Beck & Steer, 1988)	Assess degree in which individuals hold negative assumptions about their future	I can't imagine what my life would be like in 10 years
The State-Trait Anger Expression Inventory (STAXI) (Spielberger, 1996)	Measure of state and trait anger and how the person manages their anger	I boil inside but I don't show it
Dissociation Scale (DES) (Bernstein & Putnam, 1986)	Measures frequency of dissociative experiences	Some people are told that they sometimes do not recognize friends or a family member. Mark on the line to show what percentage of the time this happens to you
Impulse Behaviour Scale (UPPS) (Whiteside & Lynam, 2001)	Impulsivity measure	I like to stop and think things over before I do them

each major instance of either para-suicidal or, in this example, violent behaviour. From the assessment, the treatment targets are formulated and identified on the patient's individual diary card.

A range of structured psychological assessment tools are often useful to obtain additional clinical information and to provide some measure of change. For instance, in DBT, typically the psychometric tests listed in Table 5.2 are used within the forensic setting.

Brian: Case example

A man in his mid-thirties, he is diagnosed as having antisocial, paranoid and borderline personality disorder. He describes an unhappy childhood and paints a picture of parents that were punitive towards him, and describes little parental supervision. His brother died when Brian was 11 and he responded to this by going 'off the rails'. He began experimenting with drugs and mixing with the 'wrong crowd'. In his late teens he was sent to prison for violence and had been in prison on more than one occasion before being referred to healthcare.

At first Brian appeared to thrive on violence and gained respect and credibility from his criminal lifestyle and his peer group. His underlying beliefs about masculinity centred on men being physically and emotionally strong. He thought that the world was a dangerous place, and to survive day-to-day life meant that, as a man, it was important to portray a 'macho image', the opposite to this implied weakness and vulnerability. To reinforce and maintain his belief systems during his incarceration, he would visualize images of himself 'kicking someone's head in'; these images excited and stimulated his anger. If he thought that a person had humiliated him in some way he would fantasize about how he could take his revenge and hurt them in some way. Historically, this has involved him making sharp instruments to attack those whom he has perceived as having 'wronged' him.

Amongst the questions that the therapist may consider when assessing Brian are: Why does he need this excitement? What can he replace it with? How do these hurdles get in the way of helping him engage in the treatment process? What is reinforcing his specific behaviour? How can these behaviours be changed? What is his current stage of change? What interventions may be beneficial? What are his treatment priorities? What interventions may make him worse? What effective coping skills does he already have?

This case raises questions about his readiness to engage in treatment and to change aspects of himself. His commitment to recognize and address behaviours that will interfere with therapy should be highlighted and targeted for treatment. These behaviours may include destructive behaviours in the unit, for example secreting weapons, taking illicit substances. These behaviours have been referred to as 'offence paralleling behaviours' (Jones, 2004). Questions should be asked about what can be reasonably expected to be changed by treatment. The assessment process is pivotal to conceptualize the case and to prioritize particular treatment interventions.

Defining DBT treatment targets and diary cards

Once the assessment phase is complete, including analysis of psychometrics, background file information, preferred learning style, past therapy encounters, commitment to change and behavioural analysis of self-harm and/or violent behaviours, then treatment targets are agreed. The individual therapist is responsible for treatment planning, working with the patient on progress to decrease specific behaviours whilst helping to integrate effective skills into their life. The initial priority is the management and reduction of extreme manifestations of behaviour which pose a threat to self and others. Violent behaviours of any type are a high priority area to change and are never ignored by the therapist in DBT. The therapist needs to define what behaviours will be targeted to increase and which behaviours to decrease. Behaviours that are defined in vague terms are not sufficient, as these can be interpreted in different ways, and are not easily measured. The treatment targets (behaviours) are labelled on the patient's diary card and the individual provides daily behavioural recordings based on a Likert scale. These ratings are developed together and define specific behaviours that reflect each point on the Likert scale; this ensures accurate recording. The diary card helps both the patient and therapist to structure the session agenda and address priority behaviours.

Brian's treatment targets

In Brian's case the high priority treatment target is to reduce his violent behaviour. Violent behaviour is broken up into specific components and includes thoughts, images, urges and actions. Other associated patterns of behaviour that link to his violent behaviours include paranoid thinking, anxiety and conflict situations; these are also identified on his diary card. The daily recording of these behaviours helps him to recognize all aspects of behaviour and increases self-awareness. The list below details specific behaviours targeted for change:

1. *Violent acts.*
2. *Violent crisis behaviours; these behaviours include planning to be violent and indirect communication of violence.*
3. *Violent thoughts, images, urges, threats and talking about violence.*
4. *Violent related affect; thinking about violence can be associated with emotions of relief, feeling calm, feeling powerful, feeling excited. These feelings can reinforce violent behaviours. Therefore an important goal of DBT is to change the emotional response to those thoughts, images and fantasies.*

Actual DBT treatment

The responsibility for the application of DBT treatment is spread across different modes of therapy. The group skills facilitators are tasked with teaching skills to replace maladaptive or ineffective responses. The individual therapist is responsible for reducing high priority behaviours whilst integrating effective skills into the patient's repertoire. Individual therapists are also responsible for keeping the individual motivated and checking that they have attended group skills sessions and completed homework tasks. Patients receive a combination of group skills training and individual weekly therapy. Described below is an account of how an individual DBT session is conducted; the segment describes how the diary card is utilized to structure the session and demonstrates how the therapist applies DBT treatment interventions. Case formulation guides the interventions and the aim is that the therapist applies DBT strategies and techniques to the highest priority treatment target; the therapist has to decide where to focus the attention. What is presented on the patient's weekly diary card helps them examine where to start. For example, any behaviour in it that is high risk to self or others is targeted first, then therapy-interfering behaviour would be prioritized before quality of life issues. This structured approach helps the therapist to concentrate the session on treatment priorities rather than on what the patient thinks is important. Behavioural principles suggest that there are controlling variables to examine in each behavioural link, therefore the therapist explores thoughts, emotions and behavioural responses in great detail and considers whether the patient's response is effective or ineffective in the moment. Therefore the amount of time spent on an ineffective behaviour can span from a brief discussion to an in-depth analysis that requires a lot of work before being replaced by a more functional behaviour. In addition, the therapist must always elicit commitment from the individual to work on reducing ineffective behaviour.

How to structure an individual (agenda) session

Brian: Individual therapy session   The completed diary (see Figures 5.2 and 5.3) helps the therapist decide how to structure his session agenda and address priority behaviours. The therapist, in this instance, focuses on the point where Brian first noticed an urge to be violent. The therapist begins to examine each thought, emotion and action that prompted the urge. DBT solutions were woven into the chain to produce alternative strategies.

Brian: I scored (4) on urges to be violent, (4) on anger and (4) on paranoid thoughts.

Therapist: Can you think back to that particular situation and *describe* (mindfulness skills) when you first noticed an urge to be violent?

Brian: It happened so quickly. I was in a room with a few other patients having a chat when a patient walked into the room and said 'You're all a bunch of pricks'.

Therapist: *Describe* (mindfulness skill) your emotional reaction in that moment. What did you *observe*? E.g. heart pounding.

Brian: I noticed that my muscles tensed up and I began to stare back at him. I guess I was making lots of negative judgements about him and this increased my anger.

He went on to describe his emotional reaction. We also explored what thoughts were linked to that emotion.

		TUES	WED	THUR	FRI	SAT	SUN	MON
1.	Wise mind	TUES	(WED)	THUR	FRI	SAT	SUN	(MON)
2.	Observe : just notice	(TUES)	WED	THUR	(FRI)	SAT	(SUN)	(MON)
3.	Describe : put words on	TUES	WED	THUR	(FRI)	(SAT)	(SUN)	(MON)
4.	Participate : join in	TUES	WED	THUR	FRI	(SAT)	SUN	MON
5.	Non-judgemental stance	TUES	(WED)	THUR	FRI	SAT	(SUN)	MON
6.	One-mindfully : in-the-moment	TUES	WED	THUR	FRI	SAT	(SUN)	MON
7.	Effectiveness : focus on what works	(TUES)	WED	THUR	(FRI)	SAT	SUN	MON
8.	Objective effectiveness : DEAR MAN	TUES	WED	THUR	FRI	SAT	(SUN)	(MON)
9.	Relationship effectiveness : GIVE	(TUES)	WED	THUR	FRI	SAT	(SUN)	MON
10.	Self-respect effectiveness : FAST	(TUES)	WED	THUR	FRI	SAT	(SUN)	MON
11.	Reduce vulnerability : PLEASE	TUES	WED	THUR	FRI	(SAT)	SUN	MON
12.	Build MASTERY	TUES	WED	THUR	FRI	SAT	SUN	(MON)
13.	Build positive experiences	TUES	WED	(THUR)	FRI	SAT	SUN	MON
14.	Opposite to-mention action	TUES	WED	THUR	FRI	(SAT)	SUN	(MON)
15.	Distract	TUES	WED	(THUR)	FRI	(SAT)	SUN	MON
16.	Self-soothe	TUES	(WED)	THUR	FRI	SAT	SUN	MON
17.	Improve the moment	TUES	WED	THUR	FRI	SAT	SUN	MON
18.	Pros and cons	TUES	(WED)	THUR	FRI	SAT	SUN	MON
19.	Radical acceptance	TUES	WED	THUR	(FRI)	SAT	SUN	MON

Figure 5.2   Skills diary card

DIALECTICAL BEHAVIOUR THERAPY DIARY CARD   INITIALS: FILLED OUT IN SESSION? Y N

DATE DAY	Violent images		Conflict with others		Paranoid thoughts	Anxiety	Violent thoughts Y/N	Anger	Urges to hit out		Physical violence	Used skills
	Time	Specify	Time	Specify	(0–5)	(0–5)	(0–5)	(0–5)	Urges (0–5)	Action Yes/No	Action Yes/No	(0–7)
TUES			In the room	He called us a prick	4		4	4	4	No	No	0
WED	11pm	In Room			3	3	2	2	0	No	No	
THUR			Disagreement		2	2	0	0	0	No	No	
FRI					3	4	0	2	0	No	No	
SAT					1	1	0	1	0	No	No	
SUN				phoned home	3	3	0	2	0	No	No	
MON					1	2	0	0	0	No	No	

0 = Not thought about or used
1 = Thought about, not used, didn't want to
2 = Thought about, not used, wanted to
3 = Tried, but couldn't use them
4 = Tried, could do them but they didn't help
5 = Tried, could use them, helped
6 = Didn't try, used them, they didn't help
7 = Didn't try, used them, helped

URGE TO QUIT THERAPY (0–5): Before therapy session: ___0___   After therapy session: ___0___

Figure 5.3 An example of weekly diary card completed by Brian. Adapted from Linehan. M. (1993). *Cognitive behavioural treatment of borderline personality disorder*. The Guilford Press, New York, London.

Therapist: What emotion did you think this was?
Brian: Anger (recognizing and describing emotions).
Therapist: Was this the primary emotion or the secondary?
Brian: I think I was probably scared, I felt threatened, so I got angry.
Therapist: So how high do you think your anger was at this point, 0–5?
Brian: It was 4. I wanted to rip his head off, who the f … does he think he
                is talking to me like that?

The therapist would continue to examine the sets of behaviours. These include behavioural/cognitive/emotional and situational in order to analyse what thought was linked to which emotion, behaviour and vice versa. This process guides the selection of intervention in the moment. The behavioural analysis helps to determine what factors were instrumental in triggering and controlling his behaviour. Meanwhile the therapist will weave DBT skills and other interventions into the behavioural analysis to examine with Brian what skills he used, what worked well and then reinforce these. Attention has to be given to delivering multiple interventions in an organized way.

The session continued and the therapist focused on the urge to be violent and asked him what skills he used in that moment that helped and what hindered, whilst also examining skills to use in the moment.

The therapist went on to explore a cognitive approach in that moment.

Cognitive restructuring

Brian: I could change my thoughts, I suppose. I could think 'He's not
                talking personally about me' or 'He's not well today'.

The therapist troubleshoots the cognitive skills.

Therapist: Would this decrease your anger arousal?
Brian: No, it would probably 'wind me' up more. This approach wouldn't
                work for me when I'm angry. I get more and more thoughts and
                I wouldn't be able to just think differently, in this situation. My
                anger was too high.

The therapist explored the pros and cons (distress tolerance skill) of him applying cognitive strategies in that moment when his emotional arousal was high. We examined other alternative skills that he could use in the moment to decrease his emotional arousal to help him work out what to do next.

Brian: I need to get out of the situation, quick.
Therapist: Maybe? Would this mean that you would have to ask the person to
                move away from the door to let you through? If you imagine that
                scene, what do you see?
Brian: I see me head butting him.
Therapist: Is this a wise or skilful (mindfulness skill) option? Does this increase
                or decrease your emotional arousal in that moment? I wonder if we
                could explore other ways to get through this situation and practise
                the skills that you could use in that moment.

Behavioural responses to help reduce the urge to be violent

Brian: I could put my hands in my pocket. I've done that before. I sometimes imagine my Gran watching me from heaven. That brings me 'right down'. (Imagery and emotional regulation.) I could look away from him and take deep breaths and be one mindful. I also need to distract myself and look down, possibly at the floor, not straight at him. (Distress tolerance, crisis survival skills.)

Therapist: And this has been effective. If we explore this further and practise this in the session, we could examine these skills further, if this may help. I wonder if the thought that you may 'lose face' entered your mind?

The therapist recognized that intrusive thinking is stronger when individuals are emotionally aroused and does not judge, but encourages problem-solving skills. The goal is to encourage mindfulness skills that promote self-awareness in the moment. To notice those thoughts and to let them go without judgement and not to encourage their survival is key. A range of mindfulness, distress tolerance skills and emotional regulation skills would be rehearsed and practised just for that particular moment. The behavioural analysis would continue until the therapist was satisfied that the urge to be violent had been explored in enough breadth and depth and that enough skill had been strengthened sufficiently to be applied in the natural environment. It is against the DBT philosophy for the therapist to ignore behaviours that are targeted for change. The therapist continues to assess the patient's ability to apply skills to their environments. Some patients can appear competent whilst in the therapy session but cannot apply skills to real-life situations; it is important to not take things on face value.

Brian was in DBT for two and a half years and did not offend violently during that time. He continued his treatment and attended a violent offender treatment programme which focused on his past offending (Gordon & Wong, 2002). He is discharged from the hospital and is doing well in medium secure facilities. His substance misuse needs will be met by the medium secure service. Brian is now described as someone who can engage with others and initiate and maintain interesting conversation, he is friendly towards others and witty, and has an image of himself as a non-violent man and feels repulsed by the use of violence. He is still an anxious person and worries about minor ailments; however, he is able to recognize these signs and regulate himself appropriately. He appears to have a realistic view about his future and the difficulties he has yet to overcome.

Sequencing

The DBT skills are delivered in four modules starting with mindfulness skills (see Table 5.3). The sessions start with a mindfulness exercise followed by homework review. Each patient is expected to feed back their experience of applying the DBT skills to their own context. Each person has the same allocated time for feedback even if the person has not done any homework. If individuals have not completed their homework then the DBT facilitators will explore what happened; did they forget, attempt to do it, maybe they have not recognized that they have done some part of their homework. This is explored and facilitators help individuals to

Table 5.3 DBT modules content

Mindfulness skills	Psychological and behavioural versions of meditation. Enable individuals to observe, describe their thoughts, emotions and behaviours in a non-judgemental way.
Distress tolerance skills	Accepting, finding meaning for and tolerating distress without behaving or making the situation worse.
Emotion regulation skills	Learning to identify and label current emotions. Being able to express and regulate them effectively.
Interpersonal effectiveness skills	Ability to analyse a situation and to determine goals. Assertiveness and interpersonal problem-solving skills.

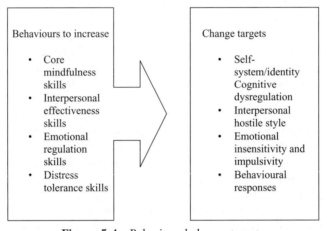

Figure 5.4 Behavioural change targets

examine what may help next time. Any effective skills utilized are reinforced positively.

Psychosocial skills are delivered in the four modules with the aim of increasing skilful behaviour and reducing maladaptive behaviours (see Figure 5.4).

Quality of life interfering behaviours

Once high risk behaviours are stabilized, quality of life behaviours can then be addressed. These are any kind of behaviours that interfere with daily living. These are wide ranging and can include substance misuse, offending behaviours, or financial debt. In the forensic setting the reduction of the risk of recidivism is interpreted as a quality of life issue in this context. This phase of work can begin when both the group and individual DBT component is complete and patients' high priority behaviours, e.g. violence, have stabilized for a period of approximately four months. This timescale is not fixed and clinical teams decide when it is appropriate for individuals to address other treatment needs. After DBT, patients usually then focus on addressing their past offending needs through offence-focused work such as the Violence Reduction Programme (VRP; Gordon &

Wong, 2002) and behaviours that may be linked to offending such as substance misuse (Orwin *et al.*, 2000) would be addressed at this stage. This work would be undertaken as a separate component to DBT; however, integration and reinforcement of the use of DBT skills is essential. Our experience to date shows that individuals who have not been in DBT and go straight into offence work often drop out of therapy due to their lack of coping skills. Offence work may take a further year before the person is able to move into stage two.

Stage two (trauma work)

If the clinical picture dictates and individuals still experience traumatic symptoms that impact significantly on their day-to-day life, then further treatment may help recovery. This stage of therapy normally occurs when first stage targets have decreased significantly, and the person has the ego strength and required skills such as mindfulness and distress tolerance skills to cope emotionally with the nature of this work. Therefore decreasing post-traumatic stress behaviours requires a more graded approach. Both Linehan (1993) and Livesley (2003a) recommend that treatment interventions that target trauma are used later on in the treatment hierarchy. This does not mean that trauma is ignored or invalidated in stage one as it will naturally surface during therapy; however, the therapist engages the person to apply a range of DBT skills to cope with distress rather than explore the trauma in depth. A range of treatment approaches can be utilized to address trauma (Foa, 1998; Ryle, 2002).

Stage 3 (relapse prevention)

Therapy in this phase might focus on creating conditions that empower individuals to make changes for themselves. Attention should be paid to progress that has been made whilst planning ahead for difficult times. Jones (2004) suggests it can be helpful to formulate individuals' offence paralleling behaviour; any behaviours that resemble in some significant way the sequence of behaviours leading up to the offence. These potential risk areas would inform the relapse prevention plan. The final phase employs approaches in the treatment of addictions and the relapse prevention model developed by Marlatt and Gordon (1985). Marlatt and Gordon recognized that many offenders relapse after the withdrawal of treatment. The relapse prevention model emphasizes the role of cognitive distortions and decision-making processes. In addition the relapse prevention model integrates nicely within a DBT framework and stresses the importance of coping behaviours. Again, principles of gaining commitment to the relapse plan whilst trouble-shooting potential barriers also complements a DBT approach.

A patient's perspective of receiving DBT: What can we learn as therapists?

In the early stage of therapy, patients often report that the therapy experience feels very negative. The specific identification and targeting of behaviours for change can appear daunting. The subsequent, in-depth functional analysis of problematic behaviours can be experienced at times as punitive or uncaring. However, in time, patients become adept at conducting 'chains' and bring them to the session for further exploration. It is important for the therapist not to detract from this process just for an easier life, or because they do not want to distress the patient.

Living in a high secure environment dictates that staff observe and report on patients' daily behaviour. This constant analysis feels intrusive and leaves patients feeling vulnerable and hopeless at times, as their behaviours are interpreted in particular ways. Even if behaviours displayed by patients are effective, staff can judge these behaviours as manipulative, thus leaving the individual confused as to how they can ever make any real change.

Concerns from patients about accurate recording on their diary card

There are several issues that therapists need to be aware of when working with patients in an in-patient forensic setting. Patients are expected as part of the therapy contract to maintain accurate records of their behaviours; these include images, urges, thoughts and actual violent episodes. These behaviours are examined in both the therapy session and, if necessary, by members of the patient's clinical team. Part of the contract negotiated is to report honestly and accurately specific behaviours. If patients report high scores on urges, or images of violence, for example, on their diary card, it is good practice for the therapist to cascade this information to the clinical team, in terms of risk management issues. The dialectical dilemma for the patient is whether to report honestly or not, and to work out the pros and cons of making a particular decision. It must be highlighted that when patients have disclosed risk issues, this can work against them, in terms of progression on from the hospital and on a day-to-day basis. It is therefore important for the therapist to work closely with both the patient and his clinical team, and to communicate regularly any new or different states of behaviour that may warrant increased concern. The dialectical dilemma for clinical teams centres on day-to-day risk and future risk.

The role of the DBT therapist is to consult with the patient rather than attempting to change or alter the environment. It can be extremely difficult to maintain this stance at times, as many factors can draw the therapist into rescuing or persecuting the patient. Many patients live chaotic lives and live in invalidating environments; the therapist can easily find themselves taking an active problem-solving role, rather than helping the patient to apply their own skills. Consulting with the patient helps the individual to take responsibility for themselves, whilst developing skills to help bring about change.

Conclusion

Complex presentations require a structured integrated response. Dialectical behaviour therapy draws from many treatment approaches and advocates that the therapist does what is needed at that particular moment. The dialectical emphasis enables both therapist and patient to look at what is being 'left out' and to explore other options. This is potentially liberating and validates the difficult nature of bringing about change.

Linehan (1993) recognizes that many individuals live in invalidating environments and that living conditions often counteract the therapy. Consulting to the patient helps to empower individuals and give them a survival 'tool kit' to cope with daily living. The therapy alone is not enough and individuals must be able to generalize their skills, particularly in high emotion situations. In this case vignette, the therapist has to consider the issue of risk of harm to others rather than to self. Therefore the ability of the individual to demonstrate that they can effectively apply a range of skills in different situations and locations is very important. Living in a high secure environment does not mirror life in the community; however, the therapist has a responsibility to create a range of dialectical dilemmas for the patient to solve.

References

Beck, A. T. & Steer, R. A. (1987). *Manual for the Beck Depression Inventory.* San Antonio, TX: The Psychological Corporation.

Beck, A. T. & Steer, R. A. (1988). *Manual for the Beck Hopelessness Scale.* San Antonio, TX: The Psychological Corporation.

Bernstein, E. M. & Putnam, F. W. (1986). Development, reliability, and validity of a dissociation scale. *Journal of Nervous & Mental Disease, 174,* 727–735.

Evershed, S. & Tennant, A. (2003). Practice based outcomes of dialectical behaviour therapy (DBT) targeting anger and violence, with male forensic patients: a pragmatic and non-contemporaneous comparison. *Criminal Behaviour and Mental Health, 13*(3), 198–213.

Foa, E. (1998). *Treating the trauma of rape: Cognitive–behavioural therapy for PTSD.* New York: Guilford Press.

Gordon, A. & Wong, S. C. P. (2002). *The violence reduction programme,* revised edition. Unpublished manual.

Heard, H. L. & Linehan, M. M. (1994). Dialectical behaviour therapy: An integrative approach to the treatment of borderline personality disorder. *Journal of Psychotherapy Integration, 4,* 55–82.

Hesslinger, B., Tebartz van Elst, L., Nyberg, E., Dykierek, P., Richter, H., Berner, M. *et al.* (2002). Psychotherapy of attention deficit hyperactivity disorder in adults: A pilot study using a structured skills training programme. *European Archives of Psychiatry and Clinical NeuroScience, 252,* 177–184.

Howells, K. & Tennant, A. (2007). Ready or not, they are coming: Dangerous and severe personality disorder and treatment engagement. *Issues in Forensic Psychology, 7,* 11–20.

Jones, L. F. (2004). Offence paralleling behaviour (OPB) as a framework for assessment and interventions with offenders. In A. Needs & G. Towel (Eds.), *Applying psychology to forensic practice.* Maldon: Blackwell Publishing.

Koerner, K. & Linehan, M. (1997). Case formulation in dialectical behaviour therapy for borderline personality disorder. In T. Eells (Ed.), *Handbook of psychotherapy case formulation* (pp. 340–367). New York: Guilford Press.

Koons, C. R. & Robins, C. J. *et al.* (2001). Efficacy of dialectical behaviour therapy in women veterans with borderline personality disorder. *Behaviour Therapy, 32,* 371–390.

Kroger, C., Schweiger, U., Sipos, V., Arnold, R., Kahl, K. G., Scunert, T. *et al.* (2006). Effectiveness of dialectical behaviour therapy for borderline personality disorder in an inpatient setting. *Behaviour Research and Therapy, 44,* 1211–1217.

Linehan, M. (1993). *Cognitive behavioural treatment of borderline personality disorder*. New York and London: Guilford Press.

Linehan, M. (2006). Randomised controlled trial and follow up of dialectical behaviour therapy vs. therapy by experts for suicidal behaviours and borderline personality disorder. *Archives of General Psychiatry, 63*, 757–766.

Linehan, M., Armstrong, H. E., Suarez, A., Allmon, D., Heard H. L. (1991). Cognitive-behavioral treatment of chronically parasuicidal borderline patients. *Archives of General Psychiatry, 48*, 1060–1064.

Linehan, M., Heard, H. & Armstrong, H. (1993). Naturalistic follow up of a behavioural treatment for chronically parasuicidal borderline patients. *Archives of General Psychiatry, 50*, 971–974.

Linehan, M. M., Tutek, D. A. *et al.* (1994). Interpersonal outcome of cognitive behavioural treatment for chronically suicidal borderline patients. *American Journal of Psychiatry, 151*, 1771–1776I.

Livesley, W. J. (2003a). *Practical management of personality disorder*. New York: Guilford Press.

Livesley, W. J. (2003b). *Handbook of personality disorders: Theory, research, and treatment*. New York and London: Guilford Press.

Lynch, T., Morse, J. Q., Mendelson, T. & Robins, C. J. (2003). Dialectical behaviour therapy for depressed older adults. *American Journal of Geriatric Psychiatry, 11*, 33–45.

Marlatt, G. A. & Gordon, J. R. (Eds.) (1985). *Relapse prevention: Maintenance strategies in the addictive behaviours*. New York: Guilford Press.

McCann, R. A., Ball, E. M. & Ivanoff, A. (2000). DBT with an inpatient forensic population: The CMHP forensic model. *Cognitive and Behavioural Practice, 7*, 447–456.

McMurran, M. & Ward, T. (2004). Motivating offenders to change in therapy: An organising framework. *Legal and Criminological Psychology, 9*, 295–311.

Orwin, R. G., Marannda, M. & Ellis, B. (2000). The effectiveness of substance abuse treatment in reducing violent behaviour. *Journal of Psychopathology & Behavioural Assessment, 22*(4), 309–324.

Ryle, A. (2002). *Introducing cognitive analytic therapy, principles and practice*. Chichester: Wiley.

Shingler, J. (2004). A process of cross-fertilization: What sex offender treatment can learn from dialectical behaviour therapy. *Journal of Sexual Aggression, 10*(2), 171–180.

Spielberger, C. D. (1996). *State-Trait Anger Expression Inventory: STAXI professional manual*. Toronto: Professional Assessment Resources, Inc.

Telch, C. F., Agras, W. S. & Linehan, M. M. (2001). Dialectical behaviour therapy for binge eating disorder. *Journal of Consulting and Clinical Psychology, 69*, 1061–1065.

Verheul, R., Van den Bossch, L. M. C., Koeter, M. W. J., de Ridder, M. A. J., Stijnen, T. & Van den Brink, W. (2003). Dialectical behaviour therapy for women with borderline personality disorder. *British Journal of Psychiatry, 182*, 135–140.

Ward, T. and Stewart, C. A. (2003). Criminogenic needs and human needs: A theoretical model. *Psychology, Crime and Law, 9*, 125–143.

Whiteside, S. P. & Lynam, D. R. (2001). The Urgency, Premeditation, Perseverance, Sensation Seeking (UPPS) impulsive behaviour scale. The five factor model and impulsivity: Using a structural model of personality to understand impulsivity. *Personality and Individual Differences, 30*, 669–689.

Wong, S. C. P. (2000). Violence reduction programme. Participant workbook. Unpublished Manuscript.

Young, J. E., Klosko, J. S. & Weishar, M. E. (2003). *Schema therapy: A practitioner's guide*. New York: Guilford Press.

Chapter Six

Cognitive Analytic Therapy (CAT): A Treatment Approach for Treating People with Severe Personality Disorder

Jackie Withers

This chapter will describe the use of cognitive analytic therapy (CAT) with high risk offenders who also have severe personality disorders. Clinical examples will be used to describe the application of CAT to this client group. As yet there is no standard treatment for individuals with personality disorder and no one treatment has been shown to be superior over any other (Bateman & Fonagy, 1999). The prevailing view for many years has been that personality disorder is not treatable but in recent years a number of therapies have been found to be of value in reducing behavioural, emotional and cognitive difficulties related to personality disorder. Borderline personality disorder (BPD) has received most research attention; however, the issue of 'treatability' remains controversial and is particularly so for those with forensic histories.

Introducing CAT

CAT was developed by Ryle (1982). As the name suggests, it is an integration of cognitive and psychoanalytic theories. As such, it draws on a broad theoretical base and has developed into a sophisticated theory of personality functioning and dysfunction. Despite this, CAT is an accessible model to many clinicians. Therapists come from all mental health disciplines but its practice does require additional formal training. Its application is based on individualized formulation and it is not a manualized treatment. Leiman (1992) integrated Vygotskian (1978) and Bakhtinian (1986) ideas into CAT theory, emphasizing the social nature of development, and how what occurs between the caregiver and infant becomes internalized as a representation of self in relation to others (Leiman, 1992). CAT has developed from an integration of psychoanalytic and cognitive approaches to become an interpersonal therapy based on a radical social concept of self (Ryle & Kerr, 2002). Interpersonal experience is seen as central to the development of self. This socially constructed 'self' is consistent with the evidence for the so-called 'non-specifics' of effective treatments. From a CAT perspective these 'non-specifics' are potentially understandable, predictable, central and specific.

The therapy has grown out of clinical practice, and draws on a wide source of empirical evidence. The multiple self-states model of personality dysfunction was proposed by Ryle (1997). The model evolved in response to difficulties encountered in understanding and formulating complex cases. Livesley (2003) developed a model for the treatment of severe personality disorder and emphasized the need to intervene across different domains, e.g. symptomatic, situational, regulatory, dispositional, interpersonal and the self system. CAT has the potential to address difficulties across all of these domains, but in relation to treating complex cases, a strength may be its explicit focus on the self system and interpersonal system.

Bateman and Fonagy (1999, 2004) emphasized the development of 'mentalization' as core to treatment, i.e. the capacity to think and interpret the actions of self and others as meaningful, with the development of a more robust sense of self being the basis of more secure relationships. When applied to complex cases a focus of CAT is the development of a self-reflective capacity, i.e. the capacity to reflect on the actions of self in relation to others.

Ryle (1982) identified a small number of themes present in persons presenting for therapy. These patterns, termed procedures, were described as traps, snags and dilemmas. In traps, negative beliefs and assumptions generate behaviours that provoke consequences that seem to confirm dysfunction beliefs and maintain the problem. Snags refer to appropriate goals being given up or undone, either in the belief that others will oppose the goals or as if the goals are forbidden. Dilemmas are options for behaving that have become dichotomized between polarized choices, each of which are restrictive or harmful in some way. These three patterns were linked in a general model of aim-directed behaviour called the procedural sequence model (PSM; Ryle, 1982). Psychoanalytic ideas were explicit, with attention to transference and countertransference issues. As the theory developed, the notion of procedure from the PSM extended, to include how procedures concerned with relationships involve the prediction or elicitation of the response of the other. The PSM developed into the PSORM and integrated ideas from Object Relations theory, the OR added to the PSM (Ogden, 1983). Reciprocal roles evolved into the construct which conceptualizes internalized representations of experience, which explain interpersonal and intrapersonal relationships.

From a CAT perspective, all problematic behaviours are viewed as reciprocal role procedures, and reciprocal roles drive both interpersonal and intrapersonal ways of behaving, thinking and feeling, i.e. self-management and relationship management. For example, the consequence of controlling behaviour from a significant caregiver would be an internalization of this experience as a controlling to controlled reciprocal role. Thus a person may develop a controlling manner with others and/or end up in relationships with controlling others. In terms of efforts to self-manage emotion this pattern may manifest as a symptom such as an eating disorder. Role procedures are maintained by the continuing elicitation from others of expected confirmatory reciprocations. In enacting a role there is a pressure on the other to reciprocate in a particular way. Consistent with Stern's (1985) attachment theory it is assumed that an individual's repertoire of reciprocal roles are acquired during early interactions, i.e. they are learned and expressed in relation to others with their origin in early relationships with caregivers.

Reciprocal roles that have been internalized form the basis of personality and, as stated above, are the source of both interpersonal and intrapersonal patterns of responding, i.e. patterns of thinking, feeling and acting in relation to self and others (Ryle, 1997). CAT does acknowledge biological predispositions toward developing difficulties but psychopathology is viewed as primarily arising from trauma and deprivation (Ryle & Kerr, 2002).

Vygotsky's (1978) activity theory is influential within CAT and explains the process of internalization. The work of Bakhtin was introduced by Leiman emphasizing the dialogic nature of the development of personality. An additional Vygotskian concept integrated into CAT is the 'zone of proximal development'. As applied by Vygotsky to child development this refers to the mother relating to the child ahead of current development but within a zone of development, i.e. the parent or teacher should not be too far ahead of the child's level of functioning. Ryle (1995) suggests therapy and the therapist should remain within the client's zone of proximal personality development throughout the therapeutic encounter.

CAT's developmental account has similarities to attachment models but differs in its Vygotskian aspects (Ryle, 1997). Early attachment relationships with caretakers are seen as the precursor of the full range of emotionally significant interactions including self-processes, e.g. self-reflection and coping with emotion. Stern's (1985) concept of attunement and development via the representation of interactions that have been generalized is consistent with CAT theory. Reciprocal roles may be further elaborated and integrated during childhood and adolescence but the initial reciprocal role patterns are viewed as robust and therefore resistant to change. Confirmation of problematic patterns occurs and reinforces the patterns of behaviour which are described as traps, snags and dilemmas (Ryle, 1997). Thus much individual behaviour can be understood as being constrained by the particular, restricted options perceived to be available to the individual.

Evidence base

As stated above, CAT has grown out of clinical practice and draws on a wide source of empirical evidence. For example, it is supported by observational and experimental studies of infants (Stern, 1985; Trevarthan, 1993; Vygotsky, 1978). Its theoretical base began with Kelly (1955) and draws on object relations theory (Ogden, 1983), and Leiman (1992, 1997) integrated the work of Vygotsky and Bakhtin. As such, CAT has developed into an interpersonal therapy that offers a focused approach to working with a wide range of complex clinical presentations (Ryle & Kerr, 2002).

There is growing support for the effectiveness of CAT and there are ongoing randomized control trials. In addition, there are a number of studies which have evaluated specific aspects of the CAT model; see Ryle and Kerr (2002) for a review. Of relevance to this chapter is support for the self-state model of personality disorder (Golynkina & Ryle, 1999; Ryle & Marlowe, 1995; Pollock, 1996, 2001). There are also a number of published case studies presenting the effectiveness of CAT with a wide range of clinical presentations (Cowmeadow, 1994; Fosbury *et al.*, 1997; Pollock, 1997, 2001), and CAT has been applied within forensic settings (Pollock, 1997; Pollock *et al.*, 2006). Of relevance to forensic clients, Pollock (1996, 1997) found support for the state shifts predicted from the self-states model of BPD; in particular the discussion focused on disavowed victim 'states' following aggressive acts, and the frequency of dissociative experiences reported before, during and after the offences. Thus CAT offers a comprehensive theoretical model which can explain a broad range of complex clinical presentations. The theoretical model is empirically derived and the evidence base has increased over the past 15 years.

Reciprocal roles and the self-state model are of particular relevance to working with forensic populations. Many therapeutic approaches emphasize either the perpetrator or victim experience of the offender but CAT explicitly incorporates both. This can enhance the possibility of increasing the client's sense of an integrated self but also (if the model is worked with by the team) can reduce the risk of staff splitting.

CAT therapy

A major aim of Ryle (1982) was to develop a therapy that could be applicable within the NHS. CAT has a collaborative style and is time-limited. The time limit originated from the pressures within the NHS to treat many clients. The time limit has become an essential component of the therapy, and is considered of particular importance when working with complex cases and when a history of rejection and abandonment has often occurred (Ryle & Kerr, 2002). For less serious presentations CAT is delivered in 16 (sometimes eight) once-weekly sessions with a follow-up after three months. More complex presentations are more often treated with 24 or 32 sessions and a longer period of follow-up is offered.

Ryle (1991) has referred to the three Rs of CAT therapy, i.e. reformulation, recognition and revision. Reformulation refers to the therapist drawing together the information gathered during early sessions and presenting this to the client in the form of a letter, that explains the development of the presenting problems in terms of significant events from their life history. Problematic patterns of behaviour (procedures in CAT terms) are represented as an attempt by the client to cope with their life experience. The reformulation letter goes on to state how the client's problematic behaviour may be enacted within therapy. It also names the therapeutic aims and the time-limited nature of the therapy and how this may impact on the therapeutic alliance.

The reformulation is also presented in diagrammatic form. This diagram, which is developed collaboratively between the client and therapist, is used throughout the therapy and is an essential tool of therapy when working with the client. The diagram is particularly useful when working with complex presentations associated with personality disorder, and specifically when there is a shifting clinical presentation. The diagram acts as a map and is a heuristic device which aids self-observation. It enables the therapist and client to recognize where they are, in terms of the reciprocal role enactments, and to work with therapeutic ruptures between the therapist and client. It can assist both in a client's awareness of currently dissociated aspects of their personality and in their obtaining control over switches between dissociated aspects of their personality.

An overall aim of therapy with complex presentations is the development of a more integrated sense of self and modification of problematic procedures or behavioural patterns. For example, when working with persons who have been aggressive but also have a history of abuse, a therapeutic aim is likely to be the integration of self both as a perpetrator and victim. When there is a clear target problem, e.g. anger, and the client is motivated to address this, then a CAT approach may have similarities with a CBT (cognitive behaviour therapy) approach but the chain of behaviour would be represented as a trap, dilemma or snag, and the client's reciprocal roles, driving the presenting procedures or problematic patterns, would inform the therapy and the therapeutic alliance.

In the middle phase of therapy, a wide range of therapeutic techniques may be used but the focus is on the recognition and revision of problematic patterns of behaving and relating to others. In the middle phase of therapy, the major task is to provide a non-collusive relationship which is focused on collaboratively agreed target problems. The diagrammatic formulation is a tool to assist with identifying reciprocal role enactments and is central to this task (Ryle & Kerr, 2002). A wide range of therapeutic techniques can be incorporated into CAT including, for example, cognitive-behavioural skills training, exposure-based assignments, gestalt techniques and cognitive restructuring. However, retaining the focus on the target problems identified at the start of therapy and the CAT formulation, within the context of a non-collusive therapeutic relationship, is the overarching goal.

Termination of therapy is emphasized and worked towards from the beginning. At the final or penultimate session, the therapist and client exchange goodbye letters. These letters are a method of reviewing the therapy, highlighting areas of further work and reflecting on the experience of termination of therapy (Ryle & Kerr, 2002). The goodbye letter represents a means of realistic appraisal of the therapy, naming what has been achieved and what has not been achieved; it allows the expression of disappointment, relief, sadness or anger about the ending, and raises issues of concern. The client is also invited to write a goodbye letter reviewing their therapeutic experience. Thus termination of therapy is on the therapeutic agenda from the start of therapy. Clients with histories of neglect, abandonment or rejection are likely to find the time limit difficult, but dealing with an ending and the threats to the therapeutic alliance is an aim of the therapy and is actively addressed within therapy (Bennett, 1998; Safran & Muran, 2000).

CAT model of personality disorder

CAT does not offer a theory of a specific disorder; it is a comprehensive theory that can explain both normal and abnormal functioning. The CAT 'self-states' model of BPD was proposed by Ryle (1997). This model evolved in response to difficulties encountered in understanding and formulating complex and shifting clinical presentations. Under normal circumstances, individuals move flexibly between their array of reciprocal role procedures in response to situational demands. The array of reciprocal role patterns consists of largely mutually compatible procedures, and transitions between them are smooth and appropriate. The CAT self-states model suggests that a client's experience will be identified with a role combining memory, affect and action. The experience of different states of mind is normal but with persons with, for example, BPD, sudden shifts between 'self-states' represent a dominance by a limited range of contrasting role patterns. Abrupt changes between 'self-states' are confusing and discomforting to the individual and others involved with him or her. Such abrupt changes may reflect role reversals or response shifts. The most disturbing pattern is when apparently unprovoked and inappropriate shifts to a different reciprocal role pairing occurs. A 'self-state' may be more or less dissociated from other 'self-states' (Ryle & Kerr, 2002).

'Self-states' are internalized reciprocal role procedures that represent more or less fragmented parts of the self. When a person has a personality disorder these different 'self-states' may be more or less fragmented. Three forms of damage are described in relation to personality disorder: harsh reciprocal role patterns, partial dissociation, and impaired or disrupted self-reflection. A 'self-state' may be experienced as either pole of a reciprocal role (Ryle & Kerr, 2002). The quality and range of reciprocal roles and level of integration is thought to be indicative of the level of psychopathology. Splitting is viewed as a failure to integrate, that continues because of an absence of a central self-observing capacity (Ryle, 1997). The 'reciprocal' nature of reciprocal roles results in the person with a personality disorder repeatedly eliciting confirmatory (of their dysfunctional personality organization and problematic behaviour) responses that can be extreme; this also explains some of the powerful, and at times negative, reactions of staff to this client group (Ryle, 1994).

Case example 1

Figure 6.1 represents the self-states described by a forensic client, assessed as meeting criteria for detention within a unit for persons with dangerous and severe personality disorder (DSPD).

This particular client met criteria for five personality disorders. As stated above, under normal circumstances individuals shift between different facets of personality which are not massively dissonant. The self-states model captures extreme shifts in clinical presentation. Clients with severely damaged personalities may present a fragmented sense of self which includes extreme shifts. The client may enact only one pole of a reciprocal role as a state and present as if this is the only pole known to him/her. Subjective experience is seemingly determined primarily by one self-state at a time. A shift in 'self-state' represents a shift in state of being, with each characterized by different thoughts, behaviours and emotions. A 'self-state' is a subjective experience of a particular role. A full state shift involves a shift to a different reciprocal role. Thus switches may occur as a shift to another reciprocal role or role reversals. Such clinical presentations are often accompanied by narrative incompetence, with an impaired capacity for self-reflection. Presentations typically

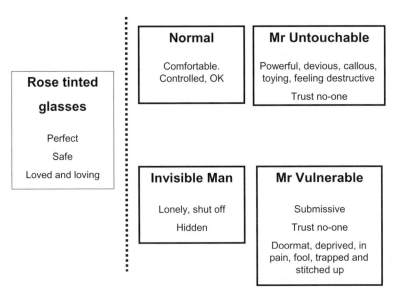

Figure 6.1 The self-states

include abrupt switches which may be observed as discontinuous behaviours. These clinical presentations are bewildering for the client and those relating to them.

The case represented in Figure 6.1 described five 'self-states'. His clinical presentation included extreme shifts. The 'Rose Tinted' state represents his ideal state where everything is perfect. What he describes as 'OK', on further exploration was an overly controlled state. 'Invisible Man' represents a state in which he feels alone and irrelevant and which he experiences as intolerable. The 'Mr Untouchable' state is often triggered from 'Invisible Man', but the client was not aware of triggers for state shifting prior to the CAT therapy. 'Mr Untouchable' and 'Mr Vulnerable' represent opposite poles of a punishing/abusing to abused/punished reciprocal role. The words he used to describe these states are striking and give a sense of the extremity of his presentation at these times, which were aggressive and sadistic versus intensely vulnerable respectively. The 'Mr Vulnerable' state, like 'Invisible Man', was experienced by him as intolerable and if he could not regain a sense of control then the likelihood of aggression increased.

This model assists by providing a coherent description of the client's presentation. Different ways of responding are likely to be effective, depending on which aspect of the client was dominant at a given time. An overall aim is to assist the client to keep in mind the different aspects of himself, i.e. when he feels 'normal' and 'in control' there are also very vulnerable and aggressive parts to him which require attention, and also to encourage dialogue about the different states. This approach can be containing for the client, therapist and potentially the treating team. The gradual increase in understanding by both the therapist and client about what triggers shifts from state to state engages the client with the therapeutic process and promotes the maintenance of the therapeutic alliance. The description of self-states as shown in Figure 6.1 is built upon to include the core reciprocal roles underpinning each self-state. Reciprocal roles are identified from the client's description of their experience, their presenting behaviour, the therapist's countertransference reaction and the client's history. The reciprocal roles assist the therapist, and eventually the client, to predict and understand therapeutic ruptures and the transference relationship, i.e. termed reciprocal role enactments within CAT.

The aim of therapy when a client is presenting in the way represented in Figure 6.1 is to contain, make sense and engage the client, i.e. it is likely to be very early in a client's treatment pathway. The client represented in Figure 6.1 completed 24 sessions of CAT with these aims. He then went on (following a break in therapy with a different therapist) to complete a second contract of CAT where the map, or diagrammatic formulation, included reciprocal roles and the mapping of problematic patterns of behaviour, and more directly focused on self-monitoring and changing behaviour, i.e. developed formulation, recognition and the beginning of revision. He then went on to dialectical behaviour therapy (DBT) where the focus was maintaining his commitment to change with regard to appropriate treatment goals and the development of coping skills. It is suggested that only then would the client be likely to be stable enough to engage with, and benefit from, specific offence-focused programmes and possibly trauma therapy.

Contextual reformulation and generalization issues

The organizational context, within which therapy is delivered, can include complex dynamics. Main (1957) talked of 'the ailment' to describe the unconscious processes operating in psychiatric hospitals and their effects on staff. Systemic or psychoanalytic theories have most often been used to understand team processes. Persons who have personality disorders often evoke strong reactions in others. These strong reactions seem to inhibit reflective thinking and have a negative impact on the reactions of staff (Bion, 1962). When working with personality disorder, Ryle and Kerr (2002) emphasize the importance of replacing reactive practice with reflected-upon responding. The utility of CAT as a method of conceptualizing complex cases, which can aid understanding of the reactions of teams to their clients, is a developing area within CAT (Dunn & Parry, 1997; Kerr, 1999; Walsh, 1996). Such an approach attempts to understand team reactions as reciprocal role enactments. A diagrammatic formulation can help the team understand their reactions, aid reflective practice and inform coordinated care plans. A CAT formulation can be used to guide general care planning so that formulations can be applied to case management. In this way, continuity of care is promoted, based on client need, which is non-collusive in terms of replicating and maintaining problematic patterns of behaviour. Thus CAT has a utility as a means of conceptualizing cases and guiding the ordering and timing of treatments.

CAT and the therapeutic alliance

A major strength of CAT is the way the model can explicitly inform the therapeutic alliance. This is particularly important given that positive outcome from psychotherapy has been found to be associated with a good therapeutic alliance (Luborsky & Auerbach, 1985). From a CAT perspective, as in other interpersonal psychotherapies, the focus of therapy is the interpersonal context of therapy as a significant vehicle for change (Benjamin, 1996; Leary, 1957). There is extensive evidence to support the importance of the therapeutic alliance as a robust predictor of treatment success. A general consensus is emerging that negative process within therapy and ruptures within the therapeutic alliance are inevitable, but that an important therapeutic skill consists of dealing therapeutically with this process via repair of the rupture (Bennett, 1998; Safran & Muran, 2000; Ryle & Kerr, 2002). It has been stated that a good therapeutic alliance is a prerequisite for change in all forms of psychotherapy (Bordin, 1979; Luborsky, 1976). Clients who have a personality disorder may have a general mistrust of others and this is likely to be enacted with mental health professionals and this general distrust is likely to interfere with constructive engagement (Livesley, 2003; Ryle & Kerr, 2002).

Exploration of what is occurring within specific interactions within a therapeutic relationship can lead to a working through of core relational themes (Bennett, 1998; Ryle & Kerr, 2002; Safran, 1993; Safran & Muran, 2000). Analytic therapy emphasizes transference and countertransference exploration but would usually view an alliance as a precondition that makes exploration of the transference possible. Cognitive behaviour therapists view a therapeutic alliance as a precondition to the tasks of therapy. However, when working with clients with personality disorder, the severe interpersonal problems can be so disruptive that building the alliance is possibly an important therapeutic task in its own right, and a model which explicitly addresses this can inform the therapeutic process. CAT, and specifically reciprocal roles, assists the therapist's work with the therapeutic relationship. Thus CAT is an interpersonal therapy which explicitly addresses difficulties in developing and maintaining a therapeutic alliance. Also CAT's contextual reformulation is a useful approach to manage team splitting. Thus it is a model to understand, predict and intervene at a level which can help to reduce collusive and iatrogenic interventions by individual staff and teams, and therefore promote positive change.

Furthermore, Bateman and Fonagy (2004) have stated that the most effective therapy for persons with personality disorders should be well structured, enhance compliance and be clearly focused. It should also have a theoretical coherence for the therapist and client, encourage a powerful attachment relationship, and be well integrated with other services available to the client. In general, treatments need to attend to engaging the client and keeping them engaged (Bateman & Fonagy, 2004; Rawlings, 2001). CAT is a model which explicitly attends to all of these aspects of the therapeutic task.

CAT is not unusual as a psychological therapy which emphasizes active collaboration, i.e. the client is required to participate actively and not be a passive recipient of therapy (Beck *et al.*, 1990; Linehan, 1993; Ryle, 1991; Young, 1994). The importance of interpersonal difficulties threatening a therapeutic alliance is a challenge. Possibly the most challenging client group are those persons classified as having significant 'psychopathic' traits. Blackburn (1998) conceptualized 'psychopathy' in interpersonal terms and it is likely that, if a therapeutic approach is going to be effective with this population, then a therapy which explicitly addresses interpersonal difficulties may be promising.

CAT's explicit collaborative style, tools and structure (for example, prose and diagrammatic reformulation) can assist a therapist to address resistance in a non-confrontational way which can enhance active participation with the therapy and address responsivity problems. The CAT model is a useful way to link problems that are inside a client's awareness with those that are outside of their awareness. Reciprocal roles provide a tool to make sense, predict difficulties and work with the relationship. They are the construct through which transference and counter-transference are understood. Indeed, it is the inevitability of ruptures to the alliance and how these are resolved which are often seen as the central therapeutic task with the overall aim being not to collude with the client's problematic inter-personal patterns while remaining within the client's zone of proximal development.

Explaining the rationale for therapy is likely to be necessary for active engage-ment. CAT focuses on jointly agreed treatment targets between the therapist and client. Reframing the meaning of therapeutic tasks in terms that are acceptable to the client is a joining intervention used by strategic and systemic approaches (Minuchin & Fishman, 1981). CAT's reformulation process serves this function. It provides a narrative for the client about how their problems have developed, are maintained and may interfere with therapeutic progress.

Case example 2

The following reciprocal roles (Figure 6.2) represent the experience of another client who met DSPD criteria, and who was assessed as having a PCL-R (Psychopathy Checklist – Revised) score over 30. This client had not previously fully engaged with therapy. He had appealed against his section, claiming he was untreatable. In terms of previous treatments, he referred to a few drug counsellors who did not help and he 'sat through' a reasoning and rehabilitation programme. He reported that, at times, he had enjoyed the programme but he was never actively engaged in attempting to change.

Reciprocal roles are described as originating in early life experience, and, as an organizing construct, determining patterns of relationships and self-management. In reciprocal role terms, playing a role always implies another person or the inter-nalized voice of another. It is suggested that both ends of the reciprocal role are

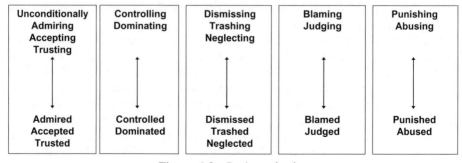

Figure 6.2   Reciprocal roles

always learnt. Therefore a victim of abuse learns both the abusing and abused poles. This does not imply all victims of abuse become abusers. Maintenance of reciprocal roles is via continued elicitation of expected confirmatory reciprocations. In enacting a role there is a pressure on the other to reciprocate. Transference and countertransference are understood in reciprocal role terms, with projective identification viewed as a particular form of reciprocal role procedure (Ryle, 1994). The client's early history was dominated by experiences of neglect and abuse (physical, emotional and sexual). During childhood there were substantial periods in care and, as an adult, much of his life has been in prison and, more recently, a secure hospital.

The totally admiring, accepting and trusting reciprocal role represents an ideal which the client strives for but relationships inevitably fail to come up to standard and he inevitably feels let down. The controlling to controlled reciprocal role is a frequent aspect of his presentation. He presents as over-controlled much of the time, and interpersonally can be very domineering and controlling. Thus others are expected to come up to high standards and, if challenged, then battles for control are likely. If a person who does not come up to his standards challenges him then he becomes trashing/contemptuous and blaming. Failings are (blamed) harshly and there is a high probability of the client feeling trashed/contemptible or the other feeling this way. The punishing/abusing to punished is avoided much of the time but there is a sense of extreme aggression. The client describes the controlling behaviour as a defence against being a victim; if this fails, then faced with a perceived threat, he attempts to stay at the powerful end of the blaming and trashing, but if the threat continues, then he will become aggressive, acting out murderous rage to avoid the victim position.

It is likely that a therapist will need to be idealized to form an initial alliance but the overall task of therapy is to provide a non-collusive relationship which, it is assumed, will be emotionally corrective. Having the reciprocal roles explicitly named allows the interpersonal enactments, which occur both within the therapy and in everyday relationships, to be more readily accessible as a therapeutic target.

Summary

In summary, CAT is a structured, focused and time-limited therapy. It can bring into awareness aspects of a person's difficulties that may have been outside of their awareness. It has components that are explicitly psychoeducational but does not reduce a therapeutic process to a didactic teaching session, and it is not deliverable as a manualized programme by clinicians without well-developed therapeutic skills. The reformulation process provides a narrative for the client of how difficulties have developed, why they are maintained, and blocks to progress. As such it is a process which promotes engagement and containment. CAT is collaborative in style and always individualized. It can be used at any stage of a treatment process, as its focus will depend on the stage of treatment. It can be integrated with other, particularly group CBT therapies, for example, individual CAT alongside skills training such as a DBT group (not full DBT), a substance misuse group or offence-focused group. Multiple therapists working with competing, and at worst incompatible, case formulations should be avoided as this is likely to lead to the staff group enacting the clients' pathology, thus maintaining or even increasing their difficulties. CAT has been applied to couples and groups, and is consistent with therapeutic community approaches.

CAT, like many therapies, emphasizes the importance of a therapeutic alliance and aims to help clients change how they experience, make sense of, and manage their lives. The importance of structuring interventions in a way that provides the person with a severe personality disorder with safety and containment, then addressing issues of control and regulation, i.e. providing stabilization of chaotic behaviour, and then moving toward further exploration and integration, has been emphasized (Linehan, 1993; Livesley, 2003). It is suggested that CAT is not only a psychotherapy that focuses on the therapeutic alliance between therapist and client; it can also target difficulties in relation to the management of emotion and behaviour, sense of self, and interpersonal relationships. It also assists clinicians' ability to be reflective practitioners. A CAT formulation can provide a structure that is containing for the care team, can inform care planning (contextual formulation), inform treatment priorities and facilitate a continuity of care. Thus CAT can be one of a range of therapies offered to a person with a severe personality disorder or it can play a central role in guiding an integrated approach to treatment. As the former, it is one of a number of promising treatments; as the latter, it offers a case conceptualization which captures personality and a range of problem areas, and has added benefit over many approaches.

References

Bakhtin, M. M. (1986). *Speech genres and other late essays.* Austin, TX: University of Texas Press.

Bateman, A. W. & Fonagy, P. (1999). The effectiveness of partial hospitalization in the treatment of borderline personality disorder – A randomized controlled trial. *American Journal of Psychiatry, 156*, 1563–1569.

Bateman, A. W. & Fonagy, P. (2004). *Psychotherapy for borderline personality disorder: Mentalization-based treatment.* Oxford: Oxford University Press.

Beck, A. T., Freeman, A. & Associates (1990). *Cognitive therapy for personality disorders.* New York: Guilford Press.

Benjamin, L. S. (1996). *Interpersonal diagnosis and treatment of personality disorder.* New York: Guilford Press.

Bennett, D. (1998). *Deriving a model of therapist competence from good and poor outcome cases in the psychotherapy of borderline personality disorder.* Unpublished doctoral thesis. University of Sheffield.

Bion, W. R. (1962). *Learning from experience.* New York: Basic Books.

Blackburn, R. (1998). Psychopathy and personality disorder: Implications of interpersonal theory. In D. J. Cooke, S. J. Hart & A. E. Forth (Eds.), *Psychopathy: Theory, research and implications for society* (pp. 269–301). Amsterdam: Kluwer.

Bordin, E. (1979). The generalizability of the psychoanalytic concept of the working alliance. *Psychotherapy: Theory, Research and Practice, 16*, 252–260.

Cowmeadow, P. (1994). Deliberate self-harm and cognitive analytic therapy. *International Journal of Short-Term Psychotherapy, 9*(2/3), 135–150.

Dunn, M. & Parry, G. (1997). A formulated care plan approach to caring for people with borderline personality disorder in a community mental health setting. *Clinical Psychology Forum, 104*, 19–22.

Fosbury, J. A., Bosley, C. M., Ryle, A., Sonkson, P. H. & Judd, S. L. (1997). A trial of cognitive analytic therapy in poorly controlled Type 1 patients. *Diabetes Care, 20,* 959–964.

Golynkina, K. & Ryle, A. (1999). The identification and characteristics of the partially dissociated states of patients with borderline personality disorder. *British Journal of Medical Psychology, 72,* 429–445.

Kelly, G. A. (1955). *The psychology of personal constructs.* New York: Norton.

Kerr, I. B. (1999). Cognitive analytic therapy for borderline personality disorder in the context of a community mental health team: individual and organisational psychodynamic implications. *British Journal of Psychotherapy, 15,* 425–438.

Leary, T. (1957). *Interpersonal diagnosis of personality.* New York: Ronald Press.

Leiman, M. (1992). The concept of sign in Vygotsky, Winnicott and Bakhtin: Further integration of object relations theory and activity theory. *British Journal of Medical Psychology, 65,* 209–221.

Leiman, M. (1997). Procedures as dialogic sequences: A revised version of the fundamental concept in cognitive analytic therapy. *British Journal of Medical Psychology, 70,* 193–207.

Linehan, M. M. (1993). *Cognitive-behavioural treatment of personality disorder.* New York: Guilford Press.

Livesley, W. J. (2003). *Practical management of personality disorder.* New York: Guilford Press.

Luborsky, L. (1976). Helping alliance in psychotherapy. In J. L. Claghorn (Ed.), *Successful psychotherapy* (pp. 92–116). New York: Brunner/Mazel.

Luborsky, L. L. & Auerbach, A. H. (1985). The therapeutic relationship in psychodynamic psychotherapy: The research evidence and its meaning in practice. In R. E. Hales & A. J. Frances (Eds.), *Annual Review,* Volume 4. Washington DC: American Psychiatric Press.

Main, T. F. (1957). The ailment. *British Journal of Medical Psychology, 30*(3), 129–145.

Minuchin, S. & Fishman, H. C. (1981). *Family therapy techniques.* Cambridge, MA: Harvard University Press.

Ogden, T. H. (1983). The concept of internal object relations. *International Journal of Psychoanalysis, 64,* 227–241.

Pollock, P. (1996). Clinical issues in the cognitive analytic therapy of sexually abused women who commit violent offences against their partners. *British Journal of Medical Psychology, 69,* 117–127.

Pollock, P. (1997). CAT of an offender with borderline personality disorder. In A. Ryle (Ed.), *Cognitive analytic therapy and borderline personality disorder: The model and the method.* Chichester: John Wiley & Sons.

Pollock, P. H. (2001). *Cognitive analytic therapy for adult survivors of childhood sexual abuse: Approaches to treatment and case management.* Chichester: Wiley.

Pollock, P. H., Stowell-Smith, M. & Gopfert, M. (2006). *Cognitive analytic therapy for offenders: A new approach to forensic psychotherapy.* London: Routledge.

Rawlings, B. (2001). Therapeutic communities for the treatment of drug users. In B. Rawlings and R. Yates (Eds). *Evaluative research in therapeutic communities,* Chapter 12. London: Jessica Kingsley.

Ryle, A. (1982). *Psychotherapy: A cognitive integration of theory and practice.* London: Academic Press.

Ryle, A. (1991). *Cognitive analytic therapy: Active participation in change.* Chichester: John Wiley & Sons.

Ryle, A. (1994). Projective identification: A particular form of reciprocal role procedure. *British Journal of Medical Psychology, 67,* 107–114.

Ryle, A. (1995). *Cognitive analytic therapy: Developments in theory and practice*. Chichester: Wiley.

Ryle, A. (1997). *Cognitive analytic therapy and borderline personality disorder: The model and the method*. Chichester: John Wiley & Sons.

Ryle, A. & Kerr, I. B. (2002). *Introducing cognitive analytic therapy: Principles and practice*. Chichester: John Wiley & Sons.

Ryle, A. & Marlowe, M. (1995). Cognitive analytic therapy of borderline personality disorder: Theory and practice and the clinical and research uses of self states SDR. *International Journal of Short-term Psychotherapy, 10*, 21–34.

Safran, J. D. (1993). Breaches in the therapeutic alliance: An arena for negotiating authentic relatedness. *Psychotherapy: Theory, Research and Practice, 30*, 11–24.

Safran, J. D. & Muran, J. C. (2000). *Negotiating the therapeutic alliance: A relational treatment guide*. New York: Guilford Press.

Stern, D. N. (1985). Affect attunement. In J. D. Galenson & R. L. Tyson (Eds.), *Frontiers of infant psychiatry*, Volume 2. New York: Basic Books.

Trevarthan, C. (1993). Playing into reality: Conversations with the infant communicator. *Journal of the Squiggle Foundation, Winnicott Studies, 7*, 67–84.

Vygotsky, L. S. (1978). *Mind in society: The development of higher psychological processes*. Cambridge, MA: Harvard University Press.

Walsh, S. (1996). Adapting cognitive analytic therapy to make sense of psychologically harmful work environments. *British Journal of Medical Psychology, 69*, 3–20.

Young, J. E. (1994). *Cognitive therapy for personality disorders: A schema-focused approach, revised edition*. Sarasota, FL: Professional Resource Press.

Chapter Seven

Schema Therapy Within a High Secure Setting

Kerry Beckley and Neil Gordon

Introduction

Schema therapy has been developing as a therapeutic intervention in the Personality Disorder Directorate (PDD) at Rampton Hospital for the past four years. The treatment pathway within the PDD incorporates a range of interventions that are aimed to treat male personality disordered offenders in a systematic but individualized way utilizing both individual and group components. As Livesley (2001) has argued in relation to the evidence base for working with personality disorder:

> Personality disorder does respond to treatment, it does not appear however that any single approach or theory has a monopoly. Instead many interventions are effective in changing at least some components of personality disorder. This suggests that an integrated approach using a combination of interventions drawn from different approaches, and selected wherever possible on the basis of efficacy, may be the optimal treatment strategy.

The challenge is to deliver diverse interventions in an integrated way when managing individual patients. Schema therapy is a core element of the pathway which is aimed specifically at modifying the cognitive, emotional and behavioural features of personality disorder. The premise is that such work is needed prior to individuals engaging in specific offence-focused work, as offending behaviour is seen as only one aspect of a repertoire of behavioural strategies that personality disordered individuals engage in to get their core needs met. In terms of schema therapy, these are conceptualized as the core emotional needs that have been unmet to a lesser or greater degree in childhood.

Using Time, Not Doing Time: Practitioner Perspectives on Personality Disorder and Risk
Edited by Allison Tennant and Kevin Howells
© 2010 John Wiley & Sons, Ltd.

Need for integrated approaches

Pragmatically in day-to-day clinical practice we are tasked with addressing the traumatic histories, psychological distress and offending behaviour of our patients whilst also trying to predict future levels of risk. This has resulted in what Jones (2002, personal communication) has described as the *Russian doll* approach to developing practice. This has involved continually adding new theoretical perspectives to inform our interpretations about patient presentations, encouraging us to develop increasingly sophisticated formulations that enable us to intervene appropriately. In some respects this seems to be a natural consequence of reflecting critically on our practice and shows our willingness, as therapists struggling with the realities of clinical work, to use theories as metaphors to help us engage with our patients' experiences and provide explanations of the causes and potential ways of reducing their behavioural problems and personal distress. Livesley (2001) describes the use of different interventions and techniques from different therapeutic approaches as *technical eclecticism*. This involves selecting the best intervention or combination of interventions in response to identified patient need. In contrast, *theoretical integration* aspires to be more than a simple combination of techniques as it seeks to create an emergent theory that is more than a sum of its parts (Norcross, 1997).

As therapists in the high secure context we are primarily concerned with the pragmatic issue of keeping the patient engaged and finding a theory that *he* can relate to and find meaningful in terms of his experiences and difficulties. This patient-centred approach has been described by Haglin (1989) as 'pragmatic blending' and rather more disparagingly by London (1986) as 'theory smushing'. We believe these descriptive terms usefully represent our use of schema therapy where we try to respond effectively to the presenting issues of our patients. The particular attraction of this approach is how it provides us and our patients with a common language, enabling us to conceptualize, work with and provide explanations of disturbing experiences, emotional distress and maladaptive behaviour patterns.

Schema therapy as an integrated approach

Young (1990) developed schema therapy to treat personality disordered patients who cannot be adequately helped by standard cognitive behaviour therapy (CBT). Schema therapy is an integrative therapy, combining aspects of cognitive, behavioural, psychodynamic, attachment and gestalt models. It sees the cognitive and behavioural aspects as vital to treatment, as in standard CBT, but gives equal weight to emotional change, experiential techniques and the therapeutic relationship. Like CBT, it is structured, systematic and specific. It follows a sequence of assessment and treatment procedures. The model outlines specific schemas, coping styles and modes. Perhaps most importantly, it normalizes rather than pathologizes personality disorders in its assumption that everyone has schemas, coping styles and modes; however, in the people we treat, they are more rigid and extreme.

Schema therapy places a greater emphasis on the childhood origins of psychological problems which is particularly relevant in this context. Young (1990) defines Early Maladaptive Schemas (EMS) as self-defeating emotional and cognitive patterns that develop early in childhood and are strengthened and elaborated throughout life. Maladaptive behaviours are thought to be driven by schemas. According to the model, schemas are dimensional, meaning that they have different levels of severity and pervasiveness. The more entrenched the schema, the greater number of situations that activate it, the more intense the negative affect and the longer it lasts. Offending behaviour can be understood as an extreme consequence of schema activation.

Young has identified 18 schemas (see appendix 1), all of which are maladaptive, and he postulates that the person develops coping strategies in order to cope with the emotional distress associated with the schema. These coping styles take the form of Schema Surrender (giving in to the schema and accepting that the resulting negative consequences are unavoidable); Schema Avoidance (avoiding triggers internally and externally that may activate the schema); and Schema Overcompensation (acting as though the opposite were true) (Young, 1990).

Case example

Robert is a man in his mid-forties who has committed numerous sexual, violent and acquisitive offences. He had received many diagnoses throughout his life, the most frequent being antisocial, borderline and avoidant personality disorders. His early history was characterized by extreme emotional and physical abuse perpetrated by his father and resulted in the core schemas of Defectiveness/Shame (I am worthless/unlovable), Emotional Deprivation (others will not meet my needs for care and nurturance) and Subjugation (others' needs will be put before mine). He developed a range of coping styles for each of these schemas. For example, he initially used surrender strategies in order to fit into a family who continually rejected and humiliated him, which resulted in increasing levels of emotional distress, thus he developed avoidance strategies in order to escape the toxic family environment, including running away from home and using drugs and alcohol. Although providing some relief from the toxic environment, the avoidance strategies serve to further reinforce his core schemas and result in a build-up of anger and shame, resulting in a range of overcompensatory behaviours such as violence and later sexual violence which are considered to be Robert's maladaptive attempts to meet his own needs for personal power, autonomy and self-worth.

The effect of the high secure environment is particularly relevant to the use of coping styles. Livesley (2003) highlights the importance of the environment in his information processing model of personality functioning. Schema theory indicates that the individual's modes and schemas will result in different observable responses, depending upon which coping strategy (surrender, avoid, overcompensate) is being used at a particular time in a particular environment. For example, a person who has experienced that others' needs take precedence over his own throughout childhood (subjugation) may surrender to this by allowing this to happen to such an extent that he overcompensates for this by meeting his needs through offending (meeting his own needs with disregard to others). When coming into an institution, this may manifest itself through the person continuing to subjugate (compliant surrendering of own needs), overcompensating by acting in an entitled or demanding manner (it's the only way to get my needs met), or avoiding getting into situations where he has to meet others' or his own needs by isolating himself or remaining emotionally detached. Each type of response, if seen over a significant period of time, and if the person tends to switch between them frequently, is likely to result in different personality diagnoses or multiple diagnoses.

One of the difficulties faced by treating professionals in high secure settings is in making accurate risk assessments as to whether someone is ready to move from a highly structured and controlled environment to conditions of lesser security, whether that is to medium or low secure services, or even community settings. If the person is assessed on their presenting behaviour alone then it may not reflect changes at a schematic level, thus the change of environment often results in changes in presenting behaviours. Jones's (2002) term of 'offence paralleling' can be used to encapsulate the behaviours which can be considered indicative of these underlying schemas.

> *Robert's behaviour within a high secure setting was more characterized by avoidance strategies as he attempted to keep others at a distance by isolating himself and minimizing the impact of his schemas. He became very focused on keeping himself busy within the workshop areas in order to distract away from distressing memories and would never ask for help or support from staff or peers. On the surface, Robert could be considered to be functioning well, and it was often commented by staff that he was the 'model patient' and was well liked. It was only through engaging in schema therapy, which he was reluctant to do at the start, that it became apparent that he was still struggling with the core schemas that had developed from his childhood experiences.*

One of the difficulties with working with individuals who have spent many years in institutional or custodial care is that they present with 'dead' stories (Spence, 1982), in that they have repeated their life history or offending history many times and consequently have become emotionally detached from it. In schema therapy this would be described as the '*detached protector*' mode, which serves to protect the person from emotional distress. Schema therapy aims to use experiential strategies which include more active techniques, such as the use of imagery re-scripting, schema dialogues and chair work. The aim is to keep the affect in the room as when the person is emotionally aroused there is more likelihood of both cognitive and emotional change.

Schema theory enables the therapist to keep the patient and his offence in mind (Gordon, 2003) in terms of offence paralleling behaviours within a secure environment. By identifying the underlying schemas/modes, and linking them to past offending behaviours and current behaviours, it is possible to see progress in terms of risk reduction through modification of the institutional behaviours in a way that is meaningfully linked to offending. It can also help establish which behaviours may not be linked to offending and may be more adaptive in terms of the person developing alternative ways of getting his needs met. For example, if someone's offending links to their propensity to subjugate their needs, and they, in turn, overcompensate at the point of offending to meet those needs, their demonstration of appropriate assertiveness could be misconstrued as 'challenging' when in fact it is an appropriate prosocial strategy for them to develop. This highlights the need for shared understanding of formulations so that staff can understand and respond to progressive changes in behaviour, in order to reduce the reinforcement of maladaptive strategies.

Schema modes

As highlighted above, many of the individuals with whom we work have multiple psychiatric diagnoses. Individuals who have severe personality disorders tend to have a greater number of core schemas and resulting coping modes. This can make formulating and treating such individuals somewhat complicated. In addition, such individuals can switch rapidly between different self-states, often within a short space of time, which can make it very difficult to help the person make sense of their schema reactions. Young *et al.* (2003) have further developed the schema therapy model to incorporate schema modes. Schema modes are defined as the 'part of the person' that is dominating their thoughts, feelings and behaviours at any given time. It has parallels to dissociative identity disorder in the most extreme cases, but in most, this represents the shifts in thinking and emotions that the person experiences in response to internal/external triggers. Young has developed 14 modes (see appendix 2), based on schema formulations of borderline and narcissistic personality disorders, that are thought to represent four categories: Child Modes (Vulnerable, Lonely, Angry, Impulsive, Happy), Dysfunctional Coping Modes (Compliant Surrenderer, Detached Protector, Detached Self-Soother, Overcompensator, Self-Aggrandizer, Bully Attack), Maladaptive Parent Modes (Punitive, Demanding) and Healthy Adult Mode (Young *et al.*, 2003). These modes are thought to be made up of differing constellations of schemas and coping strategies. The aim of therapy is to develop and strengthen the 'Healthy Adult Mode' through the relationship with the therapist, in order to meet the needs of the vulnerable/lonely child modes, set limits for the angry/impulsive child modes, and moderate the dysfunctional coping and parent modes.

Bernstein *et al.* (2007) have proposed four new dysfunctional coping modes which are thought to be present in forensic populations. These are Angry Protector Mode, Conning and Manipulative Mode, Predator Mode, and Over-Controller Mode (Paranoid and Obsessive-Compulsive Subtypes).

Although these ideas are potentially useful ways of conceptualizing the self-states of our patients, they have the potential to become as complex as using the standard schema model. However, we have found the mode model to be the most pragmatic way in which to work with our patient group due to the high numbers of schemas they tend to have. Modes can be most usefully thought of as 'convenient fictions' (Mahrer, 2004) in the sense they can be used to provide descriptors. We have tended not to be prescriptive in the use of modes as the individual tends to react against the idea of being put into preset 'boxes'. Instead, we have taken the approach of introducing the basic model of mode types to patients in order for them to develop their own individualized descriptors of their self-states. We have found this process does lend itself to broadly categorizing the person's modes under the four headings. Regardless of the method used, the main aim is to help the person to develop meaningful links between the parts of themselves that have previously felt overwhelming and contradictory.

Empirical support for schema therapy

The evidence base for schema therapy is in its infancy, in part due to the length of time it takes to conduct robust clinical trials. The first multicentre randomized clinical trial (RCT) was recently completed in the Netherlands, demonstrating patients with borderline personality disorder (BPD) making significant improvements across the whole range of personality functioning associated with this diagnosis over the course of a three-year treatment course and at 12-month follow-up (Giesen-Bloo et al., 2006). An RCT of group based schema therapy has also been shown to be an effective treatment for BPD in comparison with treatment as usual (Farrell et al., 2009).

Other indications of the efficacy of schema therapy come from smaller studies and single case designs. Hoffart et al. (2002) found that schema-focused formulations, used early in therapy, increased self-understanding and reduced emotional distress in patients with Cluster C personality traits. Ball and Young (2000) outline some positive findings in their case studies of substance-dependent individuals diagnosed with personality disorder.

Schema therapy is receiving increasing attention in forensic settings internationally, particularly in the Netherlands where there is a large RCT being conducted within their TBS clinics. Within the UK, this is particularly evident in high secure services, where there are a greater number of personality disordered offenders. In addition to our own developing service there is a clinical trial being conducted at Ashworth Hospital comparing schema therapy to treatment as usual (TAU) over an 18-month period (Dolan et al., 2005). The findings reported so far highlight the severity of personality disorder and psychopathy within the samples, which is indicative of high secure populations in general, and emerging links between psychopathy and the Emotional Deprivation schema. A study of our own pilot schema therapy group indicated positive treatment gains in terms of a reduction in reported incidents of aggression, and ambivalence over emotional expression and increases in self-esteem and empathic concern for others (Farnsworth, 2005). We are in the process of conducting further analysis on the subsequent groups as our clinical experiences indicate that differing group process, pace and personality dynamics both in patients and facilitators radically affect the delivery of the treatment and its impact.

This tension between the certainty of research-led academic thinking about practice and evidence, and the responsive pragmatism (Fishman, 2000) of the more ambivalent and sometimes sceptical frontline worker, is an issue at the heart of clinical practice in this under-researched social context. Some clinicians have developed treatment manuals based on schema therapy principles in both forensic and substance misuse settings (Ball & Young, 2000; Nauth, 2001). The development of a manual for our schema group has presented us with many challenges in creating a 'formulaic' guide to working with the complexities and idiosyncrasies of this population. This can feel somewhat reductionist, and goes against the principles of creativity and flexibility which are core to the approach. Our ambivalence is captured eloquently by Yalom and Leszck (2005):

> Many practitioners feel that manuals restrict their natural responsiveness and result in a 'herky-jerky' ineffective therapeutic process. Therapist effectiveness has much to do with the capacity to improvise as the context demands it, drawing upon both new knowledge and accrued wisdom.

PDD schema therapy programme

The programme incorporates both individual and group components, and regular teaching and supervision activities for staff in order to effectively support the application of schema therapy within this context. The aim has been to integrate the approach with the therapeutic milieu of the ward environment in order to enhance the benefits of the treatment intervention. To describe in full the range of techniques utilized within the programme is beyond the scope of this chapter. In order to illustrate schema therapy's application in a high secure context, we intend to concentrate on the use of clinical formulation, illustrative case material and the unique contribution of the group component.

Importance of formulation

> In essence a formulation says that the nature and content of your distress is personally meaningful, while a diagnosis says it is meaningless. These assumptions cannot both be true. (Johnstone & Dallos, 2006)

One aspect of the programme which aims to enhance the efficacy of schema therapy's effectiveness are clinical team formulations. These are focused sessions utilizing schema principles to understand a person's personality difficulties within a developmental context, in order to make sense of the links between personality, criminal behaviour and current behaviour. Our engagement with our patients is centred on the difficulties they have in achieving what Duggan (2002) refers to as the integration of self-states. Our patients have experienced multiple traumas in their life, both those in which they have been the victim as well as those they have inflicted on others, a fact that cannot be ignored when you begin to explore with them the damaging and abusive experiences of their chaotic lives. To formulate these experiences within a singular theoretical frame can only be limiting and unsatisfactory. Meaningful formulation consolidates the therapeutic alliance, helping the person to make sense of their own behaviour.

Clinical team formulations are also useful in helping to understand and manage the schema enactments that occur when working closely with personality disordered offenders. Developing the schema approach at a systemic level has encouraged us to create organization development programmes that focus on the dynamics of staff–patient relationships and the potential for schema enactment within them. For example, Kiesler (1983) describes the principle of complementarity whereby interactions evoke interpersonal pull in others, which generate reinforcing schema-consistent responses and prevent contradictory evidence. This often leads to ruptures in therapeutic relationships. Young and Gluhoski (1997) describe relationship spectrums (connection, power, feeling, mutuality and valuing) where people move to extreme positions on these poles when schemas are triggered in both individuals, often around issues of control and autonomy in the high secure environment. The development programme is aimed at helping staff to learn to work with this in a more psychologically informed way. Creating the opportunity for schema healing can be challenging in the restrictive environment of the institution, which limits the opportunities for individualized risk-taking and authentic therapeutic encounters. One of the core tasks of the formulation is to embed an understanding of the individual's presenting issues within the care team, to ensure that daily interactions are utilized to enhance schema healing as opposed to reinforcing maladaptive behaviour.

In our experience, individuals with narcissistic presentations can create the greatest challenges and difficulties for therapists and ward staff alike, particularly with the overlay of antisocial features and an associated criminal history usually involving the victimization of others through sexual and physical violence. Young *et al.* (2003) suggest that the narcissistic schema-driven sense of entitlement in forensic populations tends to be *fragile* as opposed to *pure*. They differentiate between these presentations through contrasting the spoilt child who has become entitled through limited boundaries and materially overindulgent parents (pure) with the compensatory responses of the defective and deprived child (fragile) who has often experienced an abusive childhood where they were exposed to significant maltreatment and deprivation. Young *et al.* (2003) also make the important point that diagnostic descriptors are predominantly focused on the (often antisocial and alienating) external adaptations the individual is employing to protect the lonely and defective inner self. They point out that this can lead to a failure of empathy and understanding on the part of treating professionals who have a limited focus on the underlying personality dynamics and psychological pain these individuals are masking through their self-aggrandizing and self-soothing detachment.

Case example

Paul is a 34-year-old man who came to the high secure setting from prison. Paul had a disrupted and traumatic childhood where he experienced extensive physical abuse and violence from his alcoholic father. A feature of these experiences was his lack of control and helplessness and his father's intention to ritually humiliate him and cause him suffering. He began drinking and got involved in petty crime before reaching his teens and over the next few years became increasingly violent and assaultive to others, both males and females. In his later teens he was involved in a serious of troubled relationships where he ended up feeling betrayed and rejected, leading to further violent behaviour, bullying and vengeful attacks on those who he believed had let him down. His index offence involved a brutal sexual and physical assault on an elderly man. Like many of our patients, Paul meets the criteria for several personality disorders; in his case these have been identified as narcissistic, borderline and antisocial, a common presenting triad in the high secure setting (Coid, 1996).

> *On one occasion, Paul was observed behaving in an intimidating and humiliating way to a member of staff who did not normally work on the ward, making reference to his weight and personal appearance and insinuating that he should move from a seat he wanted to occupy. This had made the member of staff feel intimidated and under threat and he had completed an incident form as a consequence. In a one-to-one session later that week, Paul's behaviour was explored utilizing the concept of 'offence paralleling' behaviours (Jones, 2002). Paul was originally defensive about this situation and denied any intention to intimidate or humiliate (Conning and Manipulative Mode). However, as it was explored further, he was able to acknowledge how he felt angry with this person about a room search he had conducted that morning where an item of his property had been broken. Paul was able to recognize his tendency to pick on others, particularly people he saw as abusive (Bully Attack Mode) based on his own anxieties and heightened sense of vulnerability (Lonely Child Mode).*
>
> *When Paul's Lonely Child Mode was active he tended to overcompensate by becoming demanding of the time of more senior staff members. His behaviour towards those who tried to offer help at these times was both denigrating and dismissive as his self-aggrandizing mode sabotaged his ability to meet the needs of his Lonely Child. This would often result in staff being less responsive to his requests and avoiding him at times when he needed emotional support, reinforcing his core schemas of Defectiveness and Emotional Deprivation.*

A major challenge in working with people like Paul involves the attempt to connect with the Lonely Child Mode. From his perspective, the main goals in treating the narcissistic personality through schema work are to:

- nurture the lonely child and help him to empathize and connect to others;
- confront the self-aggrandizer to reduce the person's need for approval and admiration; and
- help the detached self-soother to give up avoidant and stimulus-seeking behaviour and replace these with emotional experiences of genuine love, connectedness and intimacy.

The relationships we create with our patients are of primary importance; if we cannot connect to the humanity of those with whom we work, we are unable to help them.

Schema therapy involves a delicate interpersonal balance and issues of rapport, timing and sensitive communication are central. A strategy that has been helpful with Paul is to build up to the process of confrontation by focusing on his early experiences of physical abuse and his relationship with his father. When engaging with this area of traumatic memories and emotional pain, Paul is quickly in touch with his *lonely child* and the tone of the session shifts to one of vulnerability and self-doubt. At this point, reconnecting to current self-aggrandizing behaviours can be experienced as a defensive, self-protecting, coping strategy where Paul has a greater level of self-awareness and is emotionally connected to the therapist.

Schema therapy in a group setting

Schema therapy was designed to be delivered on an individual basis over a number of years, depending on the severity of the person's difficulties. The use of the therapist relationship to provide limited reparenting (a corrective emotional experience) is central to this approach, thus the individual modality is essential to the process. However, there is increasing evidence that the most effective approach for working with personality disorders is an integrated flexible programme, delivered within a combination of group and one-to-one work (Livesley, 2003). Yalom and Leszck (2005) point out that, although CBT therapists have tended to use groups to increase the efficiency of delivering individual treatments, they have missed the opportunity to tap in to the unique benefits inherent in group work. Both of these are central themes to the development of the schema therapy group.

Group framework

The group runs for 12–18 months and involves individuals at different stages within their individual schema therapy. It is expected that individuals will be in individual therapy for two to three years, so the group is only one part of the overall treatment. The group has four modules as outlined below.

Schema Education. This introductory module outlines the schema theory and reinforces the developmental focus. The same techniques are utilized in the group as would be used in the individual sessions (schema dialogues, imagery exercises) in order to enhance the learning experience. The aim is for all group participants and facilitators to explore how the concepts apply to themselves and others in the group in order to increase the level of trust and the equality between facilitators and patients.

The exercises are designed to activate schemas in order for the experience to become the focus of discussion. In terms of group life, this first module is focused on creating a safe environment where self-disclosure and feedback can occur. As the majority of group members have issues around mistrust/abuse and defectiveness/shame, the facilitators create sufficient safety through the use of structured experiential methods, while still emphasizing the importance of attending to interactions between participants and the emotional experiences these are creating. The relationship within individual therapy is thought to be the richest source of information in identifying schemas and maladaptive coping strategies. Within experiential group processes, this therapeutic factor is not only mimicked, it is also amplified through the intensity of relationship between group members in an emotionally charged atmosphere. Due to the nature of the second module, it is important that the group is cohesive and emotionally connected and that the 'forming' (excessive focus on the rules and structure) and 'storming' (challenging of leadership and interpersonal conflicts) phases (Tuckman, 1965) often encountered in early group processes have been managed effectively.

The second module is the *Self-Formulation* module where each individual takes the 'hot seat' within the group and gives an account of their life history. The person in the hot seat gets to choose another group member to facilitate and support them through the process. The group then uses this life history to develop a formulation of the schemas and modes, coping strategies and subsequently target behaviours for that individual. This module is again led by example as the facilitators give a 'career history' as their self-formulations. Individuals are encouraged to use their own judgement as to how much detail is given regarding their life histories as this can be the first time they have ever had to disclose such detailed personal information within the group setting. The sense of universality experienced in this module is a powerful therapeutic factor and consolidates group cohesion and high levels of empathic resonance between group members.

The third module is focused on *Schema Healing* and outlines and works with the different approaches used within the integrated therapy, including cognitive (reframing evidence, diaries, flashcards, dialogues, pros and cons), experiential (imagery, switching seats, letter writing) and behavioural (target setting role-plays, flashcards). Individuals work on their identified targets using a range of change strategies within both the group and the individual therapy. We also make use of video work within the group where individuals have the opportunity to work through schema-activating situations within the sessions and are able to see themselves 'in action', in order to reflect critically on their self-presentation and potential impact on others.

The final module is *Looking to the Future*, where the patients review the changes they have made (reformulation) and identify the ongoing needs for each group member. The aim is for the group members to empathically challenge each other, regarding their observations of progress made in the wider hospital environment, which is enabled through the strength of the group cohesion. This is framed to the group members as their opportunity to demonstrate change within a less supportive, and at times caustic, environment. The reformulations are to be presented by the patients to their clinical teams, to increase the generalization and the individual's ownership of the formulation and the work that they still have to do. It is hoped that this facilitates the individual shifting from the group as a supportive structure to a more internalized and robust self-structure that has emerged out of schema healing.

A focus on participant experience

Yalom and Leszck (2005) highlight the importance of connecting the 'here and now' experience with a capacity to reflect on these processes and explore them with the group. In the schema group, when powerful emotional experiences occur, it is imperative that we pay attention to, and narratively reflect on, these processes, enabling the patient group to retain the experience, generalize from it, and transfer that learning back into the ward environment.

Case example

Daryl was a life-sentenced prisoner convicted of murder who was considered to meet the criteria for antisocial and borderline personality disorder with traits of histrionic and narcissistic personality disorder. His strongest schemas were those comprising the Disconnection and Rejection Domain, creating a strong Vulnerable Child Mode. Daryl struggled to let others close to this aspect of him, utilizing forms of overcompensation which involved dominance and aggression. However, he had formed an intense idealized relationship with his individual therapist who was also one of the group therapists. Daryl's Vulnerable Child Mode was activated in a particular group session triggered by his therapist becoming visibly upset. Daryl experienced her distress as his fault. He responded aggressively by punching the wall and pushing a table over before he was contained by his therapist and another group member. This was later explained by Daryl to be a result of his inability to cope with the feelings of shame and responsibility for 'hurting' his therapist. This was a distressing event for all the group members but, as Yalom and Leszck suggest, the therapeutic impact and usefulness of this experience arose from the capacity of those present to talk about what had happened and how they had been affected. Daryl was able to describe the profound effect that this had had on him and how vulnerable and defective he had felt, thus exposing his Vulnerable Child Mode to the group. This proved to be a pivotal factor in Daryl's progress and led to an increased ability to generalize this learning into his behaviour in the ward environment.

Concluding remarks

In this chapter we have attempted to demonstrate how the schema model can offer insight into the complex worlds of the individuals with whom we work within a high secure context. We believe that schema therapy continues to present clinicians with exciting challenges, as it provides a framework from which we can enhance our understanding of both personality disorder and offending behaviour. Schema therapy provides us with a way of not only focusing on the 'disordered' aspects of the individuals which have resulted in them being detained within this setting, but allows us to recognize and build upon their developing strengths, which is imperative if we are to be successful in both treating the individual and protecting the public. It is hoped this chapter will stimulate further interest from others so that the effectiveness of this approach can be explored in the wider context of forensic settings.

References

Ball, S. A. & Young, J. E. (2000). Dual focus schema therapy for personality disorders and substance dependence: Case study results. *Cognitive and Behavioral Practice*, *7*, 270–281.

Bernstein, D. P., Arntz, A. & de Vos, M. (2007). Schema focused therapy in forensic settings: Theoretical model and recommendations for best clinical practice. *International Journal of Forensic Mental Health*, *6*(2),169–183.

Coid, J.W. (1996). Dangerous patients with mental illness: increased risks warrant new policies, adequate resources, and appropriate legislation. *British Medical Journal*, *312*, 965–966.

Dolan, M., Doyle, M., Cooper, K. & Povey, A. (2005, April). *Evaluation of schema therapy in a high secure personality disorder service.* Paper presented at The International Association of Forensic Mental Health, Melbourne, Australia.

Duggan, C. (2002). *Presentation to the Home Office on treatment approaches with dangerous and severe personality disorder.* Arnold Lodge and University of Leicester.

Farnsworth, J. (2005). *A pilot study evaluating the effectiveness of a schema focused therapy group intervention with personality disordered offenders.* Unpublished Masters dissertation, Coventry University.

Farrell, J. M, Shaw, I. A. & Webber, M. A. (2009). A schema-focused approach to group psychotherapy for outpatients with borderline personality disorder: A randomized controlled trial. *Journal of Behavior Therapy and Experimental Psychiatry, 40*(2), 317–328.

Fishman, D. B. (2000). *The case for pragmatic psychology.* New York: New York University Press.

Giesen-Bloo, J., Van Dyck, R., Spinhoven, P., Van Tilburg, W., Dirksen, C., Van Asselt, T. *et al.* (2006). Outpatient psychotherapy for borderline personality disorder: Randomized trial of schema-focused therapy vs transference-focused therapy. *Archives of General Psychiatry, 63*, 649–658.

Gordon, N. S. (2003). *'The swamp workers stories': An exploration of practitioners' perspectives as a foundation for the development of a context sensitive development programme in a forensic setting.* Unpublished doctoral dissertation, Metanoia Institute/Middlesex University.

Haglin, R. P. (1989). Pragmatic blending. *Journal of Integrative and Eclectic Psychotherapy, 8*, 320–328.

Hoffart, A., Versland, S. & Sexton, H. (2002). Self-understanding, empathy, guided discovery, and schema belief in schema-focused cognitive therapy of personality problems: A process-outcome study. *Cognitive Therapy and Research, 26*(2), 199–219.

Johnstone, L. & Dallos, R. (2006). *Formulations in psychology and psychotherapy.* London: Routledge.

Jones, L. F. (2002). An individual case formulation approach to the assessment of motivation. In M. McMurran (Ed.), *Motivating offenders to change.* Chichester: John Wiley & Sons.

Kiesler, D. J. (1983). The 1982 interpersonal circle: A taxonomy for complementarity in human transactions. *Psychological Review, 90*, 185–214.

Livesley, W. J. (Ed.) (2001). *Handbook of personality disorders: Theory, research and treatment.* New York: Guilford Press.

Livesley, W. J. (2003). *Practical management of personality disorder.* New York: Guilford Press.

London, P. (1986). *The modes and morals of psychotherapy,* 2nd edition. New York: Hemisphere.

Mahrer, A. R. (2004). *Theories of truth, models of usefulness.* London: Whurr.

Nauth, L. (2001). *Treatment manual for Lifetraps, the Cognitive Intervention Program (CGIP).* Wisconsin: Wisconsin Department of Corrections.

Norcross, J. C. (1997). Integrative approaches to psychotherapy supervision. In C. E. Watkins (Ed.), *Handbook of psychotherapy supervision.* Chichester: John Wiley & Sons.

Spence, D. P. (1982). *Narrative truth and historical truth.* New York: W. W. Norton.

Tuckman, B. W. (1965). Developmental sequence in small groups. *Psychological Bulletin, 63*, 384–399.

Yalom, I. D. & Leszck, M. (2005). *The theory and practice of group psychotherapy.* New York: Basic Books.

Young, J. E. (1990). *Cognitive therapy for personality disorders: A schema focused approach.* Sarasota, FL: Professional Resource Exchange.

Young, J. E. & Gluhoski, V. (1997). A schema-focused perspective on satisfaction in close relationships. In. R. Sternberg (Ed.), *Satisfaction in close relationships* (pp. 356–381). New York: Guilford Press.

Young, J. E., Klosko, J. S. & Weishar, M. E. (2003). *Schema therapy: A practitioner's guide.* New York: Guilford Press.

Appendix 1: Domains and schemas

Disconnection and Rejection
Abusive, traumatic childhoods, unstable family life, experienced rejection and humiliation, feel different and lacking in some way, long periods of insecurity and inconsistent parenting

Abandonment/Instability
Mistrust/Abuse
Emotional Deprivation
Defectiveness/Shame
Social Isolation/Alienation

Impaired Autonomy and Performance
Often over-protected and controlled as children, or neglected and ignored, left alone with no interest shown in their lives, continually undermined and made to feel incompetent, or were encouraged to be dependent on others

Dependence/Incompetence
Vulnerability to Harm
Enmeshment
Failure

Impaired Limits
Have not developed an internal sense of control, difficulty respecting the rights of others, families were very unboundaried, children did not have rules

Entitlement
Insufficient Self-Control/ Self-Discipline

Other Directedness
Experienced conditional love (i.e. I will love you only if…), family overly (continued) concerned with appearances, parents focused on their own needs

Subjugation
Self-Sacrifice
Approval Seeking/Recognition Seeking

Over-vigilance and Inhibition
Strict control by parents to gain compliance, learned to be watching all the time waiting for bad things to happen, frightened to express feelings, severe punishments

Negativity/Pessimism
Emotional Inhibition
Unrelenting Standards/ Hypercriticalness
Punitiveness

Appendix 2: Outline of Modes (based on the work of Young *et al.*, 2003 and Bernstein *et al.*, 2007)

Child Modes – involve feeling, thinking, and acting in a 'child-like' manner:

1. **Vulnerable Child** (Abandoned, Abused, or Humiliated Child) – feels vulnerable, overwhelmed with painful feelings, such as anxiety, depression, grief, or shame/humiliation.
2. **Angry Child** – feels and expresses uncontrolled anger or rage in response to perceived or real mistreatment, abandonment, humiliation, or frustration; often feels a sense of being treated unjustly; acts like a child throwing a temper tantrum.
3. **Impulsive, Undisciplined Child** – acts like a spoiled child who 'wants what he wants when he wants it', and can't tolerate the frustration of limits.
4. **Lonely Child** – feels lonely and empty, as if no one can understand him, soothe or comfort him, or make contact with him.

Dysfunctional Coping Modes – involve attempts to protect the self from pain through maladaptive forms of coping:

5. **Detached Protector** – uses emotional detachment to protect one from painful feelings; is unaware of his feelings, feels 'nothing', appears emotionally distant, flat, or robotic; avoids getting close to other people.
6. **Detached Self-Soother/Self-Stimulator** – uses repetitive, 'addictive' or compulsive behaviours, or self-stimulating behaviours to calm and soothe oneself; uses pleasurable or exciting sensations to distance oneself from painful feelings.
7. **Compliant Surrenderer** – gives in to the real or perceived demands or expectations of other people in an anxious attempt to avoid pain or to get one's needs met; anxiously surrenders to the demands of others who are perceived as more powerful than oneself.
8. **Angry Protector** – Uses a 'wall of anger' to protect oneself from others who are perceived as threatening; keeps others at a safe distance through displays of anger; anger is more controlled than in Angry Child Mode.

Maladaptive Parent Modes – involve internalized dysfunctional parent 'voices':

9. **Punitive, Critical Parent** – internalized, critical or punishing parent voice; directs harsh criticism towards the self; induces feelings of shame or guilt.
10. **Demanding Parent** – directs impossibly high demands toward the self; pushes the self to do more, achieve more, never be satisfied with oneself.

Over-Compensatory Modes – involve extreme attempts to compensate for feelings of shame, loneliness, or vulnerability:

11. **Self-Aggrandizer Mode** – feels superior, special, or powerful; looks down on others; sees the world in terms of 'top dog' and 'bottom dog;' shows off or acts in a self-important, self-aggrandizing manner; concerned about appearances rather than feelings or real contact with others.
12. **Bully and Attack Mode** – uses threats, intimidation, aggression, or coercion to get what he wants, including retaliating against others, or asserting one's dominant position; feels a sense of sadistic pleasure in attacking others.
13. **Conning and Manipulative Mode** – cons, lies, or manipulates in a manner designed to achieve a specific goal, which either involves victimizing others or escaping punishment.
14. **Predator Mode** – focuses on eliminating a threat, rival, obstacle, or enemy in a cold, ruthless, and calculating manner.
15. **Over-Controller Mode (Paranoid and Obsessive-Compulsive Types)** – attempt to protect oneself from a perceived or real threat by focusing attention, ruminating, and exercising extreme control. The Obsessive type uses order, repetition, or ritual. The Paranoid type attempts to locate and uncover a hidden (perceived) threat.

Chapter Eight

Violent Offending Treatment for Male Patients with Personality Disorder

Louise Sainsbury

Background theory and practice

This chapter provides an overview of the Violence Reduction Programme (VRP; Gordon & Wong, 2000) and details the adaptations that have been made in the process of delivering the VRP to patients with severe personality disorder as illustrated by case examples. There has been increasing focus on developing treatment programmes for violent offenders (Howells & Day, 2002; Polaschek, 2006), which have included anger management, anger treatment and other programmes with a cognitive-behavioural and psychoeducational basis. The focus on anger is based on the assumption that anger is a central component in aggression and violent offending. Anger is not associated with all violent crimes (Blackburn, 1993) and can be conceptualized as one of many potential components of violent offending (Novaco, 1997). This is consistent with the heterogeneity of violent offenders and personality disorders. This heterogeneity is likely to be more effectively addressed within treatment programmes that incorporate recent developments within the treatment literature such as individual formulation and functional analysis and combined with risk assessments that include static and dynamic factors that represent individual treatment targets (Howells *et al.*, 2004). Furthermore, a complex and difficult-to-engage patient group will require higher levels of therapist responsivity and skill to maximize treatment readiness and engagement in the patient (Howells & Day, 2006). As an illustration of the treatment of violence in personality disordered offenders, the author will describe the development and clinical challenges of delivering treatment for violence.

Using Time, Not Doing Time: Practitioner Perspectives on Personality Disorder and Risk
Edited by Allison Tennant and Kevin Howells
© 2010 John Wiley & Sons, Ltd.

The VRP is delivered within the context of a treatment pathway that had developed over several years through clinical experience and the emerging published evidence. Multiple treatments have been implemented within the treatment pathway to target the complex areas of psychopathology within personality disorders and the dynamic risk factors. Different aspects of personality disorders are frequently related to offending and there is considerable overlap between aspects of personality disorder and empirically identified dynamic risk factors for violence; for example, poor emotional control, cognitive distortions, relationship instability, poor response to stress, interpersonal aggression, etc.

The personality disorders and dynamic risk factors for violence may go some way to explain the high responsivity needs of this patient group. Responsivity considers factors that may affect or impede an individual's response to interventions, and includes two general types of factors, internal to the person (e.g. cognitive-motivational structures) and external factors (e.g. staff characteristics) (Ogloff & Davis, 2004). For example, a patient is assessed as high on emotional control deficits, cognitive distortions and impulsivity dynamic risk factors. If the cognitive distortions consist of mistrust of others, starting a new treatment with expectations that participants will make personal disclosures is likely to trigger mistrust beliefs, emotional dysregulation and behavioural urges to protect himself through habitual defences, e.g. withdrawal, hostility or aggression.

To address these difficulties, a treatment pathway was developed, to increase patients' abilities to manage their psychopathology, including their propensity to use violence, so as to be able to engage in increasingly challenging therapies. The pathway begins with an individual psychological assessment of their personality, offending and risk, incorporating structured risk assessments. Treatments are initially begun on an individual basis and group therapy is introduced when the patient has sufficient abilities to cope with the specific challenges of group work. The overall aim is to increase the patients' abilities to contain their current impulsivity, cognitive distortions and emotional dysregulation. This can increase their ability to gain some distance from their automatic defensive reactions and begin to observe self and others more accurately. These automatic reactions are frequently components in their violent behaviours, e.g. poor emotional control. Treatment at this stage is often focusing on their offence paralleling behaviours (Jones, 2004), and thus targeting dynamic risk factors. Treatment specific to their past violent offending typically comes at the end and draws together the previous treatments to focus on their index offences.

The VRP was developed using a cognitive-behavioural approach with high risk and high need offenders, for whom previous treatment approaches within the Canadian prison system had not been successful. The VRP uses a CBT (cognitive behaviour therapy) approach which is supported by the stages of change model and motivation interviewing to guide target setting and therapeutic approach. The authors developed a programme that targeted perceptions, thoughts and attitudes and emotions that drove the patients' violence within the format of a behavioural cycle; and high risk situations. Within the programme, no assumptions are made about what specific thoughts, emotions or attitudes had contributed to their violence; rather this is identified through functional analysis of past acts of violence and current patterns of aggression and violence, exploring their past violence, within the context of their psychosocial development.

The Violence Risk Scale (VRS; Wong & Gordon, 1999–2003, 2006) is a struc-tured risk assessment guide that was developed both as a risk prediction guide and as the core assessment tool for the VRP, with the dynamic risk items representing treatment targets. The VRS is administered prior to and after the treatment programme.

The VRP authors have presented the evidence base for the Aggressive Behaviour Control (ABC) programme for violent offenders, on which the VRP is based. The ABC programme was evaluated using a matched controls design, comparing 93 offenders who had completed the programme and 92 matched controls. All offenders were assessed as high risk using the VRS. The treated group had a violent reoffending rate of 37% after a minimum of 66 months on release; the matched control group had a violent reoffending rate of 67% after a minimum of 87.6 months on release. Those offenders who did not complete the programme had a 55% reoffending rate. The survival analysis showed a similar pattern of results, except no difference was found between the 'no treatment group' and those offenders who did not complete the programme; these differences were found to be statistically significant. Further analysis showed that those participants who rated their relationships with the group facilitators as strong had lower recidivism rates than those who reported poor therapeutic relationships (Wong & Gordon, 1999). Wong *et al.* (2007) have described studies on the use of the ABC programme with specific groups of inmates within the Canadian prison service and in an English prison, demonstrating similar results.

Extending the VRP for patients with severe personality disorder

Due to the depth and breadth of personality difficulties that contribute both directly and indirectly to offending, the VRP was expanded to address these needs. The focus on cognitions (perceptions, schemas, attitudes and thoughts) is consis-tent with the proposal that cognitions are the consistent core construct under-pinning all theories of personality (Livesley, 2003), and with the developing understanding of the role of core beliefs or schemas within violent offending (Baker & Beech, 2004; Beck, 1999). Identifying and working with schemas, as defined by Young's schema therapy (Young *et al.*, 2003), was explicitly incorpo-rated into the emotional baggage section, as well as implicitly throughout the VRP.

Emotions can be considered a second core structure within personality and the emotions module within the VRP has been expanded to include the dialectical behaviour therapy (DBT; Linehan, 1993) model of emotional regulation, which looks at emotional processing and content. Within this model, the concept of primary and secondary emotions is introduced. The strategies for effectively tol-erating and expressing typically suppressed emotions are incorporated into this section, drawing on the distress tolerance and emotional regulation skills from DBT. This expands and complements the emotional containment strategies within the VRP.

Personality disorders manifest predominantly in interpersonal relationships, including significant difficulties in establishing and maintaining positive relationships. Attachment theory and adult attachment styles were introduced into the relationships section of the high risk situations module, to provide a framework for understanding the relationship between their personality disorders and their violence towards others. The attachment framework provides a theory for linking their childhood experiences with aspects of their personality development and violence within a relational context. There is considerable empirical evidence that secure childhood attachments function to promote the development of healthy emotional, psychological functioning and in particular social functioning (e.g. Cassidy, 1994). It is further argued that an important evolutionary purpose of attachment is the socialization of natural aggression (Fonagy, 2003).

The Good Lives Model–Comprehensive (GLM-C; Ward & Gannon, 2006) is a recent development within sexual offending treatment that identifies the links between rehabilitation models and theories of human needs (e.g. Deci & Ryan, 2000) and sexual offending. Whilst the development of the Good Lives Model was focused on sexual offending, the theory and research on primary goods are from general psychology and philosophy and apply to all people. This model appears equally applicable to violent offenders and people with personality disorder where this disorder has a significant impact on their beliefs about and abilities to develop a 'good life'. The GLM-C provides a holistic approach to the VRP relapse prevention phase and a framework for understanding the relevance of new ways of being, to developing a 'good life' that can be a protective factor against reoffending, through strength building in areas of dynamic risk.

These developments aim to integrate and build on prior treatments into the VRP, to increase the understanding and ability to manage the multiple domains of psychopathology that constitute personality disorders (Livesley, 2003; Sperry, 2003) and contribute to risk.

The Extended Violence Reduction Programme (EVRP)

The VRP is divided into three phases: phase one, 'looking in the mirror'; phase two, 'breaking the cycle'; phase three, 'relapse prevention'. The programme is currently delivered in a combination of weekly two-hour group sessions and weekly one-hour individual sessions. The individual sessions focus on any difficulties the participants are experiencing and to work on areas in more depth. The programme runs for approximately two years, depending on the number of patients and their combined individual needs, and typically involves a total of more than 140 hours.

Phase one aims to increase the patients' abilities to effectively engage within this programme and to contain their anxieties, through transparency about the content and expectations for participants and facilitators. Participants are encouraged to disclose their behaviours that are likely to interfere with the process, through the facilitators disclosing their behaviours that may interfere and developing ideas of how others can help them to manage these behaviours. This emphasizes the group process of giving and receiving feedback and support from group members as well as facilitators. For example, when a patient disclosed his tendency to dominate discussions and requested other patients to interrupt him, he was asked if he would accept this. This feedback helped him to recognize that he needed to be aware of his response to such feedback even when he had suggested the intervention. This process begins to develop participants' abilities to accept that support is not always just reassurance or agreement, thus working on the dynamic risk factors of community support and compliance with supervision.

The second major aim of phase one is to explore patients' insights into the factors that have contributed to their violence. This process begins with the participants describing their life history up to their index offence, including their history of violence, to the group. This process frequently triggers fears of vulnerability, potential humiliation and abuse by others. It is potentially an occasion where their progress is both tested and developed further through the support of the facilitators and participants.

Life histories provide the developmental context for patients' violence and the basis for identifying patterns of behaviours relating to violence. The process of evaluation and the VRS is explained to them and the costs and benefits of accurately assessing their progress are explored, as part of developing acceptance and value in assessing themselves. The patients are then asked to identify which of the VRS dynamic risk factors are relevant to their offending.

Phase two, 'breaking the cycle', focuses on the patterns of behaviours that have led to violence, utilizing the CBT structure of beliefs, perceptions, thoughts, emotions and behaviours to understand the behavioural cycle leading to violence. This framework provides the core content of the programme, with modules on each of the components and further modules covering specific high risk situations. Participants initially develop non-offending positive and negative examples of behaviour cycles. They then provide a baseline account of their index offence or most violent offence to the group. This is repeated at the end of the module in the more detailed form of an offence cycle. Each component of the behavioural cycle is explored in relation to their offending.

The VRP has been extended by incorporating sections on schemas relating to violence. This aims to increase patients' understanding of their perceptions, thoughts and attitudes and emotional reactions that are distorted by schemas. Patients reflect on the relevance of the different schemas and discuss within the group what schemas they recognize within themselves and what perceptions and thoughts they have identified so far in the programme that may indicate specific schemas. Feedback from other patients and exploration in individual sessions is particularly important in identifying relevant schemas.

The 'emotions' module has been extended to include the emotional regulation model from DBT and the concept of primary and secondary emotions. This is a crucial aspect, as anger is frequently the secondary emotion in response to emotions of hurt, shame and humiliation, and functions to suppress these primary emotions. The focus is to develop participants' awareness of their primary emotions and the schemas associated with these emotions. This is followed by the development of abilities to tolerate primary emotions. Patterns of over- and under-controlling specific emotions are identified and emotional regulation and distress tolerance strategies from DBT are incorporated.

High risk situations include the common external factors associated with violence, such as substance misuse, negative peers and relationships. A particular feature of this client group is that their violence is frequently directed towards many targets, and there are generally a high number of participants who have been violent towards partners, thus their use of violence is a general problem-solving or coping strategy.

Within the section on relationships, adult attachment styles are explored. Attachment theory provides a model for understanding the development of emotional management, schemas and behavioural patterns to maintain personal security and their relationship behaviours (including avoidance of relationships). This section focuses on intimate relationships and friendships; exploring their attachment patterns and schemas that influence the development and maintenance of relationships; and the patterns patients have shown in past and current relationships, with a focus on the use of violence and identifying effective ways of managing their difficulties in relationships.

All of the modules in phase two focus on problem solving through identifying specific problems that support their violent offending and developing and testing effective solutions for each of the components. A brief model of problem solving is taught within the perceptions module and this is being expanded to incorporate a problem-solving structure (e.g. McMurran *et al.*, 2005).

Phase three, 'relapse prevention', takes the patients' offence cycles and organizes the new skills and abilities they have developed to address these difficulties. The GLM-C focuses the relapse prevention phase on developing a good life. The model puts offending within a functional context of trying to gain primary goods. The patients talk about how violence made them feel and what they gained from violence and its costs. From this and the previous modules primary goods are identified. Their ability to gain primary goods and the negative impact of using violence to achieve primary goods is explored. Patients have identified a range of primary goods that they have attempted to gain through their violence, e.g. achievement, autonomy, emotional expression, belonging. There was also evidence that their ability to achieve primary goods prosocially was restricted and that their methods for achieving one primary good reduced their ability to achieve another. The skills and abilities that they have been developing are then explored in terms of how these help to achieve primary goods.

Extended Violence Reduction Programme in practice: Case examples

The case examples are an amalgam of patients who have participated in the extended VRP and were developed to highlight specific points and experiences. All participants in this programme had undertaken previous therapies and in many cases had not been violent for several years. As a result, the initial issue that some participants raise is that they have already demonstrated that they are no longer violent.

Case example: Tom

Tom had been in secure settings for 10 years and had not been physically violent since his index offence. At the start of the programme he was initially dismissive of his need for the programme and maintained that he was attending as it was required to move to medium security. Tom's history of violence was characterized by under-control of his aggressive behaviour and over-control of pain and sadness at repeated abuse and rejection. His aggression was consistently triggered by perceived attempts by people or systems to put limits on him. It appeared that this pattern was being repeated within the programme. His denial of his ongoing verbal aggression having any link with his risk of future violence was noted at this stage in the programme. To quote the VRP manual, the facilitators initially 'rolled with the resistance'. Some of the other patients supported Tom's denial, creating a difficult situation where patients were supporting denial, rather than challenging each other. However, this does provide the opportunity for the participants to experience being listened to and disagreed with by the facilitators, with the facilitators maintaining the therapeutic relationships. This can be particularly important as personality disordered patients have often experienced disagreements as rapidly leading to either rejection or punishment. The development of further insight on this topic was gradually developed through the subsequent sessions, especially the autobiography, as this highlighted the severity of his violent offending combined with the increasing engagement of other patients and the reduction in their support of his denial. Key to maintaining the facilitators' patience and motivation is their understanding that resistance typically represents a coping strategy, combined with the knowledge that issues may be left to be worked with in relevant later modules.

Case example: George

George has been at the hospital for several years. He had an intermittent history of violence against both men and women. Within phase one he struggled to contribute fully. His previous dominance of interactions with others had been reduced in early personality focused interventions and he was left with fears that he would be found by others to be boring and then rejected. His previous social dominance had been formulated as a means of preventing rejection, to increase his sense of achievement and to gain a sense of belonging and acceptance. He initially informed the group of his pattern of trying to dominate discussions and strategies were agreed in the group to reduce this. He contributed little initially, which represented his alternative strategy of avoidance to prevent rejection or criticism. This process of letting go of one strategy, and finding another to meet the original function, occurred many times throughout the group, with the group providing the safe environment to test out new ways of interacting.

The presentation of their autobiographies is a significant point in the development of the group cohesion, substantially decreasing their subsequent fears of disclosing vulnerability in the group. The group became aware of the similarities within their developmental histories, both in the factual aspects, for example abuse and rejection, being placed in care, and the impact on their feelings and beliefs. In particular, they all described reaching a point where they no longer cared about themselves or others, which appeared to have triggered a significant increase in their violence.

George: *The autobiography was the first time he had been expected to disclose painful aspects of his past and this placed him in a vulnerable situation. He reported significant anxiety, including fears of not being believed, of being humiliated and rejected and being seen as weak and open to further abuse. During the preparation in individual sessions he expressed his concerns that it was too early in the programme (the presentations were to take place on sessions 12 and 13) and trying to find 'legitimate' reasons for his fears, such as the facilitators getting it wrong. Encouraging the expression and containment of these anxieties was a significant factor in George experiencing containment within the secure relationship with his individual therapist and starting to develop a secure attachment to the group.*

   Presenting his autobiography provided George with the experience of his peers valuing his disclosure of vulnerabilities and offering to help him understand his past and its effects on him. George gained a sense of achievement and acceptance from disclosing aspects of himself that he had hidden for many years through aggression and violence; as well as experiencing an alternative means of gaining the primary goods of belonging, freedom from emotional distress and acceptance.

Phase one ends with the participants identifying the dynamic risk factors from the VRS that are applicable to them.

Case example: John

John is a highly anxious and impulsive patient, whose primary coping strategy was to minimize his difficulties and work hard at convincing others he was progressing well. John found the self-assessment process overwhelming as it connected with his strong sense of inadequacy. He rated all of the dynamic risk factors as relevant, triggering a sense of hopelessness and failure. This also occurred with other patients and on the first occasion it caught the facilitators by surprise. The expectation was that patients would underestimate the number of relevant risk factors and the task over phase two would be to increase their insight. It was important for facilitators to accept and tolerate the patients' painful emotions of shame and despair from their open acknowledgement of their risks, combined with expressing hope for their future based on their abilities to engage in therapy and change. For John, this process meant blocking his impulsive tendency to prevent himself experiencing distressing emotions by minimizing their impact and focusing on an unrealistic view of his future; and preventing the group from supporting this pattern of emotional avoidance.

Phase two begins with preparation for the presentation of the baseline account of their violent offending and outlining the behavioural cycle components.

George: *George had considerable anxieties about disclosing his offence, including whether he would be able to provide a good enough account and fears that others would interrogate him to show how bad he really was. The individual sessions included a focus on eliciting disclosure anxieties and facilitating the patients in acknowledging these anxieties in the group. In the group planning for the disclosures, George initially suggested ground rules about how everyone should be respectful and support each other; at that point he was unable to explicitly acknowledge his anxieties and this was noted by the facilitators as an area to be explored within the perceptions and emotions modules.*

Within the high risk situations module, patients draw on their previous work to identify their high risk situations and the most common situations are focused on. This always includes intimate relationships, partly because many of the patients have been violent to varying degrees with partners and partly because difficulties within relationships are frequently related to violence towards others. The relationship between their violence and their attachment styles are explored within the group and changes in their attachment patterns within specific contexts are highlighted and developed. For example, the group considered participants who are highly avoidant of close relationships and support, for fear of rejection or abuse, and who had begun to rely on the group. The impact of their general attachment styles within supportive and supervisory relationships are explored and strategies are developed and role-played for increasing their abilities to contain their insecure attachment patterns to enable them to utilize support and supervision effectively.

John: *During the high risk situations sections, John's impulsivity in interactions with negative peers was deliberately triggered in a carefully constructed role-play of an occasion where he had been verbally aggressive and had a strong urge to be physically violent. The role-play was preliminarily scripted from the examination of the behavioural cycle of the incident. The aims of the role-play were to review the initial understanding of the behavioural cycle, identify key components and increase his ability to intervene earlier in the behavioural cycle. John's reaction to a specific insult from another person indicated that this was the trigger for his urge to be violent and had a specific connection to his defectiveness schema. Additionally, his strong reaction in the role-play broke down his minimization of his ongoing risk in specific situations. Further role-plays on the incident were undertaken with two other patients playing the roles of his 'old me' negative schemas encouraging him to be violent and the role of 'new me' thoughts and encouraging prosocial means of thinking about and handling himself in this situation.*

The presentation of their offence cycles is the culmination of phase two.

Case example: Ben

Ben had been a patient for several decades and had for much of this time main-tained a 'tough' reputation, which was formulated as a defence against self-beliefs of defectiveness and expected abandonment by others, and as a means of gaining respect. He had presented a somewhat vague account of his index offence at the initial disclosure, in particular not giving any information about the gender of his victim, for fear of rejection by the other patients. This fear was much stronger by the time of the offence cycles, as the group had become important attachment figures. He was encouraged to explore these issues within his individual sessions, including his assumptions about the group's reactions and the importance of making a comprehensive disclosure. Ben disclosed the gender of his victim and he was encouraged to voice his concerns about the group's potential reactions. The group responded with an acknowledgement of his anxieties and challenges to his beliefs about it being okay to offend against men, but not women, emphasizing that all offending causes harm.

The relapse prevention phase involves a significant focus on the importance of supportive relationships.

George: *For George this was an identified area of difficulty that he had started to allow the group to fulfil. This area of difficulty was brought into sharper focus for George whilst examining the relevance of the 'Good Lives' model to his offending. George identified the primary goods of achievement, belonging and freedom from emotional distress as important to him and he had tried to gain these through violence. Within the group it was identified that whilst violence had attracted a number of 'friends', there was little sense of belonging and that his violence had reduced this further as it prevented people from getting to know him fully, limiting the extent to which he was accepted for himself. At this stage in the group and individual sessions, George was able to reflect on how sharing his vulnerable side increased his sense of belonging rather than reduced it as he had believed.*

Group process became particularly tense during a period where George had felt betrayed and let down by his individual therapist who was also the group facilitator. Some of his 'old' behaviours or defences re-emerged in a weaker form, including hostile sarcasm towards his therapist in the group sessions, withdrawal in the individual sessions and a somewhat negative demeanour generally. His therapist contained the hostile sarcasm by verbally noting its occurrence in the group in a matter of fact and somewhat irreverent manner, setting a boundary that indicated it was not acceptable, but that it would be tolerated in the short term, due to recognizing the distress that was underpinning it. Other group members toler-ated and disagreed with his behaviour and supported him in engaging in the group (the group at this point was approximately 14 months into the programme). George was encouraged to talk about what he was feeling, rather than express it defensively, utilizing the behavioural cycle format to understand his reactions and behaviours and, with support from others, he acknowledged evidence against his cognitive distortions about his therapist and the role of his past 'emotional baggage' in influencing his schema reactions. Whilst the group participants managed their responses to his hostility towards his therapist well, one of the junior group facilitators discussed in supervision his feelings of anger towards George for 'attacking' the facilitator and wanting to punish George. These feelings were discussed in terms of possible transference and countertransference, drawing on the individual formulation of George's personality disorder and his childhood history of abuse. It was important that George was given the message that his behaviour would be contained and understood, but not agreed with, and that he was not 'punished' as punishment would have mirrored the response he received from his father when he was distressed as a child and this would have emotionally overwhelmed his ability to consider his own behaviour.

Key issues in the treatment of violence with personality disordered patients

The VRP is manualized in terms of defining the content and the aims and objectives of each module, with suggestions for different methods of delivery. It is not prescriptive in how the content should be delivered, nor is it detailed in the process of therapy. There are implicit assumptions, in both the manual and training, that facilitators are familiar with specific therapy approaches, e.g. motivational interviewing, cognitive behaviour therapy and group process. Thus the programme can be delivered in a variety of ways, depending on the qualifications and abilities of the facilitators/therapists, ranging from psychoeducational to an integrated combination of group and individual therapy. For the EVRP to be delivered as a therapy requires that at least some of the facilitators are experienced therapists, to be able to actively integrate the different therapies within the treatment pathway. Furthermore, whilst the VRS identifies specific dynamic risk factors as treatment targets for individuals, the VRP programme is structured using a behavioural chain format. Thus therapists need to have a good working knowledge of the dynamic risk factors and how they relate to the different components of the behavioural cycle, to able to facilitate the participants in exploring their relevant dynamic risk factors within the chain analysis format. With personality disordered patients this requires the facilitators to have significant therapy skills to manage the patients' defences and also their own reaction to what are likely to be minimizing, withdrawing or aggressive behaviours from the patients.

The task of enabling patients to integrate a range of therapies can appear to be overwhelming for all concerned. However, in practice, it appears that this has been facilitated by several factors: the shared structure of cognitions and emotions influencing behaviour underpinning all the therapies; there being a core group of psychologists and therapists who have been trained in and run the majority of these therapies; and the therapies occurring over a number of years. This is further supported by the individual sessions that form one component of all the major therapies, e.g. DBT, schema therapy, SOTP (Sex Offender Treatment Programme) and EVRP.

Personality disordered offenders have been found to have high dropout rates from treatment programmes and significant difficulties engaging in therapy. The patients' therapy-interfering behaviours and lack of treatment readiness (Howells & Day, 2007) may represent the activation of their personality disorder, e.g. paranoid/difficulties trusting others, expectations of failure, deficits in emotional and cognitive regulation, in other words the targets for treatment. Within the EVRP there is emphasis on enabling patients to examine themselves, without triggering overwhelming therapy-interfering behaviours that function to protect the patient from feelings of vulnerability. The disclosure process throughout the VRP is facilitated using a number of different approaches. Case vignettes were used at various points within the programme. They were written vaguely enough for participants to project their emotions, fears, beliefs and behaviours onto the characters. The case vignettes placed the participants in the role of investigator with the aim of developing formulations about main characters' perceptions, beliefs and emotions. This appeared to give them temporary relief from the anxiety of scrutinizing their own behavioural patterns, and increased the extent to which they are able to explore their internal world and past lives.

The GLM-C is a positive psychology model and focuses the patients on making gains, which can also protect against risk. This approach appeared to trigger less defensiveness and therapy-interfering behaviours, possibly because it focuses on meeting needs and is less directly critical. The GLM-C was developed in relation to sexual offending; its application here to violent offending appeared to resonate strongly with all the participants. They reported that the model helped to make explicit the potential links between their risk management and their personal goals.

The VRP places a strong emphasis throughout the programme on generalization of the skills and changes developed within the programme to all aspects of the patients' lives. This is an emphasis that starts with staff supporting generalization and moves towards patients focusing on how they gain help in generalizing their changes to new environments. This is explicitly undertaken when the participants are required to talk through their relapse prevention plans with a member of staff from either their ward or clinical team, who is not involved in the VRP, and to gain feedback.

There has been consistent feedback from the participants of the VRP as to the importance of having consistent and committed therapists, due to the high level of personal disclosure that is expected of the participants. This appears to reflect the patients experiencing the facilitators as a secure base, which can increase the patients' ability to use the group process.

Conclusions

Treatment for violence for high risk male patients with personality disorder, within the setting described, involves a comprehensive treatment pathway, in which different components of personality disorders, that have contributed to their violence, are targeted. The EVRP provides the format within which to further treat dynamic risk factors, including integrating previous treatments. This approach begins with developing patients' abilities to contain their current risk and personality difficulties (e.g. impulsivity, emotional control, interpersonal aggression and cognitive distortions) and provides the opportunity for patients to effectively adapt these difficulties and restructure them.

References

Baker, E. & Beech, A. R. (2004). Dissociation and variability of adult attachment dimensions and early maladaptive schemas in sexual and violent offenders. *Journal of Interpersonal Violence, 19*(10), 1119–1136.

Beck, A. T. (1999). *Prisoners of hate: The cognitive basis of anger, hostility and violence.* New York: HarperCollins.

Blackburn, R. (1993). *The psychology of criminal conduct: Theory, research and practice.* New York: Wiley.

Cassidy, J. (1994). Emotion regulation: Influences of attachment relationships. In N. A. Fox (Ed.), *The development of emotional regulation: Biological and behavioural considerations. Monographs of the Society for Research in Child Development, 59*(2–3, Serial No. 240).

Deci, E. L. & Ryan, R. M. (2000). The 'what' and 'why' of goal pursuits: Human needs and the self-determination of behaviour. *Psychological Inquiry, 11,* 227–268.

Fonagy, P. (2003). Towards a developmental understanding of violence. *British Journal of Psychiatry, 183,* 190–192.

Gordon, A. & Wong, S. C. P. (2000). *Violence Reduction Program: Facilitator's manual.* Unpublished manuscript.

Howells, K. & Day, A. (2002). Grasping the nettle: treating and rehabilitating the violent offender. *Australian Psychologist, 37,* 222–228.

Howells, K. & Day, A. (2006). Affective determinants of treatment engagement in violent offenders. *International Journal of Offender Therapy and Comparative Criminology, 50*(2), 174–186.

Howells, K. & Day, A. (2007). Readiness for treatment in high risk offenders with personality disorders. *Psychology, Crime and Law, 13*(1), 47–56.

Howells, K., Day, A. & Thomas-Peter, B. (2004). Changing violent behaviour: Forensic mental health and criminological models compared. *Journal of Forensic Psychiatry and Psychology, 15*(3), 391–406.

Jones, L. (2004). Offence paralleling behaviour (OPB) as a framework for assessment and interventions with offenders. In A. Needs & G. Towl (Eds.), *Applying psychology to forensic practice* (pp. 34–63). Maldon: Blackwell Publishing.

Linehan, M. M. (1993). *Cognitive-behavioural treatment of borderline personality disorder.* New York: Guilford Press.

Livesley, W. J. (2003). A framework for an integrated approach to treatment. In W. J. Livesley (Ed.), *Handbook of personality disorders: Theory, research and treatment.* New York: Guilford Press.

McMurran, M., Egan, V. & Duggan, C. (2005). Stop and think! Social problem-solving therapy with personality-disordered offenders. In J. McGuire (Ed.), *Social problem solving and offending: Evidence, evaluation and evolution* (pp. 207–220). New York: Wiley.

Novaco, R. (1997). Remediating anger and aggression with violent offenders. *Legal and Criminological Psychology, 2,* 77–88.

Ogloff, J. & Davis, M. (2004). Advances in offender assessment and rehabilitation: Contributions of the risk-needs-responsivity approach. *Psychology, Crime and Law*, *10*(3), 229–242.

Polaschek, D. L. L. (2006). Violent offender programmes: Concepts, theory and practice. In C. R. Hollin & E. J. Palmer (Eds.), *Offending behaviour programmes: Development, application and controversies* (pp. 113–154). New York: Wiley.

Sperry, L. (2003). *Handbook of diagnosis and treatment of DSM-IV-TR personality disorders*. London: Routledge.

Ward, T. & Gannon, T. (2006). Rehabilitation, aetiology, and self-regulation: The Good Lives Model of rehabilitation for sexual offenders. *Aggression and Violent Behavior*, *11*(1), 77–94.

Wong, S. C. P. & Gordon, A. (1999). *Unpublished outcome data for the ABC programme*. Violence Reduction Training Presentation.

Wong, S. C. P. & Gordon, A. (1999–2003). *Violence Risk Scale*. Unpublished manuscript.

Wong, S. C. P. & Gordon, A. (2006). The validity and reliability of the Violence Risk Scale: A treatment-friendly violence risk assessment tool. *Psychology, Public Policy, and Law*, *12*, 279–309.

Wong, S. C. P., Gordon, A. & Gu, D. (2007). Assessment and treatment of violence-prone forensic clients: An integrated approach. *British Journal of Psychiatry*, *190*(suppl. 49), s66–s74.

Young, J. E., Klosko, J. S. & Weishaar, M. E. (2003). *Schema therapy: A practitioner's guide*. New York: Guilford Press.

Chapter Nine

Working with People Who Have Committed Sexual Offences with Personality Disorder Diagnoses

Lawrence Jones

Introduction

The category of 'sexual offending' is a problematic one in that it can be seen to imply that the motive for the offence was a sexual one when in reality the motivations exhibited by those committing these offences are multiple and not solely or indeed, in any clear sense, primarily sexual. They are driven by a similar range of interacting biological, psychological and social factors to those that underpin violent offending (and other offending) and often cannot be meaningfully distinguished from violent offending. The category of 'personality disorder' (PD) is equally problematic (see Livesley, 2003). To put a number of individuals together and call them 'personality disordered sex offenders' is then almost meaningless; it is also impossible to assume that they are all going to have the same or similar clinical needs. Each case requires a detailed assessment and work developing an individualized formulation (see chapter 4), informed by the current evidence base and models of offending.

Initial observations of the kinds of personality disorders found amongst sex offenders suggest that they often meet the criteria for borderline and antisocial PD with a few individuals with paranoid and schizoid traits. Most exhibit 'approach explicit' (Ward & Hudson, 2000) offending; that is they were not interested in regulating their behaviour when they were in the process of offending and in the treatment setting they are often reluctant to admit that they had done anything wrong and are primarily interested in engaging in therapy as a way of moving through the system.

Using Time, Not Doing Time: Practitioner Perspectives on Personality Disorder and Risk
Edited by Allison Tennant and Kevin Howells
© 2010 John Wiley & Sons, Ltd.

Several individuals who are not explicitly categorized as sex offenders have evidenced significant sexual components to their offending both in the past and in their index offences.

Low IQ (intelligence quotient) or an unstable psychometric profile of cognitive abilities (Ray St Ledger, personal communication) is not uncommon in this population. This suggests that interventions designed for individuals of average intelligence are likely to be difficult for this group. The instability of the results suggests that cognitive capacity is state dependent and that individuals may be capable of quite high cognitive functioning when they are emotionally stable but, when they are distressed or emotionally dysregulated in some way, they lose this capacity and evidence a reduced ability.

Previous work looking at the past experiences of individuals involved with a group-based intervention delivered in the Personality Disorder Directorate at Rampton Hospital identified a range of responsivity issues in this population, including the fact that the majority of individuals had previously either not responded or dropped out of interventions (Jones, 2006) targeting their offending and consequently may have a number of difficulties embarking on a process of re-engagement.

The implications for designing interventions for this population are as follows:

1. They need to address the motivational or readiness issues of re-engagement and continue to address these as the intervention progresses.
2. The characteristic styles of responding to interventions described in the literature about borderline, antisocial, paranoid and schizoid personality disorders need to be taken into account.
3. Working on strategies for engaging and addressing the offending of those whose offending took the approach automatic offence pathway described by Ward *et al.* (2006).
4. Interventions need to be kept simple and intelligible.

The literature

A review of the literature on personality disorder incidence amongst sex offenders and attempts at addressing their treatment needs (Jones, 2006) identified a number of previous attempts at working with this client group. Few studies reporting reconviction rates actually explicitly report on the outcomes of working with sex offenders with personality disorder diagnoses. The literature suggests however that:

1. Psychopathy increases the risk of reconviction (Hart, 1998).
2. The assumption that high PCL-R (Psychopathy Checklist – Revised) scorers are made worse by intervention, as suggested by a number of researchers, is not supported by the evidence (D'Silva *et al.*, 2004).
3. Sex offenders have a high representation of borderline, antisocial, narcissistic, schizoid and avoidant personality disorders.
4. Using a whole milieu approach is important (Thornton *et al.*, 2000).

5. Making links between adverse daily social experiences, fantasy as coping and offending, or in-treatment offence-related behaviour is an important component (Buschman and Van Beek, 2003).
6. Links between sexual abuse and offending may be significant in this group but this is not the only motivation for sexual offending (e.g. Saradjian, 1996).
7. Approaches using interpersonal, schema therapy, approach goals and strengths-based perspectives may be promising with this group.

Brief literature review

Interventions with high risk offenders with high levels of personality disorder

There is little evidence for interventions impacting on sex offenders who pose a high risk of reoffending. The prison service SOTP (Sex Offender Treatment Programme) study by Friendship *et al.* (2003) found little impact for the prison service core programme on high risk offenders, who, it is argued, are more likely to be personality disordered.

Accounts of interventions with this group are mostly anecdotal and about interventions where there has been no evaluation or indeed there has been no clearly manualized treatment developed. They are nevertheless useful and appear to converge in their accounts around some core themes.

Beech and Mann (2002) argue that for high risk offenders there is a need for more intensive input (at least 360 hours). This is clearly relevant to the personality disordered sex offender population.

Willmott (2006) conducted a qualitative review of patients' reports, in the Rampton Hospital Personality Disorder Directorate, about a sex offender group using the model of attrition prevention developed by Jones (1997, 2009) and found that the strategy had been effective in holding patients in the group.

Proulx *et al.* (1994) model of personality disorder and rape

Proulx *et al.* (1994) elaborated a model for analysing the link between an individual's personality and their sexual offending. They suggest that the interpersonal and intrapersonal processes associated with their personality disorder are likely to be manifested during the offence process. The offence is conceptualized as a replication in the sexual domain of the habitual mode of relating associated with an individual's personality disorder. They go on to propose that sexual offending can be analysed in terms of affective processes. The affective function of the offence, in each case, is driven by the individual's personality disorder. The personality disorder, they argue, underpins the characteristic structure of interacting and feeling, which is played out in the offence process. They also suggest that fantasies also replay this characteristic interactive structure.

They explore a number of treatment considerations. Personality disordered offenders, they claim, typically blame others, have an external locus of control, take a victim stance and are thus difficult to engage. Typically, they suggest, they arrive into treatment due to external pressures. Cluster B dramatic personality disorder increases the chances of the individuals exhibiting seductive behaviour in the intervention; they may try to push the pace of the therapy, and attempt to challenge and control the therapy and the therapist. They warn that for this group there is a risk that they will act out in response to the therapy ending. Cluster A eccentric personality disorder is accompanied by bizarre fantasies which can be difficult for the practitioner engaging with them; they can appear to live in an imaginary world impermeable to the reality of others and can get involved with esoteric or ideological groups. Cluster C anxious personality disorder, they propose, is associated with passivity, silence, incomprehension, not doing homework; the individual tends to leave all the work to the therapist.

Proulx *et al.* (2006) developed a model of offending by individuals with sadistic personality traits. They are identified as avoidant and schizoid and consequently isolate themselves, have low self-esteem and fear rejection; the sadistic offending, it is suggested, serves to compensate for anger and humiliation experienced in daily living which is unexpressed. The victim's suffering is seen as resulting in a cathartic experience, for the perpetrator, in which the offender experiences temporary release from internal distress.

Buschman and Van Beek (2003) self-regulation pathways model

This useful framework highlights the importance of individual case formulation informed by the sex offender literature and being aware of the potential for 'pathway switching' state-dependent switches in attitude to offending between wanting to self-regulate and not wanting to self-regulate.

They propose that a number of additional 'assumptions' be 'knitted into' the self-regulation model:

1. Stress-related sexual violence occurs if the offender lacks the ability to cope with interpersonal stress in another way. They underscore the importance of fantasy in understanding the offending of personality disordered sex offenders. They suggest making links between: repeating socially difficult experiences and deviant fantasies which are, they propose, used as a strategy for undoing or reversing the aversive aspects of these experiences.
2. The cognitive distortions of the personality disordered offender 'are a result of a general explanatory model underlying the offender's overall view of the world and himself, his dominant affect and his internal motive for engaging in an offence'. Both fantasies and offending fall out of these 'explanatory models'.
3. There is an increasing rigidity in the offender's basic assumptions; originally developed in the context of 'unsafe childhood experiences and a global sense of loneliness'. They propose four 'self-confirming domains of interpersonal motivation: lust, emotional control, social positioning and power.

They develop a four-stage intervention strategy:

- Phase 1: 'Identifying the general explanatory theory underlying the behaviour of the patient'. This involves developing a case formulation using the nine steps of the pathways model as a general framework.
- Phase 2: 'Observing the offence related behavioural structures that occur in daily life'. This is seen as working on the patient's general explanatory theory as it drives behaviour in the treatment setting. Skills training is targeted at deficits identified in the daily problems experienced by the patient. Targets are set and reviewed regularly.
- Phase 3: 'Recognizing the general explanatory theory-related behavioural chains in sex offences' and 'deviant' sexual fantasies. In group therapy they address 'other issues' such as sexual identity, victim impact and their own abuse, their value systems and beliefs about life and offending. They are 'confronted about offence related behaviour that occurred during the week' and are encouraged to take responsibility.
- Phase 4: Learning how to communicate their 'underlying general explanatory theory' and how to deal with high risk factors related to it. Steps taken to self-regulate following the plan in daily living are then monitored.

Psychopathy amongst sex offenders

The literature suggests using the individual's sense of 'enlightened self-interest' if they are not capable of experiencing empathy for others. Work with 'sadistic psychopaths' needs to address the possibility that they might enjoy discussing offences, and act out sadistically in response to the intervention. Some argue that participation in treatment targeting interpersonal skills building and empathy training may lead to psychopaths using these skills to gain access to victims following release and to manipulate others more effectively and thus becoming more effective psychopaths rather than more responsible or considerate individuals. They have also suggested that psychopaths may increase their risk for reoffence through exposure to others' deviant sexual fantasies and behaviour or learning from others' 'modi operandi' during treatment.

Implication for intervention It may be important to ensure that for some offenders they are not exposed to accounts of other offenders' offences. In addition it is important that fantasies are monitored for the possible introduction of themes deriving from peer disclosures. Obviously this will not be easy for those who are reluctant to be open about their offence-related fantasies.

Schizoid personality amongst child sex offenders

The literature suggests that schizoid personality disorder is particularly associated with insecurely attached child sexual offending associated with finding children to be emotionally congruent and feeling comfortable in their presence (see Jones, 2009 for reasons).

Social and state repertoires as link between PD and offending

A number of theorists have identified two key underlying factors describing the aspects of personality associated with social functioning. These are dominance and affiliation. These factors correspond to the extraversion and agreeableness factors of the Big Five (McCrae & Costa, 1990). These two factors have also been identified in the evolutionary psychology literature as critical to survival in group contexts.

In order to render these constructs clinically useful it is important to identify ways in which these traits manifest themselves in the day-to-day lives of individuals. One key linking construct making this possible is the idea of states associated with different traits. A state is a brief episodic event whereas a trait is an enduring pattern. Some theorists have identified emotion (a kind of state) as one key linking construct between traits and behaviour. Individuals with certain kinds of traits are more likely to experience certain kinds of states.

States associated with attachment   Attachment theory suggests different ways in which an individual characteristically responds to a number of different kinds of relationship events (Jones, 2002):

- being alone;
- seeking relationship;
- being rejected in an attempt to form a relationship (exclusion pain, Baumeister *et al.*, 2007);
- forming a relationship;
- having a honeymoon period;
- maintaining a relationship;
- reacting to separations (brief and protracted);
- reacting to reunion following separation;
- becoming estranged within a relationship;
- ending a relationship;
- having a partner end a relationship;
- being faithful or unfaithful;
- experiencing a partner being faithful or unfaithful (jealousy); and
- coping with children and significant others in partner's life.

Interviewing carefully about these areas of relationship helps the clinician to get a sense of the way in which an individual's attachment style plays out in real relationships. Themes in relationship problems, often critical triggers for offending, become key targets for intervention. Building an offence-free lifestyle with 'approach goals' is likely to be more achievable if basic relationship skills have been developed, including insight into patterns of attachment and relationships breaking down.

States associated with rank status   Stevens and Price (2000) describe mania as a model of what they term agonistic behaviour associated with individuals who are attempting to establish and maintain dominance in a group context. The strategy here is to go all out to win and not to submit. It is contrasted with the submission strategy which is associated with depression and anxiety.

The personality disorders most frequently encountered in our population – antisocial, psychopathic, narcissistic and paranoid – would fall into the hostile dominant quadrant of the interpersonal circumplex. (Borderline personality disorder is associated with changeable states and as such these individuals would present at times with these states also; as indeed would individuals during the experience of some kinds of substance abuse.) Jones (2004a) argued that developing a psychology of state hostile dominance would enable clinicians to understand the kinds of state associated with psychopathy. Behaviourally, individuals characterized by the hostile dominant quadrant present as being preoccupied with establishing and maintaining dominance.

Much offending behaviour is about power and the individual's relationship with their own lack of power or their urge to abuse power. It is thus not surprising that a significant proportion of offenders evidence power and dominance-oriented interpersonal styles. Rank status theory suggests a number of different orientations to power. Evolutionary approaches to human problems highlight the links between psychopathology and normal or extremes of patterns of behaving noted in studies of social animals including humans. The following are taken from Gardner's framework (1988) for describing social roles from an evolutionary perspective.

Most dominant 'alpha' position   This is a dominant role, often oriented to being the most dominant individual. In many social groups this is a role that is fought for vigorously. An extreme manifestation of this behaviour is identified by Gardner (1988) as manic behaviour.

Individuals with this position are particularly interested in obtaining submission cues from their peers. Consequently submission of peers is rewarding for them. Jones (2004a) argues that taken to its extreme this can account for some forms of sadistic behaviour which is dependent on obtaining distress cues from others; insensitivity to distress makes it even more difficult to obtain the reassurance, of perceived submission, that an individual in an alpha position would require and could result in increasing dominance behaviour until submission cues are detected.

Followers   The alpha reciprocal role is the role of a follower in a group. This group evidence the capacity to be uncritically obedient. In offending terms this would be individuals who have been caught up in gang-based offending as 'followers'.

Submissive individuals   This is the role of an individual with a very low rank who exhibits submissive behaviour to other members of the group. In-group omegas are generally depressed in Gardner's framework. Depression is construed as concerted submissive behaviour in the context of the group. In this position obtaining status becomes very difficult as the whole orientation towards self and others is disturbed and the individual is only interested in appeasing those in dominant positions.

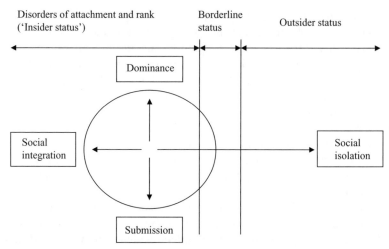

Figure 9.1 Interpersonal circumplex (based on Stevens, A. & Price, J. (2000). *Evolutionary Psychiatry: A New Beginning* 2nd Edition, Routledge, page 54)

Outsiders   This is the role of a persecuted member of an 'out-group'. This role is associated with paranoid perspectives. It can often be associated with people who come from a minority culture.

Stevens and Price (2000) develop this model using the interpersonal circumplex (see Figure 9.1).

Blackburn *et al.* (2005) argue that this circumplex captures the interpersonal aspects of personality disorder. Stevens and Price (2000) indicate that personality disorders can be seen as extremes of each position in the circumplex. Cluster A personality disorders are seen as different reactions to 'outsider' status, Cluster B as primarily hostile dominance with borderline personality switching between outsider and insider status.

Stevens and Price (2000) suggest that submission is associated with depression, shame, humiliation and anxiety; whereas dominance is associated with 'high self-esteem, hypomania, sadism, and a liability to victimise and abuse others'. This convergence of interpersonal and evolutionary theorizing in a two-dimensional model offers a simple model for clinicians to think about the state repertoires each individual experiences in the context of their particular personalities and how these might contribute both to offending and to individual responses to change initiatives.

State-dependent activation of schemas and attachment style

Having a sense of an individual's state repertoire then enables work on looking at the kinds of schemas that are activated in different states. Hostile Dominant states, for example, associated with positive affect or anger can trigger schema such as entitlement, over-confidence about not being caught, strong 'feeling of knowing' or being 'right' and an egocentric cognitive style (see Leahy's 2005 account of hypomanic cognitive distortions being the opposite of those associated with depression).

Intervention

Personality disordered sex offenders have often experienced a number of interventions. The treatment pathways model (Hogue *et al.*, 2007; Jones, 1997) based on Linehan's (1993) hierarchy of treatment targets, and more recently Livesley's (e.g. 2007) hierarchical model, advocates that interventions targeting therapy-interfering behaviour and developing the capacity to tolerate the emotional distress associated with change processes need to be completed before embarking on an intensive intervention targeting offending behaviour. Early work using DBT-informed interventions with personality disordered offenders (Jones, 1997) indicated that this had several additional advantages. Strategies and skills used in the early treatment pathway to stabilize behaviour and manage affect also served to facilitate drop-out prevention planning; moreover it was often the case that factors that lead to urges to drop out of treatment were also factors that had led an individual to renege on their commitment to maintain an offence-free lifestyle. Individuals who have completed a DBT intervention prior to starting a SOG (sex offender group) are usually able to generate options for coping with high risk situations presented to them in a way that is not evident amongst those who had not completed such an intervention.

Iatrogenic responses

Jones (2007) identifies a number of ways in which interventions in groups and individually can be potentially harmful. The key strategy with this group is to conduct a detailed analysis of responsivity issues for the individual case (Jones, 2002). This involves looking at key turning points for the individual both in terms of decreased engagement and dropping-out and looking at times when they have been able to respond well to interventions or self-management regimes (as evidenced by periods of not offending, for instance). Using the solution-focused philosophy of 'find out what works and do more of it' the individual develops an individualized 'what works' framework collaboratively with the practitioner.

Offsetting potential adverse responses

Group and individual interventions Pre-empting treatment drop-out with a group of personality disordered offenders who had previously dropped out of group-based interventions. This involved taking some of the detailed disclosure work out of the group context and working with individual offenders on offences outside the group. This strategy proved to be effective in maintaining patients in the group and enabled much more detailed offence work to take place as doing this in a group context can limit the resources allowable to individual cases. The argument that this could lead to patients avoiding dealing with critical issues was addressed by having two co-workers run these sessions, one conducting the intervention directly and the other observing for possible collusion or other process issues that might impact on the efficacy of the intervention.

Group work was used for the rest of the work. This involved detailed disclosure about long-term and proximal antecedents to the offence, and psychoeducational work on understanding constructs such as relapse and abstinence violation effects.

Change processes

Psychoeducational work

Psychoeducation is increasingly becoming a significant part of a range of cognitive behaviour therapy (CBT) intervention. When working with personality disordered sex offenders this is aimed at developing:

1. understanding of offending processes;
2. understanding of processes of coping; and
3. building knowledge about the consequences of offending on the self and on others.

The change process is one of increasing an individual's capacity to understand and make sense of both their offending and their own process of change. This approach can help for individuals who find dissonance difficult to tolerate and where the strategy is one of building new schemas rather than demolishing old ones.

Typically group-based interventions work at developing knowledge in the following areas:

- the importance of changing behaviour;
- relationships and attachment styles and offending;
- core beliefs/schema and their relationship to offending;
- 'high risk situations';
- sexual arousal;
- states (emotional and other) associated with changes in behaviour and beliefs;
- self-regulation and self-compassion skills;
- empathy for victims;
- lifestyle building through establishing positive 'goods' to aim for;
- skills for understanding and managing high risk situations; and
- pleasure skills (ways of seeking out enjoyable experiences that do not harm others or self).

Individual work typically addresses these issues but also targets:

- understanding and making sense of what happens before, during and after offending with a view to identifying alternative coping strategies and building a lifestyle that meets needs without offending;
- understanding links between abuse and offending;
- addressing pro-offending attitudes and habits;
- relapse prevention planning using 'approach goals', goals to move towards rather than just things to avoid;

- mindfulness (Segal *et al.*, 2002) and goal directedness (managing distraction from goal-oriented behaviour); and
- addressing sexual arousal to themes associated with offending.

Working in the here and now

Interventions are typically construed as work undertaken with a therapist during a session. However, it is important that all interventions maximize the extent to which the model of change includes work with problem behaviours as they emerge in the treatment setting (Kohlenberg & Tsai's (1995) 'clinically relevant behaviours'). Work in the here and now aims to bring about change by rewarding and reinforcing appropriate and strengths-based behaviour and making the individual aware of inappropriate or harmful behaviour so that they can do something about it.

Offence paralleling behaviour   Offence paralleling behaviour is behaviour that has been shown to be related to the individual's offending (cf. Daffern *et al.*, 2007). The core idea here is that if the individual has not changed then they will demonstrate their problem behaviour, or a significant aspect of it, in the here and now. Responses to it are either going to facilitate them becoming more deeply ingrained or they are going to change them. The custodial experience is likely to test even the strongest of individuals and they are likely to demonstrate their characteristic patterns of not coping when they are tested. Offence-supportive beliefs activated in the daily encounter with the custodial experience are a critical target for live intervention. Crisis management strategies can be designed to maximize this aspect of crises if they are seen as an opportunity to learn and not something to sweep under the carpet and hope that the problem will go away.

Changing beliefs

As with most other CBT interventions the emphasis is first of all on forming a collaborative therapeutic alliance. Once this alliance is established it is used to facilitate the use of standard change strategies of Socratic questioning, collaborative discovery, motivational interviewing and generating dissonance between values/needs and actual behaviour past and present. Davidson (2006) argues that changing old beliefs is more difficult than it seems and as a consequence she advocates developing new beliefs as opposed to changing old beliefs. Old beliefs are likely to re-emerge in particular states and it is important that the individual has some insight into this process and recognizes that their re-emergence is not evidence of their losing the gains they felt that they have made.

Strengths-based strategies   There is current movement towards strengths-based interventions following Seligman's (e.g. Seligman *et al.*, 2006) introduction of the construct of positive psychology. So much of the business of working with offenders and personality disorder is, at least traditionally, about identifying risks, weaknesses and deficits; recognizing strengths and abilities is important. A number of approaches make use of strengths and can be usefully incorporated in sex offender interventions (e.g. Seligman *et al.*, 2006).

Developing capacity for attachment

Through relatively long-standing therapeutic relationships, individuals can improve their capacity to form attachments and develop a sense of the value of genuine relationships that can give them a stable 'internal working model' and a 'secure base'.

Solution-focused approach

There are a number of strategies used in solution-focused (e.g. De Shazar, 1988) approaches that are particularly useful for working with offenders. The central idea is one of focusing on practical approaches to finding out what works for an individual and being specific about what needs to change. Using a narrative approach to change, it works towards re-telling the individual's story in such a way as to generate hope and a sense of empowerment.

As a strengths-based approach it highlights the utility of 'looking for exceptions', for example times when the individual has managed not to offend and to successfully self-regulate; identifying what they did that worked and then committing to doing more of it. Instead of attempting to install new skills this approach builds on and validates existing skills by entering into the individual's way of seeing the world and actively exploring what self-regulation means in their own terms.

So instead of seeing the individual as having a self-regulation problem they are seen as having expertise on what is effective for them and they are encouraged to 'find out what works and do more of it'. As offenders rarely spend all their time offending they must have alternative ways of living their lives that do not lead to offending. It is this sense of the individual as having skills, insight and ability to self-regulate that makes this approach attractive. The therapist embarks upon a collaborative exploration of 'what works' for the individual. In Maruna's terms (2001) it is about building redemption narratives and unearthing condemnatory narratives with a view to identifying what functions they served for the individual.

Case example: James

James was born in Liverpool and was very close to his mother. He remembers little of his childhood but reports that he was frequently neglected and left to fend for himself. His sister recalls that he was often beaten by his father for minor transgressions that other members of the family would be forgiven for. She also reported that on one occasion his mother had threatened to kill him, blaming him for her depression. Eventually his mother had not been able to cope with looking after all her children and had sent him into care. He experienced this as a rejection at the time. He was reported to have become very difficult to control at this time and had a turbulent experience in care. He now idealizes his mother. He protects his mother from his feelings of anger about the time when he went into care, rarely showing any of these feelings to her.

> *When James was 25 he committed a protracted assault on a partner. The offence took place in the context of a relationship breaking down and his partner saying, after several years of violent abuse, that the relationship had ended. He described feeling overwhelmed with panic and angry feelings when she ended the relationship. He had kidnapped her and subjected her to a series of sadistic acts including forced sexual acts and burning her with a cigarette.*

Hypotheses about why the offending had taken place include:

a. Core beliefs about being unlovable when triggered by current themes of abandonment in relationships leave him feeling panicky and overwhelmed with feelings of hurt. To offset these he forces potentially abandoning individuals to stay with him.
b. Angry beliefs and associated feelings about past abandonment are triggered in current relationships and lead to retaliatory punitive aggression which is sadistic in nature.
c. Pairing of violent behaviour with sexual arousal had generated an association between these two kinds of arousal (see Figure 9.2).

Predicted offence paralleling behaviour:

a. Fantasies of violence associated with sexual arousal.
b. These fantasies are triggered by both sexual arousal and by social contexts which make him feel that he is going to be abandoned or rejected (e.g. key people leaving him such as therapists and staff).
c. PPG (penile plethysmography) arousal to sadistic behaviour with women.

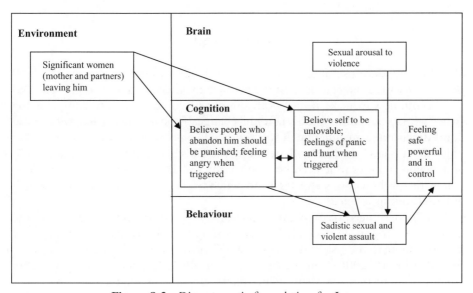

Figure 9.2   Diagrammatic formulation for James

d. Compensatory idealization (schema compensation) of some women which switches briefly, on occasion, into anger towards women.
e. Beliefs and associated behaviour about women who abandon men as being cruel and about the justification of violence in the context of punishment.

Key issues

In this case a number of key issues emerge. The themes of attachment, loss and use of dominance are key to understanding the case. Hilburn-Cobb (2003) discusses a developmental pathway in which dominance comes to be habitually used to meet attachment needs. In this case the use of sadistic punitive dominant behaviour also serves to offset fears of abandonment. This pattern may have contributed to the development of sexual arousal to sadistic dominant behaviour (aimed at soliciting submission cues from the victim). The pairing of sexual arousal with sadistic behaviour may have led to a conditioned arousal to sadistic thoughts and behaviour (perhaps no longer even requiring real threats of abandonment to trigger them). Jones (2004b) highlights the way in which intense sexual arousal can lead to intrusive thoughts and experiences of anticipatory arousal in a similar way to other intense emotional arousal such as fear arousal leading to intrusive PTSD (post-traumatic stress disorder) experiences.

Intervention in addition to the standard psychoeducational work in a group context would need to work on his ways of relating to self and others on the ward as examples of his sadistic interest emerged. A long-term piece of work with an individual therapist where he could develop an attachment that could help him to develop an ability to relate in ways other than simply the dominance mode would also be useful. Work using behavioural strategies to address sexual arousal alongside work on managing interpersonal stress without recourse to using fantasy and dehumanizing others as a way of regaining a sense of self-worth and value would be critical.

Conclusion

Working to reduce risk of reoffending with offenders who have personality disorder diagnoses is a difficult task. In the absence of an evidence base there is a need for practitioners to make use of both the personality disorder literature and the 'what works' literature. Understanding changeable states associated with social contexts eliciting, in different ways, the need for rank status and the need for attachment is critical – as is understanding the links between these changing states and coping fantasies which can be used to offset social alienation (whether associated with attachment or status loss) and which become entrenched as habits which are acted out in offence contexts.

Practitioners need also to avoid focusing on deficits and pathology at the expense of recognizing strengths and an existing reservoir of skills and values that can contribute to the task of developing a holistic rewarding lifestyle that is offence free (Ward *et al.*, 2006). This needs to see individuals developing their personality strengths and recognizing their offence management skills and their existing values that can support these aspects of themselves. Mindfulness skills (Segal *et al.*, 2002) offer much in helping the individual to regulate emotion, monitor the self and enhance positive experiences. Self-sabotaging and offending against the self (e.g. offending as stealing happiness from the future as well as from other people) need to be recognized and addressed.

References

Baumeister, R. F., Brewer, L. E., Tice, D. M. & Twenge, J. M. (2007). The need to belong: Understanding the interpersonal and inner effects of social exclusion. *Social and Personality Psychology Compass, 1*, 506–520.

Beech, A. & Mann, R. (2002). Recent developments in the assessment and treatment of sexual offenders. In J. McGuire (Ed.), *Offender rehabilitation and treatment: Effective programmes and policies to reduce re-offending*. Chichester: Wiley.

Blackburn, R., Logan, C., Renwick, S. J. D. & Donnelly, J. P. (2005). Higher order dimensions of personality disorder: Hierarchical structure and relationship with the five-factor model, the interpersonal circle and psychopathy. *Journal of Personality Disorders, 19*(6), 597–623.

Buschman, J. & Van Beek, D. J. (2003). A clinical model for the treatment of personality disordered sexual offenders: an example of theory knitting. *Sexual Abuse: A Journal of Treatment and Research, 15*(3), 183–199.

Daffern, M., Jones, L., Howells, K., Shine, J., Mikton, C. & Tunbridge, V. (2007). Refining the definition of offence paralleling behaviour. *Criminal Behaviour and Mental Health, 17*(5), 265–273.

Davidson, K. (2006). Cognitive formulation in personality disorder. In N. Tarrier (Eds.), *Case formulation in cognitive behaviour therapy: The treatment of challenging and complex cases*. London: Routledge.

De Shazar, S. (1988). *Clues: Investigating solutions in brief therapy*. New York: Norton.

D'Silva, K., Duggan, C. & McCarthy, L. (2004). Does treatment really make psychopaths worse? A review of the evidence. *Journal of Personality Disorders, 18*, 163–177.

Friendship, C., Mann, R. E. & Beech, A. R. (2003). Evaluation of a national prison-based treatment programme for sexual offenders in England and Wales. *Journal of Interpersonal Violence, 18*(7), 744–759.

Gardner, R. (1988). Psychiatric syndromes as infrastructures for intraspecific communication. In M. R. A. Chance (Ed.), *Social fabrics of the mind*. Hove: Lawrence Erlbaum.

Hart, S. D. (1998). Psychopathy and risk for violence. In D. Cooke, A. E. Forth & R. D. Hare (Eds.), *Psychopathy: Theory, research and implications for society* (pp. 355–375). Dordrecht, The Netherlands: Kluwer.

Hilburn-Cobb, C. (2003). Adolescent psychopathology in terms of multiple behavioral systems: The role of attachment and controlling strategies and frankly disorganized behavior. In L. Atkinson & S. Goldberg (Eds.), *Attachment issues in psychopathology and intervention*. Mahwah, NJ: Lawrence Erlbaum Assoc Inc.

Hogue, T. E., Jones, L., Talkes, K. & Tennant, A. (2007). The Peaks: A clinical service for those with dangerous and severe personality disorder. *Psychology, Crime and Law, 13*(1), 57–68.

Jones, L. (1997). Developing models for managing treatment integrity and efficacy in a prison-based TC: The Max Glatt Centre. In E. Cullen, L. Jones & R. Woodward (Eds.), *Therapeutic communities for offenders* (pp. 121–157). Chichester: Wiley.

Jones, L. (2002). An individual case formulation approach to the assessment of motivation. In M. McMurran (Ed.), *Motivating offenders to change: A guide to enhancing engagement in therapy*. Chichester: Wiley.

Jones, L. (2004a). *Interpersonal and affective contributions to the development of offending behaviour*. Division of Forensic Psychology conference, Leicester.

Jones, L. (2004b). Offence paralleling behaviour (OPB) as a framework for assessment and interventions with offenders. In A. Needs & G. Towl (Ed.), *Applying psychology to forensic practice* (pp. 34–63). Oxford: Blackwell.

Jones, L. (2006). *Sex offender group theory manual.* Unpublished document.

Jones, L. (2007). Iatrogenic interventions with personality disordered offenders. *Behaviour, Crime and Law, 13* (1), 69–79.

Jones, L. F. (2009). Working with sex offenders with personality disorder diagnoses. In A. R. Beech, C. A. Leam & K. D. Browne (Eds.), *Assessment and treatment of sex offenders: A handbook.* Chichester: Wiley.

Kohlenberg, R. J. & Tsai, M. (1995). Functional analytic psychotherapy: A behavioral approach to intensive treatment. In W. O'Donohue & L. Krasner (Eds.), *Theories of behavior therapy: Exploring behavior change* (pp. 637–658). Washington, DC: American Psychological Association.

Leahy, R. L. (2005). Clinical implications in the treatment of mania: Reducing risk behavior in manic patients. *Cognitive and Behavioral Practice, 12*(1), 89–98.

Linehan, M. (1993). *Cognitive behavioural treatment of borderline personality disorder.* New York: Guilford.

Livesley, W. J. (2003). *Practical management of personality disorder.* New York: Guilford Press.

Livesley, W. J. (2007). The relevance of an integrated approach to the treatment of personality disordered offenders. *Psychology, Crime and Law, 13,* 27–46.

Maruna, S. (2001). *Making good: How ex-convicts reform and rebuild their lives.* Washington, DC: American Psychological Association.

McCrae, R. R. & Costa, P. T. (1990). *Personality in adulthood.* New York: Guilford Press.

Proulx, J., Aubut, J., Perron L. & McKibben, A. (1994). Troubles de la personnalité et viol implications théoriques et cliniques. *Criminologie, 2*(27), 33–53.

Proulx, J., Blais, E. & Beauregard, E. (2006). Sadistic sexual aggressors. In W.L. Marshall, Y.M. Fernandez, L.E. Marshall, & G.A. Serran (Eds.) *Sexual offender treatment: controversial issues.* Chichester: Wiley.

Saradjian, J. (1996). *Women who sexually abuse children: From research to clinical practice.* New York: Wiley.

Segal, Z.V., Williams, J.M.G., & Teasdale, J.D. (2002). *Mindfulness-based cognitive therapy for depression: A new approach to preventing relapse.* New York: Guilford.

Seligman, M.E.P., Rashid, T., & Parks, A.C. (2006). Positive psychotherapy. *American Psychologist, 61,* 774–788.

Stevens, A. & Price, J. (2000). *Evolutionary psychiatry: A new beginning,* 2nd edition. London: Routledge.

Thornton, D., Mann, R., Bowers, L., Sheriff, N. & White, T. (2000). Sex offenders in a therapeutic community. In J. Shine (Ed.), *A compilation of Grendon research.* Aylesbury: HM Prison Grendon, Grendon Underwood.

Ward, T. & Hudson, S. M. (2000). A self-regulation model of relapse prevention. In D. R. Laws, S. M. Hudson & T. Ward (Eds.), *Remaking relapse prevention with sex offenders: A sourcebook* (pp. 79–101). London: Sage Publications.

Ward, T., Polaschek, D. L. L. & Beech, A. (2006). *Theories of sexual offending.* Wiley series in forensic clinical psychology. Chichester: Wiley.

Willmott, P. (2006). *Adapting treatment for personality disordered offenders.* Tools to Take Home conference, Birmingham.

Chapter Ten

Working with Personality Disordered Offenders Who Have Substance Misuse Problems

Glen Thomas and Jackie Withers

This chapter will focus on the treatment of substance misuse problems in male personality disordered patients within the context of forensic mental health settings. The need for a comprehensive treatment approach will be presented and an example of a manualized group programme, with a clinical example, will be presented.

Personality disorder and substance misuse

Numerous clinical studies illustrate that there is a close association between mental disorders and substance use disorders, in particular personality disorders (Coid *et al.*, 2006; Compton *et al.*, 2005). Antisocial personality disorder and borderline personality disorder appear to be those most regularly associated with substance misuse disorders (Moran *et al.*, 2006; Skodol *et al.*, 1999).

In a UK survey of four substance misuse treatment centres, Bowden-Jones *et al.* (2004) found the overall prevalence of personality disorders to be 37% in the drug service sample and 53% in the alcohol service sample. Furthermore, Coid *et al.* (2006) identified persons with comorbid mental disorder and substance misuse problems as a particularly vulnerable group. The close association between personality disorders and substance use disorders is mirrored in offender populations (Lader *et al.*, 1998; Singleton *et al.*, 1998).

Using Time, Not Doing Time: Practitioner Perspectives on Personality Disorder and Risk
Edited by Allison Tennant and Kevin Howells
© 2010 John Wiley & Sons, Ltd.

Relevance to forensic personality disorder services

Substance misuse problems are a significant issue amongst the various samples of mentally disordered populations (Blackburn *et al.*, 2003; D'Silva & Ferriter, 2003; Quayle *et al.*, 1998). Despite an increased awareness among forensic services of the high prevalence rates of substance use evident within their populations, it is relatively recently that its role as a major risk factor contributing to offending behaviour amongst the mentally disordered has been more widely acknowledged (Johns, 1997; Monahan *et al.*, 2001).

Individuals with comorbid personality disorder and substance use problems tend to commit more seriously violent offences, have a higher frequency of offending behaviour, and continued substance use is a significant predictor of violent recidivism following discharge into the community (Eronen *et al.*, 1996; Putkonen *et al.*, 2004; Scott *et al.*, 2004). Within a high secure forensic establishment, a screening of substance misuse problems found prevalence rates of 85% among male patients with personality disorders, with at least two thirds of respondents disclosing that they considered they were under the influence of substances at the time of their index offence (Thomas & O'Rourke, 2002). The true prevalence rate may be even higher given that most of the small number of respondents who refused to participate in the survey were known to have a history of problematic substance misuse.

Theoretical considerations

There is considerable evidence of an association between substance use and violence in personality disordered offenders, with alcohol intoxication being a special area of concern (Corbett *et al.*, 1998; Eronen *et al.*, 1996). Alcohol, stimulants and cannabis are all commonly abused substances of choice amongst forensic personality disordered populations. Also there is ample evidence for an association between alcohol, stimulants, and cannabis use, and violence (Boles & Miotto, 2003; Hoaken & Stewart, 2003). In addition, while heroin use is also prevalent in personality disordered populations, its links with violence are less clear. Thus complex aetiological relationships are likely to underpin the co-occurrence of personality disorder and substance misuse disorders (Verheul, 2001).

There are questions about how to make reliable and valid diagnoses given the interaction and overlap between personality disorders and substance misuse. For example, impulsivity, irresponsible behaviour and compulsive behaviour can all be critical to a diagnosis of personality disorder or substance dependency problems, and these same factors are often present in persons with a history of offending behaviour. In addition, substance misuse impacts on behavioural controls leading to impulsive and irresponsible behaviour. Substance use is also an example of impulsive behaviour and forms part of the diagnostic criteria for e.g. borderline personality disorder. As dependency develops, a compulsion to use substances becomes a diagnostic criterion. Thus attempting to separate personality disorder and substance misuse, as if they are distinct disease entities, is problematic.

Several hypotheses exist to explain the possible relationships that may exist between drug and alcohol use and violence-related behaviour. There are a number of links which are likely to be substance specific, e.g. intoxication, neurotoxic effects and withdrawal states (Hoaken & Stewart, 2003). In addition, indirect effects such as individual psychopathology, the environment and context, as well as social processes associated with drug distribution and drug acquisition are also known to influence drug-related violence (Boles & Miotto, 2003). Similarly, variables such as drinking context, rate of consumption and pattern of drinking are also known to influence alcohol-related violence (Graham *et al.*, 2000).

Personality disorder and substance misuse frequently co-occur (NICE, 2009a, 2009b). One factor common to both is trauma. The literature supports the view that an early history of physical, sexual and psychological abuse is common in many individuals who are later diagnosed as suffering from a personality disorder, especially antisocial and borderline types (Bernstein *et al.*, 1998; Bollinger *et al.*, 2000; Camacho, 2004; Coid *et al.*, 2006; Young, 1994). Furthermore, a history of trauma and abuse are common in many individuals who develop substance misuse problems, with the trauma seen as an important factor in the development of the substance misuse (Chilcoat & Menard, 2003; Stewart & Conrod, 2003).

Close associations between violence, trauma and PTSD (post-traumatic stress disorder) are also well documented (Lisak & Miller, 2003). Orth and Wieland (2006) suggested an increased risk of violence in individuals with PTSD, and many violent offenders go on to develop PTSD symptoms seemingly as a consequence of their violent offending behaviour (Gray *et al.*, 2003). Thus it is not surprising that many individuals within forensic settings experience significant problems with PTSD (Spitzer *et al.*, 2006). Therefore the relationships which exist between personality disorder, substance use, violence and trauma, including PTSD, warrant careful consideration. Many persons with personality disorder within forensic services are likely to present with a complex array of these problems, any of which may influence the individual's ability and motivation to work on their substance misuse-related problems.

Substance misuse is often a risk factor for violent offending. However, some substances may present a greater risk of violence than others. It is important that practitioners develop a formulation of how the complex array of personality disorder, substance use, and any trauma- and PTSD-related problems interact to contribute to the likelihood of violence occurring for an individual. It is also possible that the relationship between an individual's substance use and violent offending may change over time. For instance, some individuals report that using certain substances reduces their level of offending; this may be when violent behaviour is associated with antecedent emotional states such as feelings of anger and hostility, and where substances have a direct calming effect on these strong emotions (Khantzian, 1985, 1997). However, it should be noted that this effect may diminish or reverse as the individual's tolerance to the substance develops and dependence-related difficulties complicate the process. In addition, substance use is known to decrease problem-solving and behavioural controls in personality disordered offenders.

Substance use treatment options

Although the link between substance misuse and violent offending is well accepted, there is a paucity of evidence-based interventions to address substance misuse problems in forensic mentally disordered populations (D'Silva & Ferriter, 2003; Johns, 1997; Scott *et al.*, 2004). There are established substance misuse interventions provided across a variety of community and residential substance misuse services, and it has been suggested that forensic services should develop stronger working links with community drug and alcohol services (Durand *et al.*, 2006; Scott *et al.*, 2004). However, community drug and alcohol services often focus on a particular substance, i.e. heroin or alcohol, and some services only work with abstinence goals while others focus on harm reduction. In addition, the evidence base for effective interventions with, for example, problematic stimulant and cannabis use is limited (Seivewright *et al.*, 2005). Furthermore, community drug and alcohol services are under-resourced, and rarely have the resources to address the range of difficulties presented by forensic and/or personality disorder clients.

The issue of comorbid mental health difficulties in people with substance misuse problems is well known. However, it is not uncommon for underlying psychopathology not to be addressed or the behavioural manifestations of personality pathology to be interpreted as non-compliance, resistance or grounds for meeting an exclusion criteria. It is not surprising therefore that a personality disorder diagnosis is indicative of poor treatment retention and outcome in substance misuse treatment services (Bowden-Jones *et al.*, 2004; Coid *et al.*, 2006).

Despite these differences, the development of links between forensic and community drug and alcohol services should not be ruled out, although the limited resources and differing priorities and responsibilities are likely to limit effective co-working. Within secure forensic treatment settings, access to drugs and alcohol is denied and, often, forensic patients who have been substance free during their period of detention view their substance misuse problems as being a thing of the past. Not surprisingly, their understanding and motivation for the need to engage with treatment interventions focused on addressing substance misuse is usually a low priority for them. However, even minimal exposure to substance-related triggers can lead to cravings, a substance relapse, and associated risk-related behaviours. Goals such as controlled drinking and recreational drug use are a high risk option when past substance misuse has been associated with violent offending in forensic populations.

Substance use treatment in the context of forensic services

There is an increasing recognition amongst healthcare professionals within forensic services that substance misuse should be a treatment target. However, it is not always viewed as a treatment priority (Main & Gudjonsson, 2006). Sometimes there is a somewhat simplistic and over-compartmentalized approach to addressing substance misuse (Miles *et al.*, 2007). The functional link between substance misuse, mental health, personality disorder and offending behaviour problems needs to be addressed (Dolan & Kirwan, 2001).

Substance misuse treatment programme

The substance misuse programme which has been developed and refined over several years within a high security hospital is a six-module manualized group intervention (Thomas & O'Rourke, 2002). It consists of approximately 56 structured sessions, with each session lasting approximately two hours. The programme was developed following an extensive review of the literature of effective treatment approaches to working with mental disorder, substance misuse and offending behaviour problems. The programme draws on motivational interviewing, relapse prevention and broader CBT (cognitive behaviour therapy) skills training. Given the treatment setting, some cue exposure work is considered vital. In addition, some psychoeducational material on mental health and personality disorder, and substance use and offending, is included. The programme was initially developed for men with comorbid mental health and substance misuse problems. It has also been applied to male patients with a primary diagnosis of personality disorder, and it has also been used successfully in a number of medium and low secure forensic services. It is likely that the programme could also be provided and considered suitable for use within a community setting.

The programme module structure is:

1. *Substance use and offending*
   Aims to increase awareness and includes exploration of their offending history, pattern of substance use, pros and cons of use, and links their substance use with their offending behaviour.
2. *Substance use and mental health*
   Explores the links between an individual's personality disorder and their substance use. In particular topics such as anxiety, depression, suicide and self-harm, childhood trauma and PTSD, strong emotional states such as anger, shame and guilt are covered. A stress vulnerability model of mental health is introduced and participants are encouraged to reflect on how these problem areas may be associated with, and influence, any offending behaviour.
3. *Relapse prevention and cue exposure*
   This module, which concludes the first half of the programme, introduces participants to the constructs of a relapse prevention model for substance misuse and integrates this with the stress vulnerability model. Some brief cue exposure work is undertaken to help participants develop a better understanding of how substance-related cues affect them physiologically, cognitively and emotionally.
4. *Skills training*
   Focuses on reviewing a number of skills-based interventions common to many cognitive-behavioural based programmes. Participants are encouraged to examine the efficacy of these skills in the context of managing problems associated with their substance use.
5. *Skills to practise*
   This module has skill practice as its focus. It includes working through a variety of possible relapse scenarios. The key relapse areas of negative emotional states, interpersonal conflict and peer pressure are all covered in detail, through a

series of case examples, participants' own experiences and possible future risk scenarios.

6. *Developing my relapse plan*

The final module of the programme aims to consolidate learning into the development of a comprehensive individualized relapse management plan. Participants are also expected to contribute in helping identify any areas of unmet need which may have arisen as a consequence of undertaking the programme. For example, patients are often motivated to engage with trauma-focused and offence-focused interventions as a consequence of completing the substance misuse programme.

Programme philosophy, facilitation and delivery

The programme is designed to link the key areas of mental disorder, substance use and offending behaviour and learning to manage any related problems. The programme is not designed or intended to treat trauma-related problems, neither is it aimed primarily at addressing violent or sexual offending behaviour. Running a therapeutic group with personality disordered patients presents facilitators with a variety of challenges. They may find their clinical credibility being questioned and the subject matter of this group increases this, driven by a common argument that one is required to have personal experience, as well as specialist knowledge, before one can facilitate such treatment interventions. We suggest that each treatment group needs a facilitator with a good knowledge of substance misuse but this is not an essential requirement for all facilitators. Moreover, this shortfall can be addressed by the provision of good quality supervision and competency in running groups.

The underlying programme ethos is motivational and seeks to enable participants to work in partnership with the group facilitators and each other, in as supportive and open a way as the boundaries of a forensic setting allow. Key to this is the development of a sound therapeutic alliance between facilitator and participants. The process of developing and maintaining a cohesive working group which addresses the individual needs of the participants is as important as the delivery of the programme content. A key aim is to enable and empower participants to make an informed choice about their future lifestyle in relation to their substance misuse and mental health. The programme is generally delivered in two components, with modules 1–3 comprising the first part and modules 4–6 comprising the second. The first three modules focus on problem recognition and the second set of modules focuses on behaviour change.

Drop-out from the programme is minimal and is most often the result of participants being transferred to less secure services rather than a failure to engage in treatment. There is the opportunity at the start of the second part of the programme to fill any vacancies which may have arisen with participants who may require some refresher work in this area. Each treatment group of six participants is normally run with a pool of four facilitators, with at least two of them having previous experience of delivering the programme. Having this number of facilitators means that each session is normally facilitated by three individuals. This number enables good observation and feedback between facilitators following each group session. Facilitators need to work as a team, and a pool of facilitators allows the programme to run without unscheduled breaks due to sickness, annual leave and other clinical commitments. Group facilitators come from a variety of professional backgrounds, e.g. nursing, psychology, social work and occupational therapy and, whenever possible, a mix of disciplines is used to facilitate each treatment group.

Engagement

As stated previously, drop-out is low. However, fluctuations in motivation and level of engagement occur related to programme content and its impact on emotional well-being, i.e. it is demanding. There may be an hypersensitivity to substance cues, increased cravings for substances, flashbacks to trauma-related experiences which may induce strong emotional states such as anger, guilt, etc. Individuals may be vulnerable to drop-out if they have not obtained a level of stability in terms of self-harm, aggression, dissociation, etc. Undertaking therapies such as dialectical behaviour therapy (DBT; Evershed *et al.*, 2003) or cognitive analytical therapy (CAT; Pollock, 2006; Ryle & Kerr, 2002; Withers, 2008) prior to undertaking substance misuse treatment is recommended. Irrespective of what prior therapy participants have completed, it is essential that participants are made aware of the possibility that starting a substance misuse treatment may trigger some of the difficulties mentioned above. Therefore participants should be aware of this possibility and have contingency plans in the form of care plans to manage such eventualities.

Normalizing the possibility of such difficulties is crucial and enables the facilitators to demonstrate a supportive and empathic understanding of just how difficult it is for participants to undertake this work. Also participants are encouraged to relate their own experiences to the session content. This puts participants in control of what they disclose and when. Taking such an incremental approach means that the level of trust which is established in the group builds over time. Thus even patients high in narcissism with a history of treatment failure or resistance tend to engage. Although the treatment programme is manualized, its style encourages challenges to participants' attitudes, opinions, substance use goals, etc., to originate from their peer group rather than from the group's facilitators.

Case example: David

David is 30 years of age. He is currently detained within a high security hospital. He has a long history of violent offending and has spent over 10 years in young offender units or prison. He is the youngest of three brothers; he grew up with his mother and stepfather in an area where unemployment, poverty and drug use was a common feature. His home life was chaotic and included domestic violence, physical abuse and neglect. His stepfather had a significant alcohol problem and he abandoned the family when David was a young teenager. While in custodial settings, David had a history of violence. His substance use began aged nine and escalated over subsequent years and included stimulants, heroin and alcohol. His preferred drugs of choice were stimulants, cannabis and alcohol.

David was angry that he was sent to a high secure hospital. However, he recognized that he has problems with his temper and that he is prone to violent outbursts, especially when under the influence of substances. He has been diagnosed as suffering from an antisocial personality disorder and with significant features of borderline personality disorder.

David recognized that substance use had been a problem for him in the past. He had completed a drug education programme while in prison and his knowledge about the harm associated with drug use was good. He was keen to progress, and when assessed for the group he reported that he felt he had been pressured to attend the group by his clinical team. However, he did acknowledge that substance misuse was a potential risk factor in the future. He referred to the substance misuse programme in prison and said he would attend the group in order to speed up his discharge into the community.

David struggled with the content of the first module. He initially denied he was experiencing any substance-related cravings but then reported that his caffeine consumption had increased. He was having difficulty falling asleep and regularly used night sedation. A breakthrough came during an early session when he talked about his stimulant use; he became quite excited and when one of his peers commented that he appeared 'high', David disclosed that he was experiencing the same sort of physical sensations that he got prior to using speed, and that he was experiencing cravings for the drug. It was reflected back to him that cravings were to be expected and highlighted the fact that some of the triggers which were linked with his past drug use were still present, even though it had been some years since he had last used due to him being in prison.

Gradually David's level of disclosure increased, as did his level of understanding of how certain substances and particular patterns of substance use lead to an increased likelihood of him behaving violently towards others. However, he believed that cannabis and alcohol use would not be problematic, should he choose to use them in the future, his rationale for this being that moderate cannabis and alcohol use helped relax him.

Initially, David questioned the relevance of the second module but later acknowledged links between his substance use and negative emotions, and his traumatic past. He found the stress vulnerability model was a helpful way to make sense of periods of crisis in his life. David also made links between his emotions, substance use and offending behaviour. During this period there were a number of incidents on the ward which impacted on David's functioning and reduced his commitment to treatment. These experiences were used to develop David's understanding of how his motivation to engage in treatment could be affected by factors not necessarily always under his control. Linking these factors with an increase in the frequency and intensity of the cravings he was experiencing, along with the self-reported drop in motivation to work on his substance misuse, was a key point in David recognizing his own vulnerabilities. At the end of this module, David decided total abstinence from drugs was his most viable option; however, he continued to desire a return to non-problematic alcohol use.

The relapse prevention module helped David understand some of his previous setbacks. The stages of change and relapse prevention model demonstrated to David why many offenders detained in prison quickly relapse into using substances despite obtaining often long periods of abstinence. He was able to relate this information to his own personal experience. As the module progressed, he developed a more sophisticated understanding of how his mental health and substance use are associated. Notably the cue exposure sessions demonstrated to David how vulnerable he was to relapse. In each session he reported experiencing a number of cravings for different substances. His cravings surprised him and enabled him to recognize how his cognitions change when craving to focus on the positive effects of using. For the first time, David began to seriously question whether he would be able to drink alcohol in the future or if this may increase the risk of him relapsing into using other drugs.

David was keen to engage with the second half of the programme. He was keen to develop a personalized relapse management plan and, at the end, he volunteered for the violence reduction programme and was considering an abstinence goal in relation to all mood-altering substances. This case vignette illustrates the impact of the programme on choice of treatment goals, and motivation to address his substance misuse problem and wider related problems.

Furthermore, while participants may, in the first instance, feel pressured or even coerced into treatment, we believe that the programme content, its motivational style and the fact that it takes individual need into account, leads most participants to actively engage and make informed choices and take responsibility for their choice of treatment goals. It should be noted that not all participants proceed directly to the second half of the programme.

Summary

When considering violent offenders who have severe personality disorders, substance misuse is often enmeshed with the individual's other problems and cannot be treated as if it is a discrete or simple problem. Its association with violent offending should result in it being a priority treatment. Although close liaison with community services is essential, to maintain progress and prevent relapse, placing substance misuse treatment as an 'add-on' following discharge is not likely to be effective in addressing the complexity of the problem and is a high risk strategy. It should be recognized that community services may focus on a particular substance and may be tolerant of a range of goals, e.g. reduced use or abstinence. However, this may not be appropriate for people with personality disorders, substance misuse problems and violent offending histories.

The reputation of people with a personality disorder diagnosis, not to mention a history of violent offending, is that they are resistant to treatment. Also, a personality disorder diagnosis is indicative of poor treatment retention and outcome in substance misuse treatment services (Bowden-Jones *et al.*, 2004; Coid *et al.*, 2006). The treatment programme presented above attempts to address substance misuse problems via a group-based, manualized treatment programme which is motivational in style, is tolerant of fluctuating motivation and explicitly links substance misuse with other significant areas of difficulty. The manualized approach gives scope for the facilitators to respond flexibly while remaining programme adherent.

The comprehensive treatment programme was developed in response to the complex nature of the substance misuse problems in people with personality disorders with offending histories. Given the much-cited level of resistance in this population, we have found patient responsivity to be surprising and rewarding.

References

Bernstein, D., Stein, J. & Handelsman, L. (1998). Predicting personality pathology among adult patients with substance use disorders: Effects of childhood maltreatment. *Addictive Behaviours, 23*(6), 855–868.

Blackburn, R., Logan, C., Donnelly, J. & Renwick, S. (2003). Personality disorders, psychopathy and other mental disorders: Co-morbidity among patients at English and Scottish high-security hospitals. *Journal of Forensic Psychiatry and Psychology, 14*(1), 111–137.

Boles, S. M. & Miotto, K. (2003). Substance abuse and violence: A review of the literature. *Aggression and Violent Behaviour, 8*, 155–174.

Bollinger, A., Riggs, D., Blake, D. & Ruzek, J. (2000). Prevalence of personality disorders among combat veterans with post-traumatic stress disorder. *Journal of Traumatic Stress, 13*(2), 255–270.

Bowden-Jones, O., Iqbal, M., Tyrer, P., Sievewright, N., Cooper, S., Judd, A. *et al.* (2004). Prevalence of personality disorder in alcohol and drug services and associated co-morbidity. *Addiction, 99*, 1306–1314.

Camacho, A. (2004). Are some forms of substance abuse related to the bipolar spectrum? Hypothetical considerations and therapeutic implications. *Primary Psychiatry, 11*(9), 42–46.

Chilcoat, H. & Menard, C. (2003). Epidemiological investigations: co-morbidity of post-traumatic stress disorder and substance use disorders. In P. Ouimette & P. Brown (Eds.), *Trauma and substance abuse: Causes, consequences, and treatment of comorbid disorders* (pp. 9–28). Washington, DC: American Psychological Association.

Coid, J., Yang, M., Tyrer, P., Roberts, A. & Ullrich, S. (2006). Prevalence and correlates of personality disorder in Great Britain. *British Journal of Psychiatry, 188*, 423–431.

Compton, W., Conway, K., Stinson, F., Colliver, J. & Grant, B. (2005). Prevalence, correlates, and co-morbidity of DSM-IV antisocial personality syndromes and alcohol and specific drug use disorders in the United States: Results from the national epidemiologic survey on alcohol and related conditions. *Journal of Clinical Psychiatry, 66*, 677–685.

Corbett, M., Duggan, C. & Larkin, E. (1998). Substance misuse and violence: A comparison of special hospital inpatients diagnosed with either schizophrenia or personality disorder. *Criminal Behaviour and Mental Health, 8*, 311–321.

Dolan, M. & Kirwan, H. (2001). Survey of staff perceptions of illicit drug use among inpatients in a medium secure unit. *Psychiatric Bulletin, 25*, 14–17.

D'Silva, K. & Ferriter, M. (2003). Substance use by the mentally disordered committing serious offences – A high security hospital study. *Journal of Forensic Psychiatry and Psychology, 14*(1), 178–193.

Durand, M., Lelliott, P. & Coyle, N. (2006). Availability of treatment for substance misuse in medium secure psychiatric care in England: A national survey. *Journal of Forensic Psychiatry and Psychology, 17*(4), 611–625.

Eronen, M., Hakola, P. & Tiihonen, J. (1996). Factors associated with homicide recidivism in a 13 year sample of homicide offenders in Finland. *Psychiatric Services*, *47*(4), 403–406.

Evershed, S., Tennent, A. & Boomer, D. (2003). Practice-based outcomes of dialectical behaviour therapy (DBT) targeting anger and violence, with male forensic patients: A pragmatic and non-contemporaneous comparison. *Criminal Behaviour and Mental Health*, *13*(3), 198–213.

Graham, K., West, P., & Wells, S. (2000). Evaluating theories of alcohol-related aggression using observations of young adults in bars. *Addiction*, *95*(6), 847–863.

Gray, N. S., Carmen, N. G., Rogers, P., MacCulloch, M. J., Hayward, P. & Snowdon, R. J. (2003). Post-traumatic stress disorder caused in mentally disordered offenders by the committing of a serious violent or sexual offence. *Journal of Forensic Psychiatry and Psychology*, *14*(1), 27–43.

Hoaken, P. N. & Stewart, S. H. (2003). Drugs of abuse and the elicitation of human aggressive behaviour. *Addictive Behaviours*, *28*, 1533–1554.

Johns, A. (1997). Substance misuse: A primary risk and a major problem of co-morbidity. *International Review of Psychiatry*, *9*, 233–241.

Khantzian, E. (1985). The self-medication hypothesis of addictive disorders: Focus on heroin and cocaine dependence. *American Journal of Psychiatry*, *142*(11), 1259–1265.

Khantzian, E. (1997). The self-medication hypothesis of substance use disorders: A reconsideration and recent application. *Harvard Review Psychiatry*, *4*, 231–244.

Lader, D., Singleton, N. & Meltzer, H. (1998). *Psychiatric morbidity among young offenders*. London: Office for National Statistics.

Lisak, D. & Miller, P. (2003). Childhood trauma, posttraumatic stress disorder, substance abuse, and violence. In P. Ouimette & P. Brown (Eds.), *Trauma and substance abuse: Causes, consequences, and treatment of comorbid disorders* (pp. 73–88). Washington, DC: American Psychological Association.

Main, N. & Gudjonsson, G. (2006). An investigation into the factors that are associated with non-compliance in medium secure units. *Journal of Forensic Psychiatry and Psychology*, *17*(2), 181–191.

Miles, H., Dutheil, L., Welsby, I. & Haider, D. (2007). 'Just say no': a preliminary evaluation of a three stage model of integrated treatment for substance use problems in conditions of medium security. *Journal of Forensic Psychiatry and Psychology*, *18*(2), 141–159.

Monahan, J., Steadman, H. J., Solver, E., Appelbaum, P. S., Robbins, C., Mulvey, E. P. et al. (2001). *Rethinking risk assessment: The Macarthur Study of Mental Disorder and Violence*. Oxford: Oxford University Press.

Moran, P., Coffey, C., Mann, A., Carlin, J. & Patton, C. (2006). Personality and substance use disorders in young adults. *British Journal of Psychiatry*, *188*, 374–379.

National Institute for Health and Clinical Excellence (NICE) (2009a). *Antisocial personality disorder: Treatment, management and prevention*. NICE clinical guideline 77. London: NICE.

National Institute for Health and Clinical Excellence (NICE) (2009b). *Borderline personality disorder: Treatment and management*. NICE clinical guideline 78. London: NICE.

Orth, U. & Wieland, E. (2006). Anger, hostility, and post-traumatic stress disorder in trauma-exposed adults: A meta-analysis. *Journal of Clinical and Consulting Psychology*, *74*(4), 698–706.

Pollock, P. (2006). *Cognitive analytic therapy for offenders: A new approach to forensic psychotherapy*. Hove: Brunner Routledge.

Putkonen, A., Kotilainen, I., Joyal, C. & Tiihonen, J. (2004). Co-morbid personality disorders and substance use disorders of mentally ill homicide offenders: A structured clinical study on dual and triple diagnoses. *Schizophrenia Bulletin, 30*(1), 59–72.

Quayle, M., Clark, F., Renwick, S., Hodge, J. & Spencer, T. (1998). Alcohol and secure hospital patients: An examination of the nature and prevalence of alcohol problems in secure hospital patients. *Psychology, Crime and Law, 4*, 27–41.

Ryle, A. & Kerr, I. (2002). *Introducing cognitive analytic therapy: Principles and practice.* Chichester: John Wiley & Sons.

Scott, F., Whyte, S., Burnett, R., Hawley, C. & Maden, T. (2004). A national survey of substance misuse and treatment outcome in psychiatric patients in medium security. *Journal of Forensic Psychiatry and Psychology, 15*(4), 595–605.

Seivewright, N., McMahon, C. & Egleston, P. (2005). Stimulant use still going strong. *Advances in Psychiatric Treatment, 11*, 262–269.

Singleton, N., Meltzer, H., Gatward, R., Coid, J. & Deasy, D. (1998). *Psychiatric morbidity among prisoners: Summary report.* London: Office for National Statistics.

Skodol, A., Oldham, J. & Gallaher, P. (1999). Axis II co-morbidity of substance use disorders among patients referred for treatment of personality disorders. *American Journal of Psychiatry, 156*(5), 733–738.

Spitzer, C., Chevalier, C., Gillner, M., Freyberger, H. & Barnow, S. (2006). Complex post-traumatic stress disorder and child maltreatment in forensic inpatients. *Journal of Forensic Psychiatry and Psychology, 17*(2), 204–216.

Stewart, S. & Conrod, P. (2003). Psychosocial models of functional associations between post-traumatic stress disorder and substance use disorder. In P. Ouimette & P. Brown (Eds.), *Trauma and substance abuse: Causes, consequences, and treatment of comorbid disorders* (pp. 29–55). Washington, DC: American Psychological Association.

Thomas, G. & O'Rourke, S. (2002). *Mental disorder and substance use treatment programme.* Nottingham: Nottinghamshire Healthcare NHS Trust.

Verheul, R. (2001). Comorbidity of personality disorder in individuals with substance use disorders. *European Psychiatry, 16*, 274–282.

Withers, J. (2008). Cognitive analytic therapy: A therapy in a medium secure hospital for a mentally disordered offender with a personality disorder. *British Journal of Forensic Practice, 10*(3), 24–32.

Young, J. E. (1994). *Cognitive therapy for personality disorders: A schema-focused approach.* Sarasota, FL: Professional Resource Press.

Chapter Eleven

Recovery from Personality Disorder: Maintaining Change

Jackie Withers

This chapter will explore what constitutes change with regard to personality disorder. Constructs such as 'treated', 'cure', 'relapse', 'remission', 'contained' and 'managed' will be considered, and whether progress constitutes change at the level of core pathology or at that of the emotional and behavioural manifestation of the personality disorder. Discussion about what is the core pathology that results in personality disorder will be considered with particular reference to the development of mentalization or a self-reflective capacity as a treatment goal.

There will be consideration of whether progress within one treatment setting can be generalized to another setting, e.g. a less secure setting. If personality disorder can be treated and/or managed, then issues about maintaining progress arise; i.e. what contexts and support networks either support maintenance of change and generalization or prevent setbacks/relapse. Parallels will be drawn with the field of addiction alongside notions of rehabilitation and recovery. The need for formulation-based care planning to assist the maintenance of change and promote further development will be presented as a useful approach. Iatrogenic factors will be explored because the natural reactions from professionals to the difficulties of persons with personality disorder, and particularly if those individuals have a history of offending behaviour, have the potential to have an adverse effect.

Personality disorder

The term 'personality' refers to regularities and consistencies in behaviour and forms of experience. These enduring features are usually described in terms of

Using Time, Not Doing Time: Practitioner Perspectives on Personality Disorder and Risk
Edited by Allison Tennant and Kevin Howells
© 2010 John Wiley & Sons, Ltd.

traits that vary across individuals. There are many different ways of structuring the classification of personality and therefore personality disorder. Although there are criticisms of the psychiatric classification of personality disorder, it does provide a common terminology. For a classification of personality disorder, an individual should have a pattern of inner experience and behaviour which differs from their culture and their difficulties should be pervasive and inflexible, have an onset in adolescence or early adulthood, and lead to distress or impairment.

It is only when problematic personality traits are inflexible and maladaptive, and cause significant functional impairment or subjective distress, that they constitute a personality disorder. The enduring pattern should be pervasive and lead to clinically significant distress or impairment in social, occupational, or other important areas of functioning. The enduring pattern should not be better accounted for as a manifestation or consequence of another mental disorder. In addition, the enduring pattern should not be due to the direct physiological effects of a substance or a general medical condition.

Diagnostic classification systems generally represent a categorical perspective and personality disorders are viewed as qualitatively distinct clinical syndromes. A dimensional perspective suggests that a personality disorder represents maladaptive variants of personality traits that merge with normality and into one another. Early attempts to understand both normal and abnormal personality were guided by psychoanalytic theory and the early psychological approaches to studying personality concentrated on general population rather than clinical samples (Cattell, 1965; Eysenck, 1967). Historically the term 'psychopathic personality' was used to describe a generally abnormal personality. More recently the term 'psychopathic' has been narrowed and emphasizes the 'damage to society' aspect and is reflected in Hare's (1996) notion of psychopathic disorder.

An influential model that attempts to identify the fundamental dimensions which underlie normal and pathological personality functioning is the five-factor model or 'Big Five' which consists of five broad domains of personality: neuroticism, extraversion, openness, antagonism versus agreeableness, and conscientiousness (McCrae & Costa, 1996). Studies of traits defining personality disorder have revealed a structure consistent with the five-factor model. Blackburn (1998) described personality disorder as a failure of interpersonal functioning that arises as a result of a variety of psychological deficits.

A classification of personality disorder is partially based on presenting behaviour rather than core pathology. This is problematic because it includes negatively evaluated behaviour such as violence and self-harm which is often viewed, by society, as intentional and therefore 'bad', and could lead people with personality disorders to be judged as 'bad' rather than ill and needing assistance. Also behaviour judged as 'bad' may not be intentional, e.g. when there is a neurological substrate. Blackburn (1998) stated that the classification of personality disorder needs to be based on personality theory and not antisocial behaviour or moral judgements. Livesley (2001) suggested that dysfunction should be defined in terms of the basic functions of personality, i.e. a stable and integrated sense of self and others, interpersonal functioning, and ability to adapt to a social group. It should be remembered that most individuals who have a personality disorder are not involved in offending behaviour or serious crimes

(Blackburn, 2000). Personality disorder is complex and questions remain about how this distressing disorder with reference to self and/or others should be conceptualized.

Treatment of personality disorder

Until relatively recently, personality disorder was viewed as untreatable. There is now a developing evidence base with a range of psychological therapies possibly offering some benefit (Bateman & Fonagy, 2004; Beck & Freeman, 1990; Kernberg, 1996; Layden *et al.*, 1993; Linehan, 1993; Livesley, 2003; Ryle, 1997; Ryle & Kerr, 2002; Sperry, 2003; Young, 1994). A complex range of interventions are likely to be required to treat personality disorder. As yet, there is no standard treatment and no one treatment has been shown to be superior to any other (Bateman & Fonagy, 1999). With regard to forensic cases, the issue of treatability is even more contentious than it is for non-offenders; this is possibly because of moral judgements about the offending behaviour which may be a manifestation of personality disorder. As discussed in other chapters, many of the promising therapies have been applied within forensic settings. Livesley (2003) developed a model for the treatment of severe personality disorder and emphasized the need to intervene across different domains, e.g. symptomatic, situational, regulatory, dispositional, interpersonal and self-system.

Currently, some of the highest risk offenders in prison are excluded from standard treatment programmes on the basis of interpersonal, affective and behavioural characteristics that together constitute the construct of 'psychopathy'. The reasons for exclusion are that, for this subgroup of offenders, there has been concern that some interventions may have iatrogenic effects (Harris *et al.*, 1991; Ogloff *et al.*, 1990). There is also some evidence that clients, classified as 'psychopathic' and rated by staff as having made good therapeutic progress, subsequently reoffend at a very high rate (Seto & Barbaree, 1999). In addition, this subgroup of people are generally found to be less compliant with treatment, to have more security-related problems during treatment, and to be more likely to drop out of treatment (Harris *et al.*, 1991; Hobson *et al.*, 2000). Excluding this group from the promising treatments which have developed over the past 10 to 20 years is morally questionable whether one is considering the distress experienced by offenders with personality disorders or the harm and distress caused to others by their actions.

Psychopathic disorder is characterized by a constellation of affective, interpersonal, and behavioural characteristics including impulsivity, irresponsibility, shallow emotions, and lack of empathy, remorse or guilt. Although many clinicians will not attempt to treat this client group, relatively little is understood about the factors that determine whether a client will genuinely engage with psychological treatment. Whether a particular constellation of personality features indicates that an individual is untreatable is not clear. Furthermore, the critical variables that influence whether an individual is able to engage and benefit from treatment are not understood. In a review of the treatment of psychopathic offenders Hemphill and Hart (2002) concluded that they are likely to disrupt treatment, drop out of treatment and to struggle to form a therapeutic alliance.

Treatability

In the UK, treatability is a legal term in terms of the Mental Health Act (1983) but it is also a clinical concept. The status of personality disorder as an illness is contentious, therefore any notion of treatment is also contentious. Adshead (2001) suggested that treatability is a function of seven factors: nature and severity of pathology; involvement of other bodily systems; previous health and comorbidity; timing of identification and intervention; experience and availability of staff; availability of specialist units; and state of knowledge.

Treatment or intervention targeting specific problems may focus on presenting symptomatology rather than personality traits, which are generally considered to be relatively fixed. Therefore helping a person express their personality traits in more effective and acceptable ways may be a useful goal of therapy (Beck & Freeman, 1990; Livesley, 2001; Paris, 1998; Sperry, 2003). Thus interventions may provide symptomatic relief and/or the management of problematic behaviours without necessarily treating the disorder per se. If this is an accurate representation of treatment then it may be helpful to conceptualize personality disorder as a disability rather than an illness, with an emphasis on managing the enduring and chronic nature of the client's problems. A challenge is generalizing change at a symptomatic level to different contexts. Very often aftercare aims to be supportive but a longer-term approach focusing on management of problems or a disorder which may be considered to be in remission may be a useful viewpoint rather than treatment being viewed as either a failure or a success.

Although the diagnosis of personality disorder is partially based on presenting behaviour rather than core pathology, e.g. dialectical behaviour therapy (DBT) assumes a skill deficit to be of central concern, some therapies attempt to address difficulties at what might be called a core pathology level, for example, Bateman and Fonagy (1999, 2004) view developing mentalization as the core of successful treatment. 'Mentalization' refers to the mental processes by which an individual implicitly and explicitly interprets the actions of self and others. Ryle and Kerr (2002) view the development of an integrated sense of self and self-reflective capacity as the core of the treatment of personality disorder. Thus, mentalization therapy and cognitive analytic therapy (CAT) may be said to be attempting to address core pathology rather than symptomatic relief or case management.

Psychological interventions require some level of cooperation, i.e. they are largely done with, and not to, individuals. A robust finding from psychotherapy research is that positive outcomes are associated with a good therapeutic alliance (Luborsky & Auerbach, 1985). The non-specifics of therapy are also associated with positive outcomes and these non-specifics are often considered to relate to the therapeutic relationship. A long-standing finding of outcome psychotherapy research is that a stronger client–therapist alliance is associated with a better outcome (Stiles *et al.*, 1998; Zetzel, 1966). There is evidence to support the importance of the therapeutic alliance as a robust predictor of treatment success. Poor outcomes are associated with a greater evidence of negative interpersonal process, i.e. hostile and complex interactions between therapists and clients (Binder & Strupp, 1997; Coady, 1991).

It may be the quality of the therapeutic alliance rather than the therapeutic modality which is associated with positive outcomes. It has been suggested that more helpful therapists, whatever the therapeutic approach, are better able to facilitate the development of a therapeutic alliance (Luborsky *et al.*, 1997). Therefore issues about engagement and how to maintain a therapeutic relationship are likely to be critical to treatment and possibly the maintenance of progress. There is a need, when treating personality disorder, to encourage a powerful attachment relationship, i.e. generally treatments need to be engaging to the client and then keep them engaged (Bateman & Fonagy, 2004).

It has been stated that a good therapeutic alliance is a prerequisite for change in all forms of psychotherapy (Bordin, 1979). Bordin conceptualized the alliance as consisting of tasks, goals and the bond. Agreement between client and therapist about the tasks and goals of therapy is important. The bond between therapist and client is complex, dynamic and multidimensional. Ruptures can occur within the therapeutic alliance in terms of disagreements about tasks and goals, and problems in the relational bond (Safran & Muran, 2000). CBT (cognitive behaviour therapy), DBT and CAT all emphasize the need for the client to understand the treatment rationale and what is required from them during the therapy.

There is a general consensus emerging that a negative process within therapy and ruptures in the therapeutic alliance are inevitable, but an important therapeutic skill consists of dealing therapeutically with this process via repair of the rupture (Ryle & Kerr, 2002; Safran & Muran, 2000). A consequence of having a personality disorder with its interpersonal manifestation is likely to impact on the development of a therapeutic alliance and may adversely impact on the effectiveness of treatments. Therapeutic gains may be obtained, over time, through a person's involvement in stable and supportive therapeutic relationships. Indeed, it is suggested that the key task for practitioners is the creation and maintenance of a therapeutic alliance with the client (McClelland, 2006; Ryle & Kerr, 2002). When progress has occurred, it is likely that the same factors are important to maintaining progress.

Maintaining change

The engagement issues relevant to a formal intervention or treatment directed at personality difficulties may be relevant to aftercare services. In relation to personality disorder and particularly those with 'psychopathic' traits, when a setback to progress occurs during, or following, the completion of formal treatment, the client is often assumed to have not progressed and the treatment is seen as having failed. This would not be the conclusion in relation to other physical and mental health problems. For example, a client may be said to be in remission or relapsed rather than judging any previous progress as fake. When the setback involves violent behaviour then the consequence of the setback is serious, but a setback or relapse does not necessarily mean that a period of stability was not genuine and cannot be built on.

Models have been borrowed from the study of addiction and applied to other clinical problems, including offending behaviour. Such explanations of behaviour may be relevant given the comorbidity of personality disorder and addiction, personality disorder and antisocial behaviour, and addiction and antisocial behaviour. Change with regard to personality disorder could be conceptualized in a similar way to that within the field of addiction. Many clinicians working with persons with a personality disorder would not view the notion of ambivalence about change, and difficulty sustaining change in relation to a range of problem areas, as contentious. The terms 'lapse' and 'relapse' undoubtedly imply a disease process but, in relation to addictive behaviour, it has allowed for the development of focused interventions to prevent relapse, and many offender programmes have incorporated these concepts (Wong & Gordon, 1999).

The study of unaided change within addiction may also be relevant. Lindstrom (1991) summarized four hypotheses on the nature of treatment in relation to alcohol problems, i.e. effectiveness is down to technique, matching of client to treatment, non-specifics or natural healing. Change without formal intervention or spontaneous remission, as it may be called, occurs in relation to addictive behaviour. A maturational process is relevant to a discussion about the treatability of personality. Linehan (1993) noted the demographic parallel between age and borderline personality disorder (BPD) classification. If BPD characteristics decrease in severity and prevalence into middle age (Paris, 1998), then a reasonable aim of treatment may be to manage instability until the person reaches middle age, when some sort of maturation or spontaneous remission may occur naturally.

Obtaining cooperation between a support team and a client with a personality disorder, be that while waiting for a maturational process to occur or following the completion of formal treatments, is sometimes problematic because either the client's difficulties may not be viewed as a priority by a given team or non-cooperation by the client. Non-compliance with professional advice is a common phenomenon and not restricted to persons with personality disorder – i.e. individuals, whatever the context, often challenge attempts by others to influence them (Cullari, 1996). Other theories relevant to understanding resistance and adherence to professional advice come from health psychology (Ajzen, 1991). These models are likely to be relevant to maintaining change as well as beginning change, e.g. persons who commit to changing behaviour usually recognize their problems and seek help with that problem.

The transtheoretical model of change (Prochaska & DiClemente, 1986) provides a heuristic that has been applied to a wide range of clinical presentations. This model provides a useful framework when considering whether a person with a personality disorder is likely to engage with treatment. The model identifies five typical stages in a change process – precontemplation, contemplation, preparation, action and maintenance – and it has been applied to offending behaviour (McMurran *et al.*, 1998; Wong & Gordon, 1999). In relation to beginning the change process, Walters (1998) argued that change begins following a crisis, with a crisis being the point at which a person becomes aware of the discrepancy between his stated goals and current behaviours. Critical events can precipitate the decision to seek help, e.g. an actual or feared negative event (Tucker *et al.*, 1999), and Frank (1974) stated that subjective distress is likely to have motivational properties. It is likely that continued effort to maintain change will be dependent on a perception of the negative consequences of not maintaining change. Thus strategies which encourage maintenance of change will probably hold the negative consequences of not maintaining change in mind, while not undermining hope and confidence.

Continued contact and engagement with services, post completion of formal treatment, may be vital to maintaining change. As yet, little is known about the types of support services which would be of benefit. From a motivational interviewing perspective, motivation should not be viewed as residing within the individual. Motivation to change versus resistance is, at least in part, viewed as a product of the interaction between the therapist/counsellor and the client (Miller & Rollnick, 2002), with ambivalence about change being considered to be a central construct. Therefore the style of support which will best encourage continued contact with services and the maintenance of progress is likely to be more effective if a motivational approach is used.

In an attempt to explain why an individual takes action to engage in a change process, Ford (1992) developed a motivational systems theory, which defines motivation in terms of personal goals, emotions and personal agency beliefs. Karoly (1999) defined goals as imagined states, towards which people intentionally aspire and actively work, and suggested that therapeutic failures of various kinds (e.g. drop-out, resistance, relapse, etc.) can result from a failure by the therapist to appreciate the structural relation between time-limited treatment goals and life goals in general. If progress is to be maintained over the longer term, then attention to life goals is probably important. The 'Good Lives' model (Ward & Brown, 2004; Ward & Stewart, 2003) is consistent with this approach and suggests that offenders may be motivated to work on issues that are not regarded as a priority by the therapist, because, in prison settings, a treatment focus is often only on criminogenic risk factors. The 'Good Lives' model focuses on a positive approach to treatment, the relationship between risk management and good lives, the preconditions of therapy and the impact of the therapist's attitude toward offenders. 'Responsivity' refers to the style and mode of intervention that engages the interest of the client (Andrews & Bonta, 1998).

There are clinical implications in relation to how progress is conceptualized; i.e. is the personality disorder treated and potentially cured or in remission? Should progress be viewed as on a continuum, interventions (be they formal therapies or supportive in style) may enhance movement along the continuum in a positive direction. If this is an accurate description, then it is equally feasible that interventions and life events could lead to movement along the continuum in a negative direction. When setbacks occur, following treatment for problems for which there are moral overtones (e.g. addictive behaviour or offending behaviour, etc.) then, so often, the person is blamed and any previous progress is dismissed as not real. It is questionable whether change with regard to specific problematic behaviours, and a person's view of self and others, if maintained, could represent change at the level of psychopathology and not merely symptomatic change.

Iatrogenic factors: Do no harm

The therapeutic approaches that are currently considered promising with regard to treating complex cases highlight the need for a non-confrontational, respectful and collaborative approach to working with clients with personality disorder (Beck & Freeman, 1990; Linehan, 1993; Miller & Rollnick, 2002; Ryle & Kerr, 2002; Young, 1994). Linehan (1993) states that an invalidating environment is significant in the aetiology of borderline personality disorder, and that the therapist needs to balance validation with the expression of the need for change. Many clients with personality disorder have histories of extreme criticism, neglect and abuse or harsh punishment. It is likely that, if a client feels criticized or blamed for their difficulties, then they are probably less likely to remain engaged and may become more resistant with regard to efforts to help them. In CAT terms, collusion with problematic reciprocal role patterns of relating (e.g. interacting in a critical manner with a client who grew up in a harshly critical environment) would replicate past problematic relationships and be unlikely to help a client to progress (Ryle & Kerr, 2002).

It is suggested that a cycle can develop that could escalate resistance and negativity by both the client and staff member. As has already been discussed, many therapeutic approaches emphasize the behaviour of the therapist as central to forming a therapeutic alliance and similar processes are likely to be relevant to assisting clients maintain their progress.

There are well-established non-specifics of effective therapy, such as empathy, genuineness and a positive regard for the client, that suggest a general approach to responding to clients' difficulties (Rogers, 1957). However, it is often people with complex problems like personality disorder who seem to provoke otherwise caring staff to behave in unhelpful ways. Analytic theory has the most comprehensive conceptualization of this phenomenon (Klein, 1946). Indeed, Ormont (1992, p. 52) stated 'The worst therapists are those who are either out of touch with their feelings or in bondage to them to the degree that their feelings dictate their performance'. CAT conceptualizes such difficulties in terms of collusive reciprocal role enactments.

Many therapeutic approaches would suggest that staff should have a positive expectancy with regard to possible change (Linehan, 1993). Many psychological and counselling approaches emphasize the need for a client to want help. How staff react, when faced by various levels and fluctuations in the level of motivation in their clients, alongside enduring and complex clinical presentations that may include no apparent distress, is likely to influence how they respond to clients, and therefore their ability to develop and maintain a therapeutic alliance.

Staff reactions that are too rescuing, with little responsibility for change given to the client, may be problematic; also too little empathy and too much responsibility (even blame) attributed to the client is likely to be problematic and could lead to boundary violations. This is consistent with several treatment approaches. For example, within the field of addiction, '12 step' approaches caution against enabling the client to stay the same, even though the intention of the 'helper' is to provide care and/or support. DBT and CAT have a developing evidence base in terms of treating personality disorder. In DBT the quality of the therapeutic alliance is emphasized and includes a balance between validation and change strategies (Linehan, 1993). In CAT, the aim of therapy is to provide a non-collusive relationship in terms of not replicating problematic reciprocal role enactments (Ryle & Kerr, 2002). It seems logical that a warm responsiveness by staff that is based on 'reflected upon' responding in place of emotional reacting, but which includes validating the client's distress with negotiation around treatment goals, is more likely to lead to active participation by the client.

As a general stance, motivational interviewing is likely to be perceived as validating, accepting, and non-blaming. There is evidence from the addictions field that such an approach increases engagement and that confrontational styles of intervening are less effective. It is likely that this stance is as necessary when working with clients to maintain and further build on their progress as it is to beginning the change process. This is consistent with many therapeutic approaches but is in stark contrast to the manualized treatment programmes which attempt to deal with motivation in an early module and then expect it to remain as if it is a discrete and stable construct.

As stated above there is a growing literature about understanding and responding to ruptures within the therapeutic relationship (Safran & Muran, 2000). These approaches to understanding and responding to therapeutic ruptures view them as inevitable and as opportunities for learning. The reactions of all staff involved with client care, as well as therapists, are likely to be important. Linehan (1993) discusses the need to address therapy-interfering behaviours and includes therapy-interfering behaviour by the therapist. Linehan has emphasized the role of the DBT consultation group in helping the DBT team retain a positive belief. It is possible that negative staff beliefs, if communicated to the client, could be therapy-interfering. In addition, it is possible that any staff member in contact with the client could engage in therapy-interfering behaviour which could trigger therapeutic ruptures. It is becoming increasingly well accepted that staff can react in unhelpful ways in response to clients with personality disorders.

Linehan (1993) suggests unhelpful responses by staff should be addressed, when possible, via consultation with the client rather than the wider team. However, this strategy can only be used once a client has actively engaged with treatment, and team interventions may be necessary following completion of treatment to promote non-iatrogenic reactions from the team. The analytic concept of splitting of teams as representing client pathology may partly explain the different perspectives of staff in relation to particular clients. CAT conceptualizes transference and countertransference reactions by staff in terms of reciprocal role enactments. As with an analytic approach, a CAT approach could include formulated care planning with the team (Dunn & Parry, 1997), and the client may be included in the consultancy to the team. This reformulation in context not only places great importance on the responses of all persons engaging with the client but also explicitly emphasizes the need for shared understanding of the client's difficulties by the care team to prevent unhelpful and collusive reactions and team splitting (Ryle & Kerr, 2002). This type of formulation-based approach also encourages a continuity of care planning as a client moves through a care pathway.

Recovery

Over the past decade 'recovery' as a model to understand wellness in relation to mental health has been influential. Its focus is on lived experience of consumers, survivors and ex-clients. It represents a paradigm shift in relation to the meaning of a diagnosis of mental illness, particularly major mental illness such as schizophrenia, major depression or bipolar disorder. From this perspective, mental illness is not viewed as an impediment to obtaining life goals; instead hope is viewed as a reality and well-being as achievable. Ralph and Corrigan (2005) stated that recovery comprises three related constructs. Firstly, that it is a naturally occurring phenomenon, secondly, that people can recover from mental illness and, thirdly, that recovery reintroduces the idea of hope in understanding serious mental illness.

Treatments may include pharmacological interventions, psychological therapy, or social interventions, and treatment may aim to reduce symptomatology, resolve disability within any life domain, increase ability to obtain life goals or improve quality of life. However, whether 'recovery' is an outcome or a process is unclear. As an outcome, it represents a change from a previously maladaptive state to a position of 'normal' living. It represents some sort of end point, i.e. more than an improved state. Descriptions of 'recovery' as an outcome typically include obtaining life goals across important life domains. There are difficulties with this approach in terms of how many goals must be achieved to be considered 'recovered' or even how much life success is considered normal.

As a process, recovery does not necessarily mean being symptom-free or without disability. The focus is on improvement in psychological well-being while continuing to struggle with symptoms and attempting to obtain life goals. An individual would be judged as 'in recovery', which is not dependent on specific outcome criteria. This approach focuses less on measuring whether change has occurred and more on indicators that the person is engaged with the process and 'in recovery'. Recovery is complex and enduring rather than a biological end state defined by an absence of symptoms (White *et al.*, 2005). Thus recovery is a lived experience of one's disorder, and exists on a continuum of improved health and functioning.

In relation to addictive behaviour, recovery has been defined as sustained abstinence and increased emotional and relational health. When improvements are not represented by abstinence, then notions of recovery are less clear. There are many pathways to recovery and may include natural recovery, peer-assisted recovery and professionally assisted recovery.

The concept of recovery in relation to major mental illness and addiction may be as relevant to the management and treatment of personality disorder. It is also consistent with the notion that treatment should aim to assist a person express their personality traits in more effective and less problematic ways (Beck & Freeman, 1990; Livesley, 2001; Paris, 1998; Sperry, 2003). A recovery model is relevant to personality disorder treatment in terms of what constitutes being recovered. Remaining actively engaged with a plan to maintain progress may be a better indicator of maintaining change than a specific symptom-free end point or outcome. It is likely that a variety of interventions would be necessary to support progress across life domains but the shared understanding of the particular person's difficulties by the client and care team is likely to be necessary if iatrogenic staff reactions are to be avoided.

Conclusion

Despite continued debate about the classification of personality disorder, the clinical and risk presentation of persons who receive a diagnosis of personality disorder represent a significant challenge to mental health services. Until relatively recently, such a diagnosis was a reason to be excluded from treatment. However, there are now a number of promising therapeutic approaches. Given the manifest interpersonal difficulties of personality disorder and the possible aetiological role of attachment difficulties which may be the result of traumatic histories, then the importance of building and maintaining a therapeutic alliance, based on a thorough understanding (case conceptualization) of the client's personality functioning, is likely to be an important feature of any successful treatment. Ideas from the field of addiction and recovery may be useful when considering the stability of progress and maintenance of change.

Maintaining contact with persons who have successfully completed formal treatments and providing aftercare is likely to be of value. It is suggested that many of the issues relevant to beginning a change process and developing and maintaining a therapeutic alliance are likely to continue to be relevant. Formulation-based care planning which guides a continuity of care, enhances a team's understanding of a person's difficulties, promotes further change, and actively decreases the likelihood of reinforcing or colluding with past problematic ways of thinking and behaving is likely to be important to the maintenance of change.

References

Adshead, G. (2001). Murmurs of discontent: Treatment and treatability of personality disorder. *Advances in Psychiatric Treatment, 7*, 407–416.

Ajzen, I. (1991). Theory of planned behaviour, organizational behaviour and human decision. In D. A. Andrews & J. Bonta (Eds.) (1998), *The psychology of criminal conduct*, 2nd edition. Cincinnati, OH: Anderson.

Andrews, D. A. & Bonta, J. (1998). *The psychology of criminal conduct*, 2nd edition. Cincinnati, OH: Anderson.

Bateman, A. W. & Fonagy, P. (1999). The effectiveness of partial hospitalization in the treatment of borderline personality disorder – A randomized controlled trial. *American Journal of Psychiatry, 156*, 1563–1569.

Bateman, A. W. & Fonagy, P. (2004). *Psychotherapy for borderline personality disorder: Mentalization-based treatment.* Oxford: Oxford University Press.

Beck, A. T., Freeman, A. & Associates (1990). *Cognitive therapy of personality disorders.* New York: Guilford Press.

Binder, J. L. & Strupp, H. H. (1997). 'Negative process': A recurrently discovered and underestimated facet of therapeutic process and outcome in the individual psychotherapy of adults. *Clinical Psychology: Science and Practice, 4*, 121–139.

Blackburn, R. (1998). Psychopathy and personality disorder: Implications of interpersonal theory. In D. J. Cooke, S. J. Hart & A. E. Forth (Eds.), *Psychopathy: Theory, research and implications for society* (pp. 269–301). Amsterdam: Kluwer.

Blackburn, R. (2000). Treatment or incapacitation? Implications of research on personality disorder for the management of dangerous offenders. *Legal and Criminological Psychology, 5*, 1–21.

Bordin, E. (1979). The generalisability of the psychoanalytic concept of the working alliance. *Psychotherapy: Theory, Research and Practice, 16*, 252–260.

Cattell, R. B. (1965). *The scientific basis of personality.* Harmondsworth: Penguin Books.

Coady, N. (1991). The association between client and therapist interpersonal processes and outcomes in psychodynamic psychotherapy. *Research on Social Work Practice, 1,* 122–138.

Cullari, S. (1996). *Treatment resistance: A guide for practitioners.* Boston, MA: Allyn & Bacon.

Dunn, M. & Parry, G. (1997). A formulated care plan approach to caring for people with borderline personality disorder in a community mental health setting. *Clinical Psychology Forum, 104,* 19–22.

Eysenck, H. J. (1967). *The biological basis of personality.* Springfield, IL: Charles C. Thomas.

Ford, M. E. (1992). *Motivating humans: Goals, emotions and personal agency beliefs.* Newbury Park, CA: Sage.

Frank, J. D. (1974). Therapeutic components of psychotherapy: A 25 year progress report of research. *Journal of Nervous and Mental Disease, 159,* 325–342.

Hare, R. D. (1996). Psychopathy: A clinical construct whose time has come. *Criminal Justice and Behaviour, 23,* 25–54.

Harris, G. T., Rice, M. E. & Cormier, C. A. (1991). Psychopathy and violent recidivism. *Law and Human Behaviour, 15*(6), 625–637.

Hemphill, J. F. & Hart, S. D. (2002). Motivating the unmotivated: Psychopathy, treatment, and change. In M. McMurran (Ed.), *Motivating offenders to change: A guide to enhancing engagement in therapy* (pp. 193–220). Chichester: John Wiley & Sons Ltd.

Hobson, J., Shine, J. & Roberts, R. (2000). How do psychopaths behave in a prison therapeutic community? *Psychology, Crime and Law, 6*(2), 139–154.

Karoly, P. (1999). A goal systems self-regulatory perspective on personality, psychopathology and change. *Review of General Psychology, 3,* 264–291.

Kernberg, O. (1996). A psychoanalytic theory of personality disorder. In J. F. Clarkin & M. F. Lenzenweger (Eds.), *Major theories of personality disorder* (pp. 106–140). New York: Guilford Press.

Klein, M. (1946). Notes on some schizoid mechanisms. In M. Klein, P. Heimann, S. Isaacs & J. Riviere (Eds.), *Developments in psychoanalysis* (pp. 292–320). London: Hogarth Press.

Layden, M. A., Newman, C. F., Freeman, A. & Morse, S. B. (1993). *Cognitive therapy of borderline personality disorder.* Boston, MA: Allyn and Bacon.

Lindstrom L. (1991). Basic assumptions reconsidered. *British Journal of Addiction, 86,* 846–848.

Linehan, M. M. (1993). *Cognitive-behavioural treatment of personality disorder.* New York: Guilford Press.

Livesley, W. J. (2001). Conceptual and taxonomic issues. In W. J. Livesley (Ed.), *Handbook of personality disorder: Theory, research and treatment* (pp. 3–39). New York: Guilford Press.

Livesley, W. J. (2003). *Practical management of personality disorder.* New York: Guilford Press.

Luborsky, L. L. & Auerbach, A. H. (1985). The therapeutic relationship in psychodynamic psychotherapy: The research evidence and its meaning in practice. In R. E. Hales & A. J. Frances (Eds.), *Annual Review,* Volume 4. Washington, DC: American Psychiatric Press.

Luborsky, L., McLellan, A. T., Diguer, L., Woody, G. & Seligman, D. A. (1997). The psychotherapist matters: Comparison of outcomes across twenty-two therapists and seven patient samples. *Clinical Psychology: Science and Practice, 4,* 53–65.

McClelland, N. (2006). Beneficence in ethical practice in diagnosis and treatment of personality disorder. *Therapeutic Communities, 27*(4), 477–493.

McCrae, R. R. & Costa, P. T. (1996). Toward a new generation of personality theories: Theoretical contexts for the five-factor model. In J. S. Wiggins (Ed.), *The five-factor model of personality: Theoretical perspectives* (pp. 51–87). New York: Guilford Press.

McMurran, M., Tyrer, P., Hogue, T., Cooper, K., Dunseath, W. & McDaid, D. (1998). Measuring motivation to change in offenders. *Psychology, Crime and Law, 4,* 43–50.

Miller, W. R. & Rollnick, S. (2002). *Motivational interviewing: Preparing people for change,* 2nd edition. New York: Guilford Press.

Ogloff, J. R. P., Wong, S. & Greenwood, A. (1990). Treating criminal psychopaths in a therapeutic community setting. *Behaviour Sciences and the Law, 8,* 180–190.

Ormont, L. (1992). *The group therapy experience.* New York: St Martin's Press.

Paris, J. (1998). *Working with traits.* Northdale, NJ: Jason Aronson.

Prochaska, J. & DiClemente, C. (1986). Toward a comprehensive model of change. In W. Miller and N. Heather (Eds.), *Treating addictive behaviours* (pp. 2–37). New York: Plenum.

Ralph, R. O. & Corrigan, P. W. (2005). *Recovery in mental illness: Broadening our understanding of wellness.* Washington, DC: American Psychological Association.

Rogers, C. R. (1957). The necessary and sufficient conditions of therapeutic personality change. *Journal of Consulting Psychology, 21,* 95–103.

Ryle, A. (1997). *Cognitive analytic therapy and borderline personality disorder: The model and the method.* Chichester: John Wiley & Sons.

Ryle, A. & Kerr, I. B. (2002). *Introducing cognitive analytic therapy: Principles and practice.* Chichester: John Wiley & Sons.

Safran, J. D. & Muran, J. C. (2000). *Negotiating the therapeutic alliance: A relational treatment guide.* New York: Guilford Press.

Seto, J. H. & Barbaree, H. E. (1999). Psychopathy, treatment behaviour, and sex offender recidivism. *Journal of Interpersonal Violence, 14*(12), 1235–1248.

Sperry, L. (2003). *Handbook of diagnosis and treatment of DSM-IV-R personality disorders.* Hove: Brunner-Routledge.

Stiles, W. B., Agnew-Davies, R., Hardy, G. E., Barkham, M. & Shapiro, D. A. (1998). Relations of the alliance with psychotherapy outcome: Findings in the second Sheffield Psychotherapy Project. *Journal of Consulting and Clinical Psychology, 66,* 791–802.

Tucker, J. A., Donovan, D. M. & Marlatt, G. A. (1999). *Changing addictive behaviour: Bridging clinical and public health strategies.* New York: Guilford Press.

Walters, G. D. (1998). *Changing lives of crime and drugs: Intervening with substance abusing offenders.* Chichester: Wiley.

Ward, T. & Brown M. (2004). The Good Lives Model and conceptual issues in offender rehabilitation. *Psychology, Crime & Law, 10,* 243–257.

Ward, T. & Stewart, C. (2003). Criminogenic needs and human needs: A theoretical model. *Psychology, Crime, & Law, 9,* 125–143.

White, W., Boyle, M. & Loveland, D. (2005). Recovery from addiction and from mental illness: Shared and contrasting lessons. In R. Ralph & P. Corrigan (Eds.), *Recovery in mental illness: Broadening our understanding of wellness* (pp. 233–258). Washington, DC: American Psychological Association.

Wong, S. & Gordon, A. (1999). *Violence Risk Scale (Version 2), manual.* Regional Psychiatric Centre (Prairies), Correctional Services of Canada.

Young, J. E. (1994). *Cognitive therapy for personality disorders: A schema-focused approach,* revised edition. Sarasota, FL: Professional Resource Press.

Zetzel, E. (1966). The analytic situation. In R. E. Litman (Ed.), *Psychoanalysis in America* (pp. 86–106). New York: International University Press.

Chapter Twelve

Adult Learning and Personality Disorders

Perdita Jackson, Clare Thurlow and David Underwood

Historical influences

To date, there has been little, if any, theoretical or empirical research related to adult learners diagnosed with severe personality disorders who pose a high risk of serious offending. Working in the education department of a unit for personality disordered male adults has provided the insight for this chapter, where the focus is on understanding effective methods of teaching and learning.

Until fairly recently, there has been relatively little investigation and writing about adult learning, yet some of the great teachers of ancient times – Aristotle, Socrates and Plato in Greece; Hebrew augurs in biblical times – were all teachers of adults, not children. The concept of adult education has also been devoid of a defining theory until the early 1970s when Knowles, the 'father of adult learning', introduced the notion that children learn differently to adults. Knowles considered that a successful approach to adult education should be via the route of situations, not through passive reception of conveyed information, as adult learners use their life experiences to solve problems, assume new roles and apply new knowledge (Knowles et al., 1998). Personality disorder is also an extremely old concept dating back some 2000 years (Tyrer et al., 1991). The formal characterization of personality, although limited, can be traced back to Aristotle who used literary characterology to describe personalities (Livesley, 1995). In the 17th, 18th and 19th centuries, clinical developments were made, with regard to assessments and descriptions of personality disorders. However, it was not until the early 20th century

Using Time, Not Doing Time: Practitioner Perspectives on Personality Disorder and Risk
Edited by Allison Tennant and Kevin Howells
© 2010 John Wiley & Sons, Ltd.

that the first influences of the classification of personality disorders were felt. By the 1980s, researchers had developed self-report inventories and structured interviews to diagnose and assess types of personality disorder, yet the paradigm shift in attitudes about the treatability of personality disorders was not evident until the 1990s (Sperry, 2003).

The effects of personality disorder on individuals

Personality comprises of individual traits that determine how a person relates to others as well as to themselves, how an individual develops goals and ambitions in life, codes of conduct and styles of behaviour and how a person adjusts to the problems and challenges that face human beings on a daily basis (Fontana, 1977). Personality disorder is a problematical pattern of inner experiences and behaviour that deviates significantly from the expectations of an individual's culture. The enduring problems create clinical distress or impairment in social, educational, occupational or other areas of functioning. Problems are also persistent, having been present since early adulthood or adolescence, and pervasive, where they are inflexible in both personal and social situations (American Psychiatric Association, 2000). Individuals who present a high risk of committing serious offences as a result of a severe personality disorder 'can be challenging, confrontational and manipulative in their behaviour. They can be expected to test boundaries and to identify and exploit weaknesses that may exist in the operational system, or in working relationships' (Home Office, Department of Health & HM Prison Service, 2005, p. 18). As academic achievement is based on personal functioning and not just intelligence, the role of education has a large part to play in the treatment of individuals with severe personality disorders.

The role of education

Education plays a triple role in society. It manages the production and distribution of knowledge, supports freedom from illiteracy and innumeracy, and acts as an instrument for socialization (Field, 1992). Generally, teachers operate according to theories of learning and within the context of a philosophy of what education should essentially be about (Moore, 2000). Within the milieu of adult education, teaching should aim to fulfil academic, social and moral learning. However, staff in a unit for high risk offenders diagnosed with severe personality disorders must operate within the context of the unit's aims, which in general terms are to reduce the risk of serious offending of each individual through building and maintaining motivational engagement, in as productive a way as possible, with the therapeutic regime. The role of education in these units can be viewed as being different to that of educators in other establishments, as a result of the need to work within the context of a therapeutic regime whilst maintaining the principles of education.

The education department's involvement in improving social proficiency and personal development is a major contributor to the treatment process. However, education can be involved in areas of work where the activity is seen to add to the therapeutic programme but is not always viewed as belonging within the normal boundaries of education; for example, delivering courses aimed at developing and practising skills learned in therapeutic programmes. In such instances the subject matter and methods of teaching and learning are educational; however, the objectives can be considered to lie outside the parameters of education. Combining models of adult learning and current initiatives in adult education with individual, tailored treatment plans, based on functional analysis of offending behaviour and risk, supports the foundations for education to provide an up-to-date, purposeful and effective service, within a unique and pioneering programme for offenders diagnosed with severe personality disorders.

Cognitive development

As the modern world is dominated by both spoken and written words, literacy is considered to be the most vital basic skill fundamental to an individual's progress. Adults who have not benefited from the educational opportunities available to them as children are very likely to have poor literacy skills and, consequently, their ability to respond to information, solve problems and develop concepts will be restricted. Many of the individuals referred to units for high risk offenders diagnosed with personality disorders have a history of social exclusion, including unstable home backgrounds and experiences of failure in schools, which, in some cases, has included non-engagement in formal education since primary school. There are certain periods during childhood that are critical in the development and progression of intellectual growth. As learning is understood to be a cumulative process where the framework is dependent on preceding learning, individuals who disengage from formal schooling, particularly at an early age, affect not only their level of cognition but their ability to communicate and integrate into society. This notion is supported by the work of Bruner (1960), a social psychologist engaged in researching the process of education and lifelong learning. He considered that environmental and experiential factors play a role in developing intellectual ability. Bruner suggested that the basic understanding of any subject can be grasped if children are provided with new experiences which allow them to develop personal construct and meaning from the activities, providing them with a structure of learning, where earlier learning renders later learning easier. Disengaging from school at an early age prevents the facilitation of this process and the ability for individuals to construct their own learning. Although individuals learn to cope and 'get by' with limited cognitive abilities, their capacity to respond to information, solve problems and develop ideas and concepts is restricted.

The assessment phase

Using the profile of learners

The assessment period in a unit for offenders diagnosed with severe personality disorders is a very challenging time, for both individuals referred to the unit, and staff. During this phase, numerous assessments are completed by different disciplines and education is no exception, as there is an expectation of the depart-ment to develop a structured process that will provide comprehensive information on the educational needs of all individuals referred to the unit. Within all colleges, prisons and other further educational establishments in England and Wales, the Basic Skills Agency (BSA) initial assessments are used to determine the literacy and numeracy levels of individuals. Hurry *et al.* (2005) stated that, despite the BSA initial assessments being 'fairly crude tests', they show reasonable reliability and validity in that the tests are highly predictive of an individual's performance. The BSA initial assessments are standardized tests and very useful tools in assisting tutors understand the general level of ability of an individual. Information obtained through the BSA assessments in literacy revealed that 46% of learners in a high secure unit for severe personality disordered offenders had reading, writing and spelling skills below that expected of 11-year-olds. This means these individuals are unable to read and write very well and have difficulty completing simple tasks such as reading a report, writing a letter or filling in a form. The information obtained by the BSA tests is used by education staff to ensure work is provided for individuals at an appropriate level and is also relayed to other disciplines as a means of raising awareness for support.

Although an individual's social report may be available for education staff, there are often many gaps in the educational history, which gives an inconsistent and unhelpful account, when trying to build an accurate picture of previous schooling experiences. Initial educational assessments provide key information on academic standards in literacy and numeracy; however, interviews, conducted by education staff with individuals, are beneficial in gaining an understanding of a person's educational, vocational and recreational background. When individuals are trans-ferred from other prison or hospital units, liaising with education staff from these units is equally as important, as it can offer the triangulation necessary to complete the overview of an individual's interests, academic ability, social skills, motivational triggers and previous educational targets. Gathering information from various sources has proven to be of paramount importance because there have been instances when an individual's perception of his educational development is unre-alistic, being either an over- or underestimate of his ability. This pretence of competence appears to be a defence mechanism used to maintain personal stability and kudos in the eyes of others. Although this façade can easily be detected by experienced tutors who have a good understanding of levels of ability, dealing with such cases requires careful handling and sensitivity, particularly with individu-als diagnosed with personality disorders who have difficulties in changing their patterns of thinking.

Providing educational programmes to assessment-based individuals is vital, as it allows education staff to familiarize learners with courses on offer and build sound working relationships. These relationships have been found to be of prin-cipal importance if individuals are to trust staff to support them in an area of their life where many have experienced failure.

Learning style preferences

Experience of working with individuals diagnosed with severe personality disorders indicates that a flexible approach to teaching is necessary, if teaching and learning is to be effective. Many offenders come from diverse educational backgrounds and exhibit a wide range of skills, therefore their preferred method for receiving learning support may be different for specific learning situations, including a traditional classroom setting, independent study or individual learning with tutor support. Individual learning has proven to be the most popular model of learning, particularly for learners with lower skills in reading and writing, because a traditional classroom setting has been said to 'reinforce bad school experiences', particularly those associated with intimidation and embarrassment.

As well as gaining information about learners' basic skills in literacy and numeracy, it is important to gain an understanding of learning styles. Having an understanding of the different learning styles of individuals (for example, visual, auditory or kinaesthetic) can help when planning individual or group lessons in both educational and therapeutic interventions. In general, primary school education focuses on a multisensory approach to teaching and learning where many visual and kinaesthetic activities are used to stimulate and engage pupils. As pupils progress through the education system into secondary, further and higher education, more auditory approaches to teaching and learning are adopted – for example, lectures. Possibly due to many offenders not having completed formal schooling, the learning style preferences of individuals corresponds mainly to the visual and kinaesthetic models. Although teaching should not be entirely structured around an individual's preferred style of learning, as this can have weaknesses in not providing the learner with opportunities to develop their full learning potential, there are advantages in teaching to their perceptual strengths, particularly in relation to engaging and motivating this group of learners who would otherwise quickly disengage.

Education in practice

Curriculum flexibility

The core principles of dangerous and severe personality disorder (DSPD) programmes are to work with individuals to identify appropriate treatment goals and for individuals to engage with their multidisciplinary team to undertake the process of change. Motivation is not viewed as being static but is seen as being a changeable factor, therefore a motivational environment should aim to engage individuals, encourage new behaviours and teach new skills. In an attempt to meet the aims of the DSPD programme, the education department needs a curriculum that provides a high standard of education by including functional skills provision, general and academic education, programmes that enhance therapeutic interventions and leisure/recreational activities. Overall, the curriculum should meet the interest of individuals, be varied, flexible and provide opportunities for gaining academic qualifications, areas for social learning and be consistent with regard to boundaries and support. These qualities reflect those suggested by the Offenders' Learning and Skills Unit, established in 2001 with the Department for Education and Skills. According to the priorities of the Offenders Learning and Skills Unit (2005), offender education should be of the same high standard as that for all other adult learners and should aim to provide reliable and appropriate advice and guidance for individuals whilst supporting the principle of lifelong learning.

Functional skills development

Functional skills including English, mathematics and ICT (information and communication technologies) provide the basis and foundation for lifelong learning and offer individuals opportunities for progression as well as addressing aspects of attitude, self-esteem and motivation. For individuals to understand, organize and transmit their thinking, using both oral and written methods, it is necessary for their literacy to have reached adult level 1, which equates to the GCSE grades D–G. Evidence by Lewis (2003) suggests that participation in functional skills learning can contribute to a reduction in reoffending of about 12% and prisoners who have not participated in education whilst in prison are three times more likely to be reconvicted than those who had participated in learning. Presently, there is no empirical evidence to link participation in functional skills education of individuals diagnosed with severe personality disorder to a reduction in their risk.

Functional skills provision aims to contribute in assisting learners improve their interpersonal functioning and long-term ability to engage in lifelong learning. Experience of working with individuals diagnosed with severe personality disorders suggests that many are very good at hiding their lack of functional skills and, given the choice, will not participate in group educational programmes aimed to improve functional skills. This refusal to engage may be related to the general attributes of individuals with personality disorders which include a negative self-image, refusal to engage in situations where rejection or failure may recur, high emotional vulnerability, rigid patterns of thinking and understanding as well as poor social skills that are consistent and persistent. Providing educational support to individuals diagnosed with severe personality disorders is vital if they are to gain the most from the multidisciplinary therapeutic programme and progress through the treatment pathway. The core elements of functional skills education include problem solving and the use of oral and written skills, all of which are necessary for participation in therapies. An efficient curriculum planned to meet the needs of learners should take account of learners not wishing to engage in group educational programmes. This difficulty can be addressed by offering different styles of learning support – for example, individual learning with tutor support or embedded and personalized learning.

General and academic education

Literacy underpins most branches of learning and therefore can be taught through general education, including subjects such as history, health studies, food and nutrition, art, English, maths, religious education, sociology, ICT, music and technology. Embedded learning has benefits in that it provides learners with the opportunity to learn about a subject of interest whilst providing them with cognitive development. A 'small steps' model of learning is an ideal approach to use with most individuals diagnosed with personality disorders if they are to develop cognitively, experience success, build on positive learning and progress; for some this will be through the acquisition of formal qualifications. The small steps model allows for success to be a very gradual process so that learners progress at a pace they can accept without causing distress or anxiety.

Individuals detained in secure units can access higher academic education through correspondence and Open University courses. These courses are ideal for developing academic skills and, as many are based on a credit system, they provide a progressive structure. Some of the more able learners have the general aptitude to comprehend material in Open University courses but often they have little understanding of academic writing or study skills. With these individuals the challenge lies in broadening their thought processes to include the skills of analysing and synthesizing texts as well as keeping to the strict time scales given for the study and completion of these courses.

Education to enhance therapeutic interventions

The provision of education for individuals with severe personality disorders means there will be occasions when teaching will deviate from the normal boundaries of educational practices. Sometimes it may be necessary to deliver programmes of learning that support or enhance the aims of therapeutic interventions. Structured treatment activities are offered to individuals to address the problems each person experiences, in terms of their personality difficulties and offending behaviour. These treatments are presented in a sequential manner, so as to optimize engagement and identify therapy-interfering behaviours, before addressing the longer-standing problems of mood swings, violence, self-harm or social difficulties. Experience suggests that some individuals have found it difficult to understand the fundamental principles of certain treatment processes and consequently have struggled to appreciate and use them effectively, thus making it difficult for them to progress along the treatment pathway. Introducing educational programmes into the curriculum, which enhance therapeutic interventions, has provided individuals with opportunities to learn key change approaches included in specific therapeutic processes, such as behaviour shaping and problem solving, through the use of varied learning resources, using preferred learning styles. Individuals have responded positively to the introduction of these programmes, stating that lessons have been stimulating and have provided them with reinforcement strategies such as self-monitoring.

Leisure and recreational activities

Many individuals diagnosed with severe personality disorders have never had the opportunity to engage in recreational activities and many welcome the chance to gain a new interest. Attendance and participation at leisure and recreational activities should be encouraged and offered to individuals after assessing their stability and current level of risk. Activities such as guitar, computer literacy, historical board games, creative writing, electronic music and computer-aided design, where individuals can select specific sessions of their choice, can be used to increase motivation and engagement, develop social skills and learn new coping strategies. Recreational activities that can be completed or practised in different areas of the unit, not just within the education department, have the benefit of providing individuals with an activity that can counter maladaptive behaviours.

Key issues

Teaching learners diagnosed with severe personality disorders has similarities to teaching in general; for example, the provision of a suitable curriculum and the use of different teaching approaches to meet varied learning styles. However, education within secure units is different, where the main disparities include the environment, learners, the teaching approach and the role of personalized learning.

The learning environment

Teaching in any secure unit means that security is an absolute necessity for the safety of all individuals. Security can impact on the effectiveness of the educational curriculum because security reduces the opportunity to present learning tasks experienced by learners in non-secure environments. As stated earlier, Bruner (1960) suggested that topics can be understood if taught through experiential learning and engagement in different learning environments with interesting and appropriate resources. The provision of such resources in secure units can be limited and is always subject to the risk associated with each individual at any time. Using inferior resources limits individuals in the development of personal construct and meaning, and therefore creativity, in both teaching methods and effective resources, is very challenging for teachers in secure settings.

The firm but fair approach to teaching

One of the key issues regarding teaching in a unit for offenders diagnosed with personality disorders is the approach that teachers should take if they are to get the best out of their learners. Teachers have to be flexible in their approach and working with these learners is no different; however, the impact of being both too caring and 'soft' or too punitive can have much more of an effect on these individuals and the teacher–learner relationship because of the nature of personality disorder.

As stated earlier in this chapter, countless offenders are a product of failure within the education system. There are many reasons for non-engagement in education but there are also factors that can have positive influences on learners and their desire to learn. Research by Brown (2005) found that specific teacher behaviours can help create lifelong learners; these include teachers who desire learners to succeed, meet students' academic needs and, most importantly, are caring and create a positive atmosphere and a trusting relationship in the classroom. Individuals diagnosed with personality disorder have difficulties in forming positive working relationships and, as stated by the Home Office *et al.* (2005, p. 18), individuals with personality disorder 'can be expected to test boundaries' and 'exploit weaknesses in working relationships'. If teachers working in the education department of secure units are to gain the best from their learners whilst maintaining structure and safety, they need to have clear boundaries with clarity and consistency where the 'firm but fair' approach is necessary in order to provide a positive working educational environment.

Individual learning plans

Individual learning plans (ILPs) are structured documents that outline differentiated steps and teaching requirements needed to help each learner achieve identified specific targets. ILPs should take into account results from the initial assessments, interviews and information gained from other disciplines as well as preferred learning styles and learning support. Plans should aim to support each learner's educational needs and be used to promote effective planning, monitor progress and raise achievements. Targets that are set should be 'owned' by each individual and be relative to their needs at a particular point in time. Such targets may need to be 'soft' targets, if engagement or improvement in attendance is the objective, or very small targets, for example to accept one positive comment per lesson, or more structured and academic and related to a learning objective. Experience of working with personality disordered individuals suggests that targets set should be reviewed regularly, be varied and related to key areas including: communication, functional skills, the development of social interactions such as the working relationship with education staff and/or other learners, and behaviour modification. Individual learning plans should also take into account the clinical or therapeutic needs of each individual as this will ensure that educational targets support each individual's overall treatment goals.

Personalized learning

However old a learner, each one brings their own ideas and experiences, confidences and insecurities, preferences and aversions that help make each one an individual. The art of teaching is to take these individuals and provide them with new knowledge and skills, in ways they find accessible and easy to retain. Personalized learning is not only about subject content nor is it solely about the skills of learning; it is a combination of the two. In schools and colleges, personalized learning has the potential to make every young person's learning experience extensive, creative and successful, where the drive is to tailor the curriculum and teaching methods to meet every individual's need, interest and aptitude. For personality disordered offenders, personalized learning, from an educational perspective, also has the potential to provide learning that meets the needs of each individual where learning can be motivating and meaningful. However, individuals with severe personality disorders present with a multitude of clinical and risk-related needs which require a range of different interventions provided by many disciplines. Each individual has a treatment plan that provides a comprehensive summary of these needs, including those related to the risk of future behaviour, therapeutic interventions necessary for treatment, educational targets, and occupational goals. For these individuals, a holistic approach to therapy is needed, where the treatment plan is a multidisciplinary concern. In this setting, personalized learning takes on a new meaning because the focus for each individual is not just to learn new subject matter or new skills but to learn new behaviours, coping strategies, thinking skills, social interactions and emotional responses in relation to the individual's treatment plan.

The following case study of Sean (pseudonym) describes some of the long-standing difficulties experienced by an individual and how his emotional and behavioural problems impacted on his engagement in educational and therapeutic programmes. With support and the provision of a personalized teaching programme, Sean was able to progress slowly and overcome some of the anxieties he had related to learning. Eventually, this had a positive impact on his self-esteem and engagement in his overall treatment programme.

Case example: Sean

Sean is a 40-year-old man who has been detained in a high secure unit for individuals diagnosed with severe personality disorders for the past 22 months. During the assessment phase, Sean refused to engage in educational group sessions, making excuses each week for non-participation. His excuses included health problems such as headaches, eye strain, toothache and injuries from sports activities. He even arranged family visits to coincide with educational sessions. Although Sean was always pleasant and polite with education staff and entered into discussions where he articulated his opinions and thoughts very well, he never completed any written work; this included his refusal to complete the BSA initial assessments in literacy and numeracy. Sean stated he had 'done them' in the unit he had been transferred from and he had 'no intention of doing them again'. Education staff contacted this unit to gain information about Sean's academic ability and interests but there were no records confirming Sean had participated or even requested educational activities with them. Problems started to arise as Sean progressed through the assessment phase. Without warning, he suddenly refused to attend some of the group therapies, giving no explanation for his change in attitude towards engagement. He continued to refuse educational activities, despite education staff offering him individual support. Eventually, through perseverance and a building of trust, education staff were able to encourage Sean to discuss his educational past and his present feelings about learning. Sean confirmed the social reports about his personal and educational history stating that he was taken into care at the age of seven and spent the following nine years in various residential children's homes. Sean remembers feeling very isolated and lonely and refused to accept his situation. He desperately tried to reunite himself with his family, regularly absconding from the various homes; consequently his education beyond the age of seven was severely disrupted. Sean said he learned very little beyond the age of seven as his emotional state made learning virtually impossible. By the time Sean reached school-leaving age, he had no formal qualifications, he could not read or write at the level expected of an 11-year-old and had no interests in vocational or recreational activities. Sean left residential care only to spend time in and out of young offender institutes and prisons. He refused education in prison because Sean believed it would have made him 'vulnerable to other prisoners', had they found out he could not read or write very well. Sean said he feels shame at having poor literacy skills yet anxiety at the thought of learning to read and write; possibly related to his memories of school when he was ridiculed and humiliated in front of other pupils for getting answers wrong. Although Sean learned to 'get by in life', he admits that he focused his attention on learning strategies to avoid situations that involved literacy, particularly writing. In preference to seeking help, for example, he would rather steal than be faced with having to fill in forms at the job centre. It was not until he reached the age of 30 that he realized the importance of being literate. Sean spent the next eight years trying to teach himself to read and write and, although he felt his reading improved, he continued to find it very difficult to read material with long, descriptive text. His main concern was writing, as he knew his ability to spell was very poor. Sean discussed these difficulties with education staff and also spoke about his anxieties regarding education and how he hated the thought of learning in a classroom setting, particularly with groups of individuals, as his peers would get to know his weaknesses. At this point Sean stated that he wanted to 'come clean' and let staff know the reason he had withdrawn from some of the group therapies, revealing that, as the focus of the sessions had moved from being discussion based to involving written work, he could not cope with the embarrassment of possibly having to write in front of others. Sean said that, when he walks into a room and sees pens and paper, he feels anxious and panics; he finds it easier to refuse groups, thus maintaining his pretence of being literate. Sean agreed to work with education staff on an individual basis where the focus was on literacy, predominantly spellings and sentence structure. Sean was involved with creating his individual learning plan where his initial targets were focused on regular attendance and the formation of a positive and trusting working relationship with education staff, progressing to more detailed literacy-based targets. To stimulate and engage Sean at the start of his educational programme education staff used many visual resources, as this corresponded with his preferred learning style. In order for Sean to develop his full learning potential other resources were gradually introduced, promoting learning using other styles. Personalizing learning for Sean provided him with new knowledge and skills but, more importantly, new positive learning experiences that helped him overcome his previous negative educational encounters and allowed him to experience success. Initially, success was something Sean found very difficult to accept. Encouragement, positive comments and achievements can be very difficult to acknowledge for individuals diagnosed with personality disorder, particularly if they are used to failure and disapproval, as this means they have to change their patterns of thinking and their behaviour in order to deal with optimism. Progress also takes individuals out of their 'comfort zone' and into the 'unknown' which can make some individuals feel very anxious and defensive. Like most individuals diagnosed with severe personality disorders, Sean has good days and bad days which affect both his attendance and his behaviour. During such 'bad' periods, Sean finds it difficult to concentrate and to absorb and retain new work. Reviewing, reflecting and over-learning are useful processes to use to overcome difficult learning phases so the educational experience is not lost and new material does not have to be the focus. Although Sean has persevered with education for the last 16 months, he has not found learning easy, possibly due to his lack of formal schooling from an early age. Sean's capacity to respond to information and to solve problems and build on ideas is limited, therefore education staff have to be very creative and flexible in their teaching. Despite Sean's limitations, he has progressed well, particularly in developing strategies for reading and writing, raising his awareness of his own learning potential and also building his self-esteem and confidence. Sean has re-engaged with group therapeutic programmes and has completed some of the interventions necessary for his progression through the unit. By developing his literacy skills, Sean has been able to cope with some of his anxieties related to reading and writing and has even completed written work in a group setting. For Sean, the collaborative multidisciplinary regime has been very beneficial. Sean has recognized how he can transfer his knowledge, understanding and skills developed in education to support his progress and ability to cope within other treatment areas and, similarly, how his progress in other disciplines has supported his self-esteem and confidence and promoted his desire to continue to learn.

Summary

Providing education to individuals diagnosed with severe personality disorders in secure settings is very challenging. Given the educational history of most of these individuals, engaging and motivating them in education programmes is even more demanding. If an individual experiences rigid and inflexible thought processes, social inhibitions, varied mood swings as well as impulsivity and negative self-image, daily living can be very difficult and the learning of new subjects or skills may be considered by the individual as being almost unattainable. To make learning achievable, a safe, supportive and positive learning environment is needed, where teachers focus on encouragement and motivation, through the provision of individual learning plans, with appropriate and specific targets. Restrictions incurred within a secure environment create a particular need for teachers to be creative, flexible, understanding and supportive, with lessons being associated (as far as possible) with realism, in order for them to be meaningful and encouraging of lifelong learning.

As in all educational establishments, the curriculum is of vital importance for supporting and promoting teaching and learning. Within secure units for individuals diagnosed with severe personality disorders, evidence suggests that an effective curriculum is one that meets the needs of each person, is flexible, offers a variety of accredited and recreational programmes and is reviewed regularly so as to accommodate the changing needs of learners as they progress along the treatment pathway. Personalized learning means adopting teaching and learning approaches that use appropriate and stimulating resources, at the same time as focusing teaching at the correct academic level for each individual, using preferred methods of learning support whilst also working within the realms of a multidisciplinary milieu. This may require the education department to provide alternative approaches to teaching and learning, if individuals diagnosed with severe personality disorders are to develop new ways of thinking and learn new skills and behaviours through reinforcement activities. Such approaches may include working outside the normal parameters of education, but as there is currently very little evidence to support 'what works', new ideas and adaptations to general educational practices are necessary, if teaching and learning is to be effective.

References

American Psychiatric Association (2000). *Diagnostic and statistical manual of mental disorders, 4th edition (DSM–IV–TR)*. Washington, DC: American Psychiatric Association.

Brown, D. (2005). The significance of congruent communication in effective classroom management. *Clearing House, 79*(1), 12–15.

Bruner, J. (1960). *The process of education*. Cambridge, MA: Harvard University Press.

Field, J. (1992). Utopia and adult education. *Oswiata Doroslych Jako Ruch Spoleczny,* Wroclaw, 141–156.

Fontana, D. (1977). *Personality and education*. London: Open Books Publishers.

Home Office, Department of Health & HM Prison Service (2005). *Dangerous and severe personality disorder (DSPD) high secure services for men. Planning and delivery guide.* London: Home Office.

Hurry, J., Brazier, L., Snapes, K. & Wilson, A. (2005). *Improving the literacy and numeracy of disaffected young people in custody and in the community.* London: National Research and Development Centre.

Knowles, M. S., Holton III, E. F. & Swanson, R. A. (1998). *The adult learner*, 5th edition. Woburn, MA: Butterworth-Heinemann.

Lewis, J. (2003) *Initiatives: Skills for life (literacy, language and numeracy)*. London: DfES, Offender Learning and Skills Unit.

Livesley, W. J. (Ed.) (1995). *The DSM-IV personality disorders*. New York: Guilford Press.

Moore, A. (2000). *Teaching and learning. Pedagogy, curriculum and culture*. London: RoutledgeFalmer.

Offenders Learning and Skills Unit (2005). *Initiatives: A new delivery service for learning and skills*. Retrieved 7 July 2005 from www.dfes.gov.uk/offenderlearning

Sperry, L. (2003). *Handbook of diagnosis and treatment of DSM-IV-TR personality disorders,* 2nd edition. New York: Brunner-Routledge.

Tyrer, P., Casey, P. & Ferguson, B. (1991). Personality disorder in perspective. *British Journal of Psychiatry, 159*, 463–471.

Chapter Thirteen

The Boundary Seesaw Model: Good Fences Make for Good Neighbours

Laura Hamilton

A fundamental dilemma faced by clinicians working in forensic in-patient treatment services is how to achieve balance or synthesis between the oft-competing agendas of care (treatment) and control (security). A 'common factors' approach to this dilemma may help, and one such commonality between security and treatment is the value and emphasis placed upon building and maintaining a relationship with our patients. For instance, 'relational security is concerned with a detailed knowledge of the patients, their backgrounds and the reasons behind their admissions to a high-security hospital, and this comes from therapeutic relationships' (Department of Health, 1994). Treatment research views the quality of the therapeutic relationship as predictive and fundamental to positive treatment outcome (Horvath & Bedi, 2002; Horvath & Greenberg, 1994; Livesley, 2003; Meier et al., 2005). Indeed it could be argued that the therapeutic relationship is the nub of effective security and treatment.

The term relational security is ubiquitously used in forensic circles; however, it is poorly conceptualized and often dealt with as an operational aside. For instance, the Tilt Report (Tilt et al., 2000) in its 'comprehensive review of security in high secure hospitals' made 50 general recommendations: three quarters were about procedural security, a quarter about physical security and relational security was scarcely mentioned (cited in Exworthy & Gunn, 2003). This significant omission of the relational component of security is in stark contrast to the treatment literature, where researchers and clinicians have spent decades investigating the therapeutic relationship. In a seminal paper, Edward Bordin (1979) synthesized the therapeutic relationship literature to produce a 'pan-theoretical' model of the therapeutic relationship which had three primary components:

Using Time, Not Doing Time: Practitioner Perspectives on Personality Disorder and Risk
Edited by Allison Tennant and Kevin Howells
© 2010 John Wiley & Sons, Ltd.

1. a bond – creation of a connection between client and staff member;
2. goals – clear objectives for the interaction; and
3. tasks – methods or activities through which the goals will be achieved.

Using Bordin's pan-theoretical model, it is clear that the goals and tasks in the therapeutic relationship from a security and treatment perspective may be different, i.e. information gathering versus facilitating change. A commonality in the relational components of security and treatment is this notion of creating a therapeutic bond with our patients. The limits of this therapeutic bond provide a demarcation between professional and personal relationships, and these limits are hereafter referred to as 'the relational boundaries'.

The relational boundaries of the therapeutic bond are formally articulated in professional codes of conduct, organizational policies and specific psychological treatment modalities. However, unqualified staff are not required to register with professional bodies and the majority of staff within high secure treatment services are not trained in specific psychological treatments. Nevertheless, it is these unregistered staff who are at the heart of the therapeutic milieu, developing bonds and managing the relational boundaries on a daily basis, within the unstructured ward environment. This mismatch between knowledge, training and role expectation is disturbing. For instance, relational boundaries set the limits of power, authority, trust and dependency in the therapeutic and containment process, and adaptive management of the relational boundaries represents a corrective emotional experience for many severely personality disordered offenders (McLean & Nathan, 2007; Peternelj-Taylor & Yonge, 2003). Indeed, one personality disordered patient wrote:

> I really appreciate your consistency. I didn't always like it, and lots of times I did things just to make you inconsistent. It didn't work very often and that was good. I've never had a stable relationship before, and it helped me to be more stable and develop boundaries.

Even though relational boundaries are crucial to human survival, growth and safety, what is clear is that there are no textbook answers telling us how to set and manage the relational boundaries. Research provides some insight into major relational boundary violations; in particular dual relationships, physical abuse and sexual exploitation perpetrated by 'professional carers' (review Gutheil, 2005 and Council for Healthcare Regulatory Excellence, 2008a, 2008b). Little consideration has been given to less serious boundary problems, such as boundary crossings and boundary shifts, and little interest has been paid to how the majority of professional carers effectively manage relational boundaries on a day-to-day basis, in sometimes very extreme circumstances.

From observing staff's everyday relational boundary management with severely personality disordered offenders, it seems this social exchange involves a complex interweave between formal and informal rules, social forces and personal and professional attitudes, values and ideas about relating. Kitchener (1986) wrote that 'staff often sit with chaos, uncertainty and anxiety and the conflicting emotions, pain and dissatisfaction that this may trigger'. Anecdotal evidence supports this proposition, as staff were observed on a daily basis endeavouring to contain intense feelings of chaos, anger and anxiety projected by very 'damaged' patients, who had regularly experienced and engaged in significant boundary transgressions. In practice this complex and emotionally intense interweave is often managed by individuals, teams and organizations by adopting models based on 'pet theories', professional and theoretical orientation or unconscious working models developed from personal experiences of relating. Leaving relational boundary management down to chance and individual choice is problematic, as it leaves our patients at the mercy of a relating lottery and in institutions it can create confusion, chaos and conflict as the multiple ideas compete for the title of how best to contain and/or treat. Moreover, preliminary research suggests that these pet theories or individual working models may be particularly skewed amongst staff working with severely damaged patients (Bowers, 2002; Elliot *et al.*, 1997).

This lack of theoretical grounding and unsystematic approach to relational boundary management is a major issue that needs to be addressed by organizations planning to contain and treat mentally disordered offenders, in particular personality disordered offenders. Developing a collective conceptualization of how the limits to the therapeutic bond should be set and maintained would provide an important starting point. Often this collective conceptualization is worked towards through the operational policies and the organization adopting a core psychological treatment model. However, having a single psychological treatment model may not be possible when working with severely personality disordered offenders, as currently it is unknown which treatments will be most effective and narrow treatment approaches are known to be ineffective (Livesley, 2001, 2003). Another solution to this requirement for a collective conceptualization of how to set and maintain relational boundaries would be to adopt a generic boundary model.

A generic boundary model was developed by the author by building upon the work of Karpman (1968) and NCSBN (1996) and using a quasi ground theorizing approach (Glaser, 1992, 1994) to analyse and make sense of everyday observations of boundary activities engaged in by staff working with severely personality disordered offenders. This information was eventually conceptualized using ideas from cognitive analytic therapy (CAT; Ryle, 1997; Ryle & Kerr, 2002) and dialectical behavioural therapy (DBT; Linehan, 1993), as these were the core personality treatments offered on the unit.

From exploring the boundary roles taken by staff, it was clear that there were some common themes in how staff set and manage relational boundaries. For example, one patient referred to the three ward nursing team leaders as 'the Pacifier, the Mediator and the Punisher'. There was also a fourth role described by patients, 'The Abuser', which represented boundary violations and often related to childhood experiences of physical and sexual abuse when in institutional care. A number of nursing staff reflected on the roles that they and others take as the 'Security Guard, Super-Carer and Negotiator'. Overall three distinct relational boundary management roles could be distinguished in staff's daily relating and these roles are labelled and described using a mixture of staff and patient terminology.

1. *The Security Guard.* Common relating characteristics of Security Guards were emotional coolness, formal, judgemental and controlling. In terms of work orientation they are particularly concerned about rules, regulations, tasks, risk management, and may hold negative attitudes about treatment and bonding with patients.

They were mainly focused on the 'offender' part of the patient and managing the associated dangers.

A fundamental assumption underpinning the Security Guard stance is that safety and healing occur through separation, control and unambiguous boundaries, therefore inflexible and impermeable boundaries are required. The only exception to this rigid application of boundaries should be emergency situations. These ideas are reflected in the boundary literature in writings by Langs (1976), Gabbard (1994) and Gutheil (2005), and the notion of distance and unambiguous boundaries reflects the traditional psychoanalytic approach to the therapeutic relationship.

The security guard role and the risks attached are represented diagrammatically in Figure 13.1 using the idea of reciprocal roles from cognitive analytic therapy (CAT). In CAT, reciprocal roles refer to the dualistic nature of a relationship and how taking one role elicits a corresponding response in another person. For instance, the Security Guard assumes that safety and treatment are achieved by controlling, judging and emotional distance; however, this elicits a reciprocal position in another in which they feel controlled, judged, emotionally neglected and vulnerable. To manage the vulnerability, the patient then pushes the relational boundaries to regain some sense of control, thereby moving the staff member(s) into the more vulnerable position. A typical Security Guard response to boundary pushing may be to restate and tighten the relational boundaries. A battle for control may ensue, resulting in both parties episodically feeling vulnerable and safe. This control trap or vicious circle can be broken by negotiation, escalation of control demonstrations leading to abuse or de-escalation after one party submits by flipping to a more placatory position (e.g. Pacifier role).

The applicability of this emotionally distant and rigid approach when working with severely personality disordered offenders and managing a ward environment is questionable. Personal experience and staff accounts suggest that a dominance of 'Security Guards' can increase the risk of patient neglect, patient compliance, seclusions and power struggles. For instance, in response to inflexible and impermeable relational boundaries an avoidant sexual offender could comply with the will of the clinical team because they feel powerless to do anything else, and consequently it becomes difficult to distinguish between compliance effects and genuine risk reduction or treatment effect. Inflexible and impermeable boundaries also seem to encourage the more antisocial and narcissistic patients to find less adaptive ways to express their autonomy. For instance, narcissistic patients may engage in a concerted complaining campaign against a targeted individual or the psychopathic patient may manipulate a vulnerable other to act aggressively towards the targeted member of staff. If the response to these maladaptive attempts to assert independence is more control through tightening the boundaries, then an escalating cycle of power struggles is likely to occur.

2. *The Pacifier.* Common relating characteristics of the Pacifier are placating, indulging, overly accepting, self-sacrificing, emotional closeness and a very involved approach to relational boundary management focused on the patient's needs. Pacifiers tend to be very much focused on the victim part of the patient and try to make up for the patient's past traumas or woes by giving unconditional care or rescuing them. The containment and treatment assumptions underpinning the

Pacifier stance is that risk is reduced and healing occurs through an unconditional connection created via a flexible and permeable approach to boundary management. These treatment ideas are reflected in the boundary literature in writings by Lazarus (1994a, 1994b), Williams (1997) and Zur (2001) and the assumptions reflect a more humanistic and client-centred approach to the therapeutic relationship.

The Pacifier role and the risks attached are represented diagrammatically in Figure 13.1 using the idea of reciprocal roles from cognitive analytic therapy. By taking a Pacifier role in a therapeutic relationship, the member of staff positions themselves in an indulging, protecting and accepting role, which then elicits a reciprocal position in the patient of indulged, accepted but vulnerable, as they are (co)-dependent on a benevolent other. The intent behind the patient's response to this reciprocated role will be influenced by their psychopathology, but the behaviour is likely to involve some sort of pushing for more or to find the limits of benevolence. Regardless of intent, by pushing the boundaries the patient then places the staff in the more vulnerable position at the bottom of the reciprocal role. Pacifiers tend to respond to this vulnerability by changing or loosening the boundaries to meet the patients' needs, and over time this can result in a vicious circle or placating trap in which boundaries become confused, overly flexible and permeable. Major boundary erosion from this placating trap can result in a shift to a personal relationship in which there is an enmeshment between staff and patient needs; however, given the member of staff's position this can be construed as abuse and exploitation under the Sexual Offences Act 2003. Alternatively, either party may reach the limits of what they are prepared to give, and may feel trapped if more is requested and this may cause a flip to a more controlling position to ensure safety (e.g. Security Guard role).

Although client-centred approaches have been strongly advocated when working with mental health service users, the applicability of this unconditional and flexible stance to management of the ward environment and forensic personality disordered patients is questionable (Doren, 1987). For instance, one highly psychopathic patient recounted targeting Pacifiers 'as you always get what you want', and a paranoid patient reported avoiding Pacifiers 'as nobody's that nice, they suck you in and then kick you in the teeth'. Moreover, the risks attached to this Pacifier position can be inconsistent boundary management and at worst boundary erosion, enmeshment and the abuse of patients and staff.

3. *The Negotiator role* represents a synthesis of the less extreme versions of the Security Guard and the Pacifier roles, i.e. relational boundary management involving care and control components. Common relating characteristics of the Negotiator are openness, being contained, balanced and respectful and having explicit 'no go' areas yet maintaining a responsiveness to patients' need. Negotiators are focused on both the offender and victim parts of the patient and can respond accordingly to both the risk posed and vulnerability experienced by their patients. The assumption underpinning the negotiator role is that risk is contained and healing is brought about in others by developing a collaborative professional relationship or bond that is neither too close nor too distant. In practice, there are areas where negotiators will allow variation (flexible and permeable boundaries) and other areas where they allow no variation (inflexible and impermeable

boundaries). These inflexible and flexible boundaries are maintained by staying in tune with the ongoing process and applying professional judgement which considers both the immediate and long-term consequences of boundary movement (Johnston & Farber, 1996; Ryle & Kerr, 2002; Taylor, 1998).

The Negotiator role and the risks attached are represented diagrammatically in Figure 13.1 using the idea of reciprocal roles from CAT. The Negotiator assumes that safety and treatment are achieved by setting explicit limits and managing other boundaries in a nurturing, respectful and negotiated way. This way of relating elicits a reciprocal position in another, in which the patient feels contained and safe as there are some static limits which provide predictability, combined with other flexible boundaries that allow patients to assert independence and influence over their environment which leave them feeling empowered and respected. Anecdotal accounts indicate a positive response from staff and patients to inflexible and flexible boundary management style, which is hardly surprising, as modelling this approach in relationships with our patients is likely to challenge one of the core deficits associated with personality disorder and offenders, i.e. being able to set and work within adaptive relational limits (McLean & Nathan, 2007). Even though the negotiator's boundaries are fair and consistent, personality disordered patients are unlikely to accept these as genuine, primarily because respectful and equitable treatment is likely to be unfamiliar. The intention behind patients' choice or urge to push against fair treatment is likely to depend on their psychopathology. For instance, the narcissistic patient may expect to be indulged as they view themselves as 'special' and are therefore likely to engage in behaviours which attempt to draw Negotiators into more placating roles. The antisocial patient may expect to be controlled and therefore is likely to engage in behaviours which attempt to draw Negotiators into more controlling and controlled roles. These pulls and pushes which draw Negotiators into less effective boundary management roles often happen through processes of persistent and unfair complaining or seduction through 'chronic niceness' and avoidance of difficult issues.

From exploring the individual boundary roles taken by staff in their professional relating, it became clear that there was a series of traps and dilemmas that caused poor staff–patient relations. A contextual reformulation diagram was developed in an attempt to formulate these staff–patient interactions and understand reciprocal role enactments between the staff and patients, which may both represent and maintain the patients' difficulties (Ryle & Kerr, 2002). The contextual reformulation diagram (Figure 13.1) reflects the Security Guard control trap, the Pacifier placating trap and the risks attached to prolonged use of these roles such as abuse through boundary erosion, boundary rigidity or boundary inconsistency caused by staff flipping between controlling and placating positions.

When the three individual boundary roles were shared with ward teams during the awareness events and during real-time reflection on boundary issues, these ideas were found to have clinical utility. Ward staff reported that training on these three boundary roles helped simplify the complex process of relational boundary management. They reflected that it helped them understand how their personal patterns of relating could elicit responses from another and the boundary roles provided a language in team meetings for talking about differences in boundary management stances. The clinical utility of the contextual reformulation diagram was less obvious as the majority of ward staff found it complex and difficult to

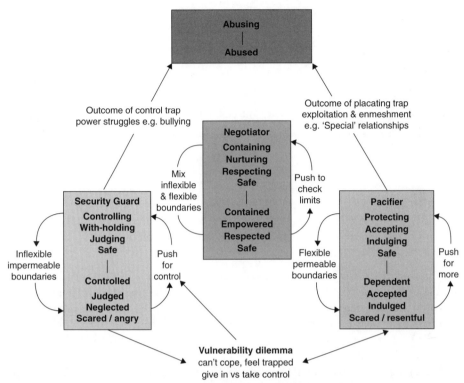

Figure 13.1   Contextual reformulation of staff–patient relationships with dangerous and severe personality disorder patients

comprehend. Nevertheless, this helicopter view of the relational boundary management process was useful as a ward psychology model for reflecting on the ward culture, team dynamics and ward dynamics, and with additional on-the-job reflection, many staff began to find the ideas in the contextual reformulation more accessible.

Given the comprehension problems associated with the contextual reformulation diagram, a more accessible framework was developed for awareness workshops, and the Boundary Seesaw Model was conceived. The Boundary Seesaw Model drew from dialectical behavioural therapy (Linehan, 1993; Talkes & Tennant, 2004), the continuum of professional behaviour developed by the American Nursing Council (NCSBN, 1996), cognitive analytic therapy and the literature on types of boundary movement. The Boundary Seesaw Model conceptualized the dynamic nature of boundary management on a seesaw with a care and control continuum straddling the pivot (Figure 13.2). The model also attempted to assimilate and reflect the identified boundary roles and associated risks.

From Figure 13.2 it is evident that the Boundary Seesaw Model has no definitive lines separating the boundary management roles; rather there is a gradual transition or melding along the care and control continuums. Managing relational boundaries in the white zone keeps things reasonably balanced; however, stepping out of the 'white zone' tips the seesaw and reflects the 'slippery slope'

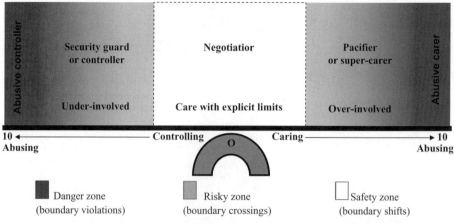

Figure 13.2   Boundary Seesaw Model (Hamilton, 2009)

into boundary crossings and boundary violations, unless, of course, the seesaw is rebalanced. Therefore the key to inflexible and flexible boundary management is to know the non-negotiables (seesaw pivot) for oneself, the team and organization and recognize movement away from these baselines. Being able to recognize small boundary shifts could prevent more serious boundary problems and aid rapid repair of relational issues.

Managing boundaries in the grey zone represents movement along the continuum to a more controlling or placating position in response to external (e.g. pressure from other staff) or internal events (e.g. strong emotions). This shifting from the white to the grey zone represents a significant shift away from normal everyday practices. However, when working with severely personality disordered patients who are deemed a grave and immediate danger to the public and have experienced extreme relational problems, boundary crossings or working at the boundary edge may be a significant part of the containment and treatment process (Gordon, 2009). Indeed, within high secure settings, in response to immediate physical aggression or threats staff occasionally take very controlling positions by putting the patient in physical restraints and placing them in a purposely designed seclusion room. This aspect of staff's work could be conceived as a boundary crossing or working at the boundary edge, as these events involve management of high risk situations which are also important therapeutic moments which can facilitate corrective emotional experiences. However, if boundary crossings are truly important therapeutic moments, then they should be rare, recognized, supported by peer review, thought through and, as soon as possible, there should be processes that allow both parties to return to a centred position on the seesaw. For instance, a patient with borderline personality disorder and a severe history of physical abuse by men in authority reported being shocked at staff's response to his physical aggression.

> all staff did when I kicked off was restrain me, put me in seclusion for a couple of days until I'd calmed down and then they got me up and asked me to work out why I behaved the way I did … I've never had this before, I always got a good kicking for not doing what I was told.

In addition to the white role (Negotiator) and grey roles (Security Guard and Pacifier), there are two black roles on the Boundary Seesaw Model that represent boundary violations, i.e. the Abusive Controller and Abusive Carer. These roles reflect the extreme end of the care and control continuums, and are easily identified as breaches of professional, technical, organizational and ethical codes of conduct. Staff members engaging in these black roles manage relational boundaries in such a way that meets their dysfunctional relationship needs and desires. For instance, the Abusive Controller misuses their authority and trusted position to exert excessive power and control over vulnerable others, by for example hitting patients, falsifying records and non-consensual sexual activity. The Abusive Carer prevents autonomy by encouraging co-dependency and may further exploit the patient by gratifying their sexual desires.

The colour coding scheme on the Boundary Seesaw Model reflects the three types of boundary movements discussed in the literature, i.e. boundary shifts, boundary crossings and boundary violations. Table 13.1 represents a non-exhaustive list of examples of boundary movement events which are evident in the literature and/or have been observed when working with personality disordered offenders.

It is evident from Table 13.1 that not all types of boundary movement are harmful, and indeed some boundary shifts are adaptive and beneficial, such as changing shifts to attend a patient's progress review meetings. However, often there is no formula for identifying if boundary movement is helpful or unhelpful; rather each situation needs to be individually considered on the basis of the situation and those involved in it (see Aiyegbusi & Clarke-Moore, 2009). Paying attention to boundary shifts and making sure that boundary crossings are well considered and documented could resolve many boundary issues before they get to a point where the patient and/or staff member is harmed, exploited or seriously abused.

In summary, developing a collective conceptualization of relational boundaries, and disseminating this through awareness events, has helped create a mental map and common language amongst many staff working on the unit and, anecdotally, this seems to take some of the emotional energy out of the discussions around relational boundary issues. However, this is only one approach which needs to be considered within a systemic framework which aims to support good relational boundary management. Other systemic initiatives which could enhance good relational boundary management are as follows:

- A clear description of the organization's core values, which are translated into guidelines on professional relating and transparent procedures for dealing with boundary mismanagement. These core values and procedures will provide a clear indication of the organization's relational ethos and non-negotiables (seesaw pivot), and could act as a baseline against which the organization can reflect on its own boundary management style. This reference point can also be used to generate a list of warning signs or red flags which suggest movement away from the core ethos and balanced relating position.
- Shared social responsibility for boundary management between patients and staff, e.g. daily business meetings, community meetings and ward activity schedules.

Table 13.1 Examples of boundary shifting, crossing and violations

Boundary shifting	Boundary crossing	Boundary violation
Become defensive about patient or staff member or regularly criticize a patient or a staff member(s).	More extreme or regular boundary shifts.	Personal relationship.
Starting to think about or treat a patient differently.	Member of staff comes to work when off-duty or changes duties to be with the patient.	Staff member enmeshed with patient's family.
Patient tried to be around a specific staff member.	Patient singled out for special attention, e.g. care or punishment or ignored.	Sexual relationship with current or previous patient.
Giving gifts or donating items to patients.	Believe you are the only person who can understand and meet the patient's needs, e.g. staff member is very protective or possessive about patient and regularly sides with patient's position.	Passing of contraband.
Member of staff changes duties/shift to attend patient's meeting, e.g. Care Programme Approach.	Staff member fails to acknowledge or do anything about sexual attraction to patient.	Breaching physical and procedural security, e.g. giving the patient access to your keys, aiding escape or absconding, etc.
Selective feedback to rest of team.	Keeping secrets from team or emphasizing negative information about a patient to rest of team.	Neglect and emotional abuse – ignoring patient distress or preventing patient's access to fresh air.
Swearing, improper language, sexual innuendo or off-colour jokes.	Staff member believes they are immune from fostering a non-therapeutic relationship.	Financial abuse – taking patient's money.
Terms of endearment or nicknames.	Self-disclosure common rather than rare, and disclosure not clearly connected to patient's problems or will support client.	Verbal abuse, e.g. 'winding up' patients, insulting, threatening, exploiting, etc.
Thinking about patient away from work.	Not adhering to basic unit procedures.	
Feelings of sexual attraction.	Dressing for a particular patient.	
Feeling irrationally guilty or responsible for patient's inappropriate behaviour or progress.	Taking or giving secret gifts.	
Changing dress style or make-up for work.	Excessive physical intimacy, e.g. routine hugs.	
Ignoring offending history or any victim issues.	Seeing the patient as a friend.	
Occasional self-disclosure to help patient make sense of an issue.	Retaliating for a previous affront or because a patient's interpersonal style is seen as abhorrent, e.g. highlighting only negative information to Medium Secure Assessor.	
De-escalation techniques.	Excessive direct intervention in the patient's life, e.g. telling patient what to wear, jewellery to order.	
Helping patient express point of view to other team members.	Physical restraint.	
Occasional relaxing of rules on special occasions or dealing with intensely distressing life events, e.g. death of a parent.	Extending care limits in emergency situations, e.g. touching patient who has self-harmed, putting an arm around a distressed patient or to move them away from aggressive incidents.	
Therapy which exceeds normal length.		
Therapeutic drift – shifting style and approach to a given client, lack of goals and reflection on progress in therapy.		
Occasional touching but for a specific therapeutic purpose, e.g. injections.		
Holding grudges for past slights.		

- Including relational boundary management awareness sessions on induction and annual mandatory training programmes. Increasing awareness of personal boundary style could also be combined with client group-specific psychopathology awareness training, social problem-solving skills and training and training emphasizing the importance of everyday communication in facilitating change, especially in personality disordered patients.
- Processes that allow regular review of boundary management and mismanagement, such as unidisciplinary and multidisciplinary team meetings, line management meetings, individual clinical supervision, support meetings and opportunity for personal counselling, if required. This is likely to encourage more on-the-job reflection about relational boundary issues which are likely to be the most effective method of facilitating good boundary management.
- Monitored Meaningful Activity Schedules to reduce the amount of unstructured time on the wards, which is thought to be a high risk time for inappropriate boundary movement.

If forensic treatment services are to adopt some of the aforementioned strategies for improving relational boundary management, then organizations, teams and individuals must get a sense that the benefits attached to adopting these strategies are outweighed by the costs attached to change. A brief review of the literature would suggest that adaptive management of relational boundaries could create a safer and more therapeutic workplace. For instance, boundary management has been associated with:

- workplace aggression (Almvik, 2008; DoH, 2002; Home Office, 1995; Larkin *et al.*, 1988; Urheim & VandenBos, 2006);
- public inquiries (Boynton, 1980; DoH, 1994; Fallon *et al.*, 1999; Home Office, 1991, 1995; Kerr-Haslam Inquiry, 2005; Tilt *et al.*, 2000);
- perpetuating cycles of abuse (Garrett & Davis, 1998; Gonsiorek, 1995; Schoener, 1995; Sheets, 2000; Wright & Denise, 2006);
- staff burnout, emotional exhaustion, increased feelings of inadequacy and depersonalization, poor staff retention and morale (Armstrong & Griffin, 2004; Bowers, 2002; Lambert & Hogan, 2007);
- the potential to maximize a service's opportunity to provide ethical, safe and therapeutic care to personality disordered patients who have also offended.

Finding the balance between treatment (care) and security (control) is no mean feat, particularly when working with patients detained in high secure forensic treatment services. Rather it is a complex and sophisticated process in which staff create a bond with very damaged and dangerous offenders. In their daily relating staff have to then set and manage the relational boundaries which separate this professional bond from a personal one, and often it is the staff with the least formal training in developing and managing professional relationships who spend the most time with our patients undertaking this task. This mismatch between knowledge and role expectation is an area that needs greater consideration, as does educating our staff about the significant impact their daily relating has on the safety and growth of those they are paid to look after. One approach considered in this chapter was the use of collective conceptualization and awareness workshops to encourage adaptive relational boundary management. Awareness workshops for staff on the Boundary Seesaw Model, types of boundary movement and the reasons for this movement have been a useful strategy to at least increase staff confidence and personal awareness. It has also created a common language for discussing boundary management style and seems to reduce the emotional intensity in this dialogue. It is hypothesized that, by adopting a more systematic and systemic approach, we could further enhance the exceptional containment and treatment work that is undertaken by all disciplines working with this very complex patient group on a daily basis.

References

Aiyegbusi, A. & Clarke-Moore, J. (Ed.) (2009). *Therapeutic relationships with offenders: An introduction to the psychodynamics of forensic mental health nursing.* London: Jessica Kingsley Publishers.

Almvik, R. (2008) *Assessing the risk of violence: Development and validation of the Brøset Violence Checklist.* PhD thesis. Retrieved 29 February 2008 from http://ntnu.diva-portal.org/smash/record.jsf?searchId=1&pid=diva2:123543

Armstrong, G. & Griffin, M. (2004). Does the job matter? Comparing correlates of stress among treatment and correctional staff in prison. *Journal of Criminal Justice, 32,* 577–592.

Bordin, E. S. (1979). The generalisability of the psychoanalytic concept of the working alliance. *Psychotherapy, Theory, Research and Practice, 16*(3), 252–260.

Bowers, L. (2002). *Dangerous and severe personality disorder: Response and role of the psychiatric team.* London: Routledge.

Boynton, Sir J., Department of Health and Social Security (1980). *Report of the Review of Rampton.* London: HMSO.

Council for Healthcare Regulatory Excellence (CHRE) (2008a). *Clear sexual boundaries between healthcare professionals and patients: Responsibilities of healthcare professionals.* Retrieved 29 February 2008 from www.chre.org.uk

Council for Healthcare Regulatory Excellence (CHRE) (2008b). *Learning about sexual boundaries between healthcare professionals and patients: A report on education and training.* Retrieved 29 February 2008 from www.chre.org.uk

Department of Health (1994). *Report of the Working Group on High Security and Related Psychiatric Provision* (The Reed Report). London: Department of Health.

Department of Health (2002). *2000/2001 Survey of reported violent or abusive incidents, accidents involving staff and sickness absence in NHS trusts and health authorities in England.* London: Department of Health.

Department of Health (2004). *Committee of Inquiry Independent Investigation into how the NHS Handled Allegations About the Conduct of Clifford Ayling* (Ayling Inquiry). Norwich: HMSO.

Doren, D. M. (1987). *Understanding and treating the psychopath.* Chichester: John Wiley & Sons.

Elliot, R. L., Wolber, G. & Ferriss, W. (1997). A survey of staff attitudes toward ethically problematic relationships with patients. *Administration and Policy in Mental Health, 24*(5), 443–448.

Exworthy, T. & Gunn, J. (2003). Taking another tilt at high secure hospitals. The Tilt Report and its consequences for secure psychiatric service. *British Journal of Psychiatry, 182,* 469–471.

Fallon, P., Bluglass, R., Edwards, B. *et al.* (1999). *Report of the Committee of Inquiry into the Personality Disorder Unit, Ashworth Special Hospital.* London: HMSO.

Gabbard, G. (1994). Teetering on the precipice: A commentary on Lazarus's 'How certain boundaries and ethics diminish therapeutic effectiveness'. *Ethics and Behavior, 4,* 283–286.

Garrett, T. & Davis, J. (1998). The prevalence of sexual contact between British clinical psychologists and their patients. *Clinical Psychology and Psychotherapy, 5,* 253–256.

Glaser, B. G. (1992). *Basics of grounded theory analysis.* Mill Valley, CA: Sociology Press.

Glaser, B. G. (Ed.) (1994). *More grounded theory methodology. A reader.* Mill Valley, CA: Sociology Press.

Gonsiorek, J. (1995). *Breach of trust: Sexual exploitation by health care professionals and clergy.* Thousand Oaks, CA: Sage.

Gordon, N. (2009). The 'unthought known': Working with men with personality disorder in a high secure setting. In A. Aiyegbushi & J. Clarke-Moore (Eds.), *Therapeutic relationships with offenders: An introduction to the psychodynamics of forensic mental health nursing.* London: Jessica Kingsley Publishers.

Gutheil, T. G. (2005). Boundary issues. In J. M. Oldham, A. E. Skodol & D. S. Bender (Eds.), *Textbook of personality disorders.* Washington, DC & London: American Psychiatric Publishing.

Hamilton, L. (2009). *Boundary Seesaw Model. Training manual.* Available from: Laura.hamilton@nottshc.nhs.uk

Home Office (1991). *Prison disturbances April 1990. Report of an Inquiry (Cm 1456).* London: HMSO.

Home Office (1995). *Review of prison service security in England and Wales and the escape from Parkhurst Prison on Tuesday 3rd January 1995 [the Learmont Inquiry].* London: HMSO.

Horvath, A. O. & Bedi, R. P. (2002). The therapeutic alliance. In J. C. Norcross (Ed.), *Psychotherapy relationships that work: Therapist relational contributions to effective psychotherapy.* New York: Oxford University Press.

Horvath, A. O. & Greenberg, L. (Eds.) (1994). *The working alliance: Theory, research and practice.* New York: Wiley.

Johnston, S. H. & Farber, B. A. (1996). The maintenance of boundaries in psychotherapeutic practice. *Psychotherapy, 33,* 391–402.

Karpman, S. (1968). Fairy tales and script drama analysis. *Transactional Analysis Bulletin, 7*(26), 39–43.

Kerr-Haslam Inquiry (2005). *HM Government Full Report Kerr-Haslam.* Norwich: HMSO.

Kitchener, K. S. (1986). Teaching applied ethics in counselor education: An integration of psychological processes and philosophical analysis. *Journal of Counseling and Development, 64,* 306–310.

Lambert, E. G. & Hogan, N. L. (2007). This job is killing me: The impact of job characteristics on correctional staff job stress. *Applied Psychology in Criminal Justice, 3*(2), 117–142.

Langs, R. (1976). *The bipersonal field.* New York: Aronson.

Larkin, E., Murtagh, S. & Jones, S. (1988). A preliminary study of violent incidents in a special hospital (Rampton). *British Journal of Psychiatry, 153,* 226–231.

Lazarus, A. A. (1994a). How certain boundaries and ethics diminish therapeutic effectiveness. *Ethics and Behavior, 4,* 255–261.

Lazarus, A. A. (1994b). The illusion of the therapist's power and the patient's fragility: My rejoinder. *Ethics and Behavior, 4,* 299–306.

Linehan, M. M. (1993). *Cognitive-behavioural treatment of borderline personality disorder.* New York: Guilford Press.

Livesley, W. J. (2001). *Handbook of personality disorders: Theory, research and treatment.* New York: Guilford Press.

Livesley, W. J. (2003). *Practical management of personality disorder.* New York: Guilford Press.

McLean, D. & Nathan, J. (2007). Treatment of personality disorder: Limit setting and the use of benign authority. *British Journal of Psychotherapy, 23*(2), 231–246.

Meier, P. S., Barrowclough, C. & Donmall, M. C. (2005). The role of the therapeutic alliance in the treatment of substance misuse: a critical review of the literature. *Addiction, 100*(3), 304–316.

National Council of State Boards of Nursing (NCSBN) (1996). *Professional boundaries: A nurse's guide to the importance of appropriate professional boundaries.* Chicago, IL: NCSBN.

Peternelj-Taylor, C. A. & Yonge, O. (2003). Exploring boundaries in the nurse–client relationship: Professional roles and responsibilities. *Perspectives in Psychiatric Care,* Apr–Jun.

Ryle, A. (1997). *Cognitive analytic therapy and borderline personality disorder: The model and the method.* Malden, MA: John Wiley & Sons.

Ryle, A. & Kerr, I. B. (2002). *Introducing cognitive analytic therapy: Principles and practice.* Malden, MA: John Wiley & Sons.

Sexual Offences Act (2003). Section 39–44: Care workers for persons with a mental disorder. London: HMSO.

Schoener, G. (1995). Assessment of professionals who have engaged in boundary violations. *Psychiatric Annals, 25*(2), 95–99.

Sheets, V. R. (2000). Staying in the lines. *Nursing Management, 31*(8), 28–34.

Taylor, P. B. (1998). Setting your boundaries. *Nursing, 28*(4), 56–57.

Talkes, K. & Tennant, A. (2004). The therapy seesaw: Achieving therapeutically balanced approaches to working with emotional distress. *British Journal of Forensic Practice, 6*(3), 3–12.

Tilt, R., Perry, B., Martin, C. *et al.* (2000). *Report of the Review of Security at the High Security Hospitals.* London: Department of Health.

Urheim, R. & VandenBos, G. R. (2006). Aggressive behavior in a high security ward: Analysis of patterns and changes over a ten-year period. *International Association of Forensic Mental Health Services, 5*(1), 97–104.

Williams, M. H. (1997). Boundary violations: Do some contended standards of care fail to encompass commonplace procedures of humanistic, behavioural, and eclectic psychotherapies? *Psychotherapy, 34*(3), 238–249.

Wright, L. & Denise, R. N. (2006). How do you set boundaries in your relationships with patients, and what's the penalty if you cross the line? *Nursing, 36*(3), 52–54.

Zur, O. (2001). Out-of-office experience: When crossing office boundaries and engaging in dual relationships are clinically beneficial and ethically sound. *Independent Practitioner, 21*(1), 96–100.

Chapter Fourteen

Afterthoughts on Personality Disorder and Risk: Tasks for the Future

Richard Howard and Kevin Howells

This book is primarily aimed at practitioners, people who 'do things', who have a coalface responsibility to assess and work therapeutically with a patient group that remains poorly understood from a scientific perspective and for whom which treatments will prove effective or ineffective is as yet unknown. Many mental health professionals in this field are likely to aspire to work in a way which is scientifically grounded and based on a reciprocal relationship between practice and research. This is an aspiration, for example, explicitly expressed in the 'scientist-practitioner' model espoused within clinical psychology training and practice. Such models of practice stress the need to ground practice within theories which have scientific support and, for treatment, to be consistent with empirical research relating to treatment outcomes.

However, within the scientist-practitioner model, reciprocity in the science–practice relationship also implies that problems, developments, ideas and findings in clinical practice should also inform and shape future theoretical ideas and research questions. Arguably, one illustration, from another field, of the possibility of the latter can be found in the sparking of the 'cognitive revolution' in clinical psychological theory and research by the early clinical findings of practitioners such as Aaron Beck (1976). This latter aspiration, to an influence of clinical practice on science, is particularly important in the context of personality disorder (PD) and risk. The learning and new ideas derived from intensive clinical work with this population in recent years are important and need to be acknowledged and captured, so they can have an influence on future developments. Hopefully, the clinical contributions to the present volume form part of this process.

Using Time, Not Doing Time: Practitioner Perspectives on Personality Disorder and Risk
Edited by Allison Tennant and Kevin Howells
© 2010 John Wiley & Sons, Ltd.

Conceptual problems and the three pillars of DSPD

Although the renewal of interest in personality disorder and risk extends more widely than the DSPD (dangerous and severe personality disorder) initiative (see chapter 1), the latter does illustrate some of the conceptual problems in the field that will need further consideration in the future. The DSPD Programme had the great merit that, perhaps for the first time, explicit criteria were laid out by which to evaluate whether someone was admissible as 'dangerous and severely personality disordered'. The DSPD edifice rested on three pillars: high risk of violence (at least a 50% risk of harm to oneself or another); a severe personality disorder, with a strong admixture of 'psychopathic' traits; and a functional, i.e. presumably causal, link between the two.

The first pillar, that of risk, has been well covered by Daffern (chapter 2, this volume). As well as problems with applying risk assessments to the individual case, risk assessment is seriously flawed by the high margins of error observed at the individual level (see also Hart *et al.*, 2007; Mullen, 2007). Daffern points out that what is sorely lacking is risk assessments that track the ebb and flow of risk from minute to minute, hour to hour and day to day. Most measures of risk, including the Psychopathy Checklist (PCL),[1] are static and unchanging. Not surprisingly, where the PCL and other risk measures have been evaluated, e.g. in the UK Prison Cohort Study (Coid *et al.*, 2009), they have not fared very well, compared with measures that simply record past violence. We need to bear in mind that it may be that no risk measure will ever be more than about 70% accurate, given the essential unpredictability and instability of human behaviour. Whether new technologies, for example, dynamic brain measures (Howard, 2009), will do as well as, or better than, psychometric measures in predicting violence remains to be seen.

Severity of personality disorder is the second pillar supporting the DSPD edifice. This is a difficult construct to operationalize – just what is a *severe* personality disorder? One has first to define what a personality disorder is, and this is difficult enough (see, for example, Howard & Duggan, 2009). The DSPD severity criteria – there are three disjunctive criteria – are unsatisfactory for a number of reasons. First, they conflate a dimensional measure of psychopathic traits (PCL-R [Psychopathy Checklist – Revised]) with categorical (DSM [Diagnostic and Statistical Manual of Mental Disorders]) measures of personality disorder – as Duggan and Howard (2009) put it, these criteria mix up apples with oranges. Second, it assumes that all of the personality disorders are equally associated with the likelihood of violence. An individual, for example, who just satisfies criteria for dependent and avoidant personality disorders can be designated as having a 'severe personality disorder' according to DSPD. Yet, as Duggan and Howard point out, there is no evidence that the presence of dependent and avoidant traits is likely to lead to violent behaviour – in fact the evidence is to the contrary (see Coid, 1992). Conversely, an individual who meets all the criteria for paranoid personality disorder might behave violently, yet fail to meet the DSPD 'severity' criteria. The DSPD literature offers no guidance as to how this dilemma should be resolved. Indeed, it cannot be resolved until a clearer understanding emerges about the nature of the relationship between personality disorder and violence, including how any such relationship is mediated. Duggan and Howard (2009), in their review of this relationship, found no good evidence for a unidirectional causal relationship between PD and violence, and suggested that the role of possible third variables in mediating the relationship needs to be thoroughly investigated. Regarding severity, they concluded:

> Defining it through sheer aggregation of PDs is not acceptable, since it has become clear from recent research that while some PDs – namely antisocial, paranoid, borderline, narcissistic, histrionic – are associated with criminal, including violent, offending, others – in particular obsessional-compulsive – are inversely related to antisociality ... The definition of 'severe personality disorder' needs to be far more nuanced. (p. 34)

How might a more nuanced definition of severity be achieved? Attempts have been made to grapple with the concept of PD severity and to operationalize it using continuous rating scales (e.g. Tyrer & Johnson, 1996), and this offers a promising approach. Tyrer and Johnson originally suggested a 0–3 scale, anchored at the low severity end by 'no personality abnormality' and at the high end by 'diffuse personality disorder' – two or more personality disorders from different clusters. This was later modified to include a fourth, higher level of severity that included, in addition to level 3, the presence of marked antisocial traits, i.e. a definite diagnosis of antisocial PD must be present. Our research group at the Peaks Unit has expanded the Tyrer and Johnson scale to include a fifth and highest level of severity that includes, in addition to those meeting criteria for level 3, those who meet the criteria for PCL psychopathy. This would capture those who, in addition to meeting criteria for antisocial PD, also meet criteria for psychopathy (the 'deviant and disinhibited'). It is known that this antisocial PD plus psychopathy combination is associated with a greater degree of violence than is antisocial PD alone (Kosson *et al.*, 2006).

Another possible measure of severity in the context of DSPD is the co-occurrence of antisocial and borderline PDs, whose prevalence is known to be disproportionately represented in high secure forensic settings and is particularly high in those who meet DSPD criteria (see e.g. Duggan & Howard 2009, Figure 2). Over 50% of male DSPD patients show this co-occurrence, and in females it is even higher, up to 80%. Both antisocial and borderline PD load on a higher-order 'psychopathy' factor derived from factor analysis of International Personality Disorder Examination (IPDE) items (Howard *et al.*, 2008), and it should in principle be possible to derive a cut-off score on this factor to differentiate the 'dangerous and severe' from other PDs.

The third and final pillar supporting the DSPD edifice is the so-called functional link between severe PD and dangerousness. The notion of a functional link turns out to be considerably more problematic than might be initially supposed. In their critical examination of the concept Duggan and Howard (2009) found little credible evidence to support a simple unidirectional causal relationship between PD and risk of violence. We are left with a relationship whose nature is unclear and which may be less robust than commonly assumed (although few would doubt that some sort of relationship exists, the epidemiology suggests as much).

Howells (in press) has proposed that the uncertainties about the strength and nature of the functional link have major implications for the process of formulation of the individual patient (see Jones, chapter 4, this volume). Formulation involves the clinical identification of antecedent (causal) factors for violence for the purpose of specifying treatment targets. It is likely that the formulation task is far broader, more detailed and more demanding than one of identifying which personality disorder(s) the individual might have (Howells, in press; Jones, chapter 4, this volume) and that an 'individual/functional' as opposed to a 'structural/diagnostic' approach may be more useful (Daffern & Howells, 2009).

It is likely that future accounts of the causation of violence and other high risk behaviours in the personality disordered will be multifactorial. For example, Howard (2009) has suggested that there are three critical links in the causal chain linking PD with violence: the first is a history of conduct disorder during child-hood; the second is a history of excessive alcohol (and other drug) use during adolescence that fundamentally impairs the prefrontal cortex of the brain, such that – and this is the final link in the chain – those brain mechanisms that are critically involved in emotional self-regulation are impaired. An advantage of such conceptualizations is that they may enable us to relate 'abnormal' violence (the sort committed by our high risk personality disordered patients) to everyday, common-or-garden violence ('normal' violence), rather than assuming that vio-lence in the personality disordered is fundamentally different (Howells *et al.*, 2004). Most violence is committed by people who, while they may be temporarily unbalanced mentally, are perfectly sane, and who are young, male and poor. It is possible, even likely, that similar risk factors operate in those whose violence we pathologize by describing it as 'functionally linked' to a severe personality disorder (or indeed to any psychological disorder). If the increased risk (see above) con-ferred by personality disorder in general is indeed modest (Duggan & Howard, 2009), there are dangers of the functional link being overstated in order to justify the (continuing) detention of individuals considered too dangerous to be at large in the community.

New treatment directions

Many treatments currently being delivered in personality disorder/high risk units or in the community have been imported from other fields – see, for example, the various therapeutic programmes described in preceding chapters. There are very few treatments that were initially developed to meet the particular requirements or characteristics of these severely personality disordered patients. This would apply, for example, to dialectical behaviour therapy (chapter 5), schema therapy (chapter 7) and cognitive analytic therapy (chapter 6). In a sense, many such treat-ments are several steps ahead of our understanding of the underlying processes that are deficient in these patients. Offending-focused interventions (see chapters 8, 9 and 10) have been derived from similar programmes delivered to non-personality disordered (or at least not formally diagnosed) offender populations, within the risk–needs–responsivity framework (Hollin & Palmer, 2006). The problem for such programmes, as commented on by several contributors to this book, is how to ensure they meet the responsivity principle (Andrews & Bonta, 2006).

There is a need for novel treatment approaches that are targeted at the patients' characteristics and that are grounded in an understanding of the underlying processes and mechanisms thought to be deficient. Increasing evidence suggests, for example, that information-processing deficits characterize psychopathic individuals, particularly when they are processing affective information (e.g. Howard & McCullagh, 2007). These deficits involve largely unconscious and automatic processes, and new treatment approaches need to address this fact.

Increasingly the concepts of self-regulation and response modulation are invoked to describe this processing deficit in psychopathic individuals. Their impaired ability to self-regulate appears to stem from a failure to engage an automatic attention mechanism when they receive information telling them that they have made an error (Varlamov *et al.*, in press). From this perspective, the problem with psychopaths lies not in their ability to process information consciously and elaboratively, but in their inability to attend (automatically and unconsciously) to cues telling them that their responses are erroneous or maladaptive. Only once these cues are captured in the attentional 'spotlight' can they be processed elaboratively.

Wallace and Newman (2004) have proposed a treatment regimen aimed at compensating for this information-processing deficit. This regimen has several components: a motivational component, aimed at getting patients to engage in treatment; and a behavioural intervention component, to increase pausing and self-reflection, particularly in the context of strong emotional arousal, and to evaluate response options and select appropriate behavioural alternatives. A cognitive component aimed at changing beliefs and attitudes, while present in this treatment package, plays a relatively minor role, since the problem for psychopaths does not, according to this treatment model, lie primarily at this level.

Other novel and promising, though not proven in this context, treatment approaches that have not as yet been applied to the dangerous and severely personality disordered population include mindfulness (Howells *et al.*, in press) and neurofeedback (Howard, 2009). Both these interventions are aimed at overcoming what is seen as a fundamental deficit in severely personality disordered patients, an inability to self-regulate, particularly emotionally. As mentioned earlier, it has been suggested that one of the critical links in the chain connecting personality disorder and violence is *emotional dysregulation*. Personality disordered patients may have an inherent tendency to excessively up-regulate or down-regulate their emotional states, either positive states such as exhilaration and excitement, or negative states such as anger. Mindfulness and neurofeedback represent very different approaches – psychological and neuro-psychophysiological – to increasing the ability to control violent impulses, but the underlying brain mechanisms are thought to be the same. At the end of the day, the relative merits of these or any other new interventions might turn on their relative cost effectiveness, in terms of expenditure on manpower and equipment, rather than on their relative therapeutic effectiveness.

In summary, there are several novel treatment interventions waiting in the wings, all of which address a particular underlying deficit that has been uncovered through experimentation. A Baconian[2] revolution is needed in the treatment of severe personality disorders, to ensure that treatments are generated inductively, based on sound empirical evidence regarding the targets of treatment, rather than deductively ('it works with patients of type X, so therefore it might work with patients of type Y').

The problem of integration of treatment components

It is apparent from the large number of treatments discussed in this book that a personality disordered individual could be exposed to a number of treatment interventions, either simultaneously or (more likely) sequentially. In the Personality Disorder services at Rampton Hospital, for example, the clinical strategy involves a series of sequential interventions through which the individual is expected to move. This might commence with introductory group and individual programmes to enhance motivation and engagement, followed by dialectical behaviour therapy and/or cognitive analytic therapy, treatments intended to address underlying personality problems. These are followed by offending-focused programmes (see chapters 8, 9 and 10 in this book) focused on violence, sex offending and substance use-related offending. Eventually the individual moves to interventions concerned with minimizing the difficulties involved in the transition to less-secure environments. It is the richness and multiplicity of such interventions that constitute the strength of the overall treatment programme, but which also can be a weakness. While the offending programmes share a broad cognitive-behavioural theoretical orientation, both dialectical behavioural therapy and, even more so, cognitive analytic therapy have distinctive theoretical backgrounds, assessments, formulation approaches and therapeutic methods. Typically, a different group of staff will deliver each programme type. In such a system, the opportunities for confusion and inconsistency as to therapeutic aims, terminology, targets and general direction are many, for both patients and staff. On the other hand, some have advocated that just such an approach – 'pragmatic eclecticism' – is exactly what is required for those with personality disorders (Livesley, 2003, 2007).

Livesley advocates a multifaceted but integrated approach, with three components: an eclectic use of diverse therapeutic models and strategies, based on their demonstrated effectiveness; delivering treatments in an integrated way; and focusing treatment efforts on producing integration and coherence of personality functioning. Thus integration is a core construct and one which needs to be unpacked and operationally defined in clinical practice. Integration may be achieved through the non-specific aspects of treatment, including the therapeutic alliance, an emphasis on motivation and engagement and having a clear structure for the various treatments delivered (Livesley, 2003, 2007). A critical task in achieving integration would seem to be developing a shared, service-wide, formulation of the individual case – no easy task for professionals with different professional roles and theoretical orientations (Howells & Jones, 2009). In an ideal world it would be desirable to formally compare treatment outcomes for a therapeutic regime which was entirely integrated, in the sense of all staff having one shared theoretical model and approach (for example, a whole service based exclusively on a schema therapy model), and a multifaceted approach of the Livesley sort, where integration of separate components has to be achieved.

Evaluation

A number of future challenges have been identified in delivering therapeutic services for individuals with severe personality disorders and who are deemed to pose a high risk (Howells *et al.*, 2007). These include the challenge of the potential reluctance of the persons so categorized to engage in therapy (see chapter 3); the challenge, particularly in high security settings, of maintaining staff morale and a therapeutic climate; and the challenge of evaluation. It is with discussion of this third challenge that we wish to conclude this chapter. The case has already been briefly made above that scientific evaluation of outcomes is critical in the development of these services. McMurran (2009) makes the point very clearly:

> It is imperative to research the effectiveness of treatments so that services can be developed on the basis of empirical evidence, thus giving mental health professionals the confidence to work with people with personality disorder, the judiciary the confidence to direct people with personality disorder into treatment, and the client the confidence to work therapeutically on his or her problem, to effect lasting change. (p. 14)

The treatments being developed may be highly plausible in the sense that they have been demonstrated to have a positive impact with other populations, including serious offender populations or personality disordered people without high risk behaviours, but there is scant evidence as yet as to their impact on personality disorder in combination with high risk (Duggan *et al.*, 2007). Thus there is a compelling argument that all interventions, including those described in this volume, should be delivered in clinical services *only if* their delivery is being formally evaluated in an ongoing way. That is, we would suggest, treatments should not be delivered if evaluation of effectiveness is seen as hypothetical and as being conducted only in the long term. The notion that 'our treatment' will eventually be evaluated in the dim and distant future, when a local university takes an interest or when a grant is obtained, is common in our experience but it is neither satisfactory nor ethical. Single case methodology (discussed below) may be particularly suited to the ongoing evaluation task.

It is possible to distinguish three types of evaluation in this context: regime evaluation, treatment evaluation and programme quality evaluation. The regime is the aggregate of the treatment interventions offered in the service. As discussed above, this may comprise a range of different treatments, activities and educational inputs being offered as well as the multitude of non-specific factors such as therapeutic climate, the social environment and therapeutic relationships with staff. An obvious evaluation question is whether regimes in prison or criminal justice settings differ in their effectiveness from regimes within mental health services. The implementation of the high secure DSPD services (two in the prison system, two in mental health services), theoretically, provided an opportunity for a 2 × 2 design experiment in which two variables (type of treatment and type of milieu) and their interactions could have been investigated. Outcomes in any regime evaluation would need to include long-term adjustment and functioning in less secure and community settings, as well as reduced risk as measured by recidivism.

Treatment evaluation is concerned with assessing the impact of a particular intervention, such as dialectical behaviour therapy (DBT), and determining whether it is more effective than an alternative therapy being offered or with 'treatment as usual' without DBT. This is likely to be a difficult task in practice because patients may be receiving multiple treatments at any one time (see above) or because they move rapidly through a treatment sequence, with little time to assess the impact of one treatment before the next is assessed. In many settings it will be impossible to assess the independent impact of any one treatment on longer-term outcomes such as transition to less secure care or to the community because of the multiple treatments experienced in the overall regime. Thus the focus would need to be on immediate outcomes such as incidents, behaviour on wards, mental health factors and cognitive and affective states.

Randomized controlled trials (RCTs) are clearly potentially very relevant to both regime and therapy evaluations. The major difficulties RCTs pose, particularly randomization, for clinical services, however, can make them a daunting though not impossible prospect, particularly in the short term. The difficulties are conceptual as well as practical (Hollin, 2006) and have led some to consider the potential contribution of other designs, particularly controlled single case methodology (Bloom *et al.*, 2003; Davies *et al.*, 2007). It is likely such work will expand in the future, though dealing with threats to internal and external validity is an important consideration.

Programme quality evaluations are generally less problematic for clinical services. Evaluation of the quality of a programme through accreditation mechanisms, comparison with best standards guidelines, integrity checklists and the like are familiar activities, particularly within criminal justice services, where particular methodologies have been developed (Goggin & Gendreau, 2006). Accreditation and programme quality checklists appear to be less prevalent in mental health systems in general and within personality disorder services in particular. This is clearly an area of evaluation requiring further development.

In conclusion, the development of significant and intensive programmes for individuals with severe personality disorder and high risk of violence has a relatively short history (see chapter 1, this volume). This book has been concerned predominantly with new clinical developments and has been produced mainly by practitioners involved in such work, at the coalface. As services become established and clinical expertise developed, it is timely, we hope, to have reminded the reader of the gaps in our knowledge and of what might be required as we move towards a scientific understanding of causal factors and of the effectiveness of treatments.

Finally, there is a need to be prepared for the ground moving under our feet. Scientific advances are likely to be made in understanding the core psychological and neurophysiological processes involved, which may require us to reconsider our practice. The concept of personality disorder itself is likely to change, particularly with the advent of DSM-V, and with it our approach to assessment, treatment and the provision of services. Public and governmental perceptions and priorities are never stable and these factors, ultimately, will also shape the future.

Notes

1. The PCL was not developed as a measure of risk, but as a way of assessing psychopathic traits.
2. Francis Bacon (1561–1626). Bacon's contribution to philosophy was his application of the inductive method of modern science. He urged full investigation in all cases, avoiding theories based on insufficient data.

References

Andrews, D. & Bonta, J. (2006). *The psychology of criminal conduct*, 3rd edition. Cincinnati, OH: Anderson.

Beck, A. T. (1976). *Cognitive therapy and emotional disorders*. New York: International Universities Press.

Bloom, M., Fischer, J. & Orme, J. G. (2003). *Evaluating practice: Guidelines for the accountable professional*. Boston: Allyn & Bacon.

Coid, J. (1992). DSM-III diagnosis in criminal psychopaths: A way forward. *Criminal Behaviour and Mental Health, 2*, 78–94.

Coid, J., Yang, M., Ullrich, S., Zhang, T., Sizmur, S., Roberts, C. *et al.* (2009). Gender differences in structured risk assessment: Comparing the accuracy of five instruments. *Journal of Consulting and Clinical Psychology, 77*, 337–348.

Daffern, M., & Howells, K. (2009). The function of aggression in personality disordered patients. *Journal of Interpersonal Violence, 24*(4), 586–600.

Davies, J., Howells, K. & Jones, L. (2007). Evaluating innovative treatments in forensic mental health: A case for single case methodology? *Journal of Forensic Psychiatry and Psychology, 18*, 353–367.

Duggan, C. & Howard, R. C. (2009). The 'functional link' between personality disorder and violence: A critical appraisal. In M. McMurran & R. Howard (Eds.), *Personality, personality disorder and risk of violence* (pp. 19–37). Chichester: Wiley.

Duggan, C., Huband, N., Smailagic, N. *et al.* (2007). The use of psychological treatments for people with personality disorder: A systematic review of randomized controlled trials. *Personality and Mental Health, 1*, 95–125.

Goggin, C. & Gendreau, P. (2006). The implementation and maintenance of quality services in offender rehabilitation programmes. In C. R. Hollin & E. J. Palmer (Eds.), *Offending behaviour programmes: Development, application and controversies*. Chichester: Wiley.

Hart, S. D., Michie, C. & Cooke, D. J. (2007). Precision of actuarial risk assessment instruments: Evaluating the 'margins of error' of group v individual predictions of violence. *British Journal of Psychiatry, 190*(suppl. 49), 60–65.

Hollin, C. R. (2006). Offending behaviour programmes and contention: Evidence-based practice, manuals and programme evaluation. In C. R. Hollin & E. J. Palmer (Eds.), *Offending behaviour programmes: Development, application and controversies* (pp. 33–67). Chichester: Wiley.

Hollin, C. R. & Palmer, E. J. (Eds.) (2006). *Offending behaviour programmes: Development, application and controversies*. Chichester: Wiley.

Howard, R. (2009). The neurobiology of affective dyscontrol: Implications for understanding 'dangerous and severe personality disorder'. In M. McMurran & R. Howard (Eds.), *Personality, personality disorder and risk of violence* (pp. 157–174). Chichester: Wiley.

Howard, R. C. & Duggan, C. (2009). Mentally disordered offenders: Personality disorders. In G. Towl & D. Crighton (Eds.), *Forensic psychology*. Oxford: Oxford University Press, in press.

Howard, R. C., Huband, N., Mannion, A. & Duggan, C. (2008). Exploring the link between personality disorder and criminality in a community sample. *Journal of Personality Disorders*, *22*, 589–603.

Howard, R. C. & McCullagh, P. (2007). Neuroaffective processing in criminal psychopaths: Brain event-related potentials reveal task-specific anomalies. *Journal of Personality Disorders*, *21*(1), 100–117.

Howells, K. (in press). Distinctions within distinctions: The challenges of heterogeneity and causality in the formulation and treatment of violence. In M. Daffern, L. Jones & M. Shine (Eds.), *Offence-paralleling behaviour*. Chichester: Wiley.

Howells, K., Day, A. & Thomas-Peter, B. (2004). Treating violence: Forensic mental health and criminological models compared. *Journal of Forensic Psychiatry and Psychology*, *15*, 391.

Howells, K. & Jones, L. (2009). Commentary on formulations of a case of problem behaviour in an older adult. In P. Sturmey (Ed.), *Clinical formulation: Varieties of approaches* (pp. 227–240). Chichester: Wiley-Blackwell.

Howells, K., Krishnan, G., & Daffern, M. (2007). Challenges in the treatment of dangerous and severe personality disorder. *Advances in Psychiatric Treatment*, *13*, 325–332.

Howells, K., Tennant, A., Day, A. & Elmer, R. (in press). Mindfulness: Does it have a role in forensic mental health? *International Journal of Mindfulness*.

Kosson, D. S., Lorenz, A. R. & Newman, J. P. (2006). Effects of comorbid psychopathy on criminal offending and emotion processing in male offenders with antisocial personality disorder. *Journal of Abnormal Psychology*, *115*, 798–806.

Livesley, W. J. (2003). *Practical management of personality disorder*. New York: Guilford.

Livesley, W. J. (2007). The relevance of an integrated approach to the treatment of personality disordered offenders. *Psychology, Crime and Law*, *13*, 27–46.

McMurran, M. (2009). Personality, personality disorder and violence: An introduction. In M. McMurran & R. Howard (Eds.), *Personality, personality disorder and risk of violence* (pp. 3–18). Chichester: Wiley.

Mullen, P. E. (2007). Dangerous and severe personality disorder and in need of treatment. *British Journal of Psychiatry*, *190*, suppl. 49, 3–7.

Tyrer, P. & Johnson, T. (1996). Establishing the severity of personality disorder. *American Journal of Psychiatry*, *153*, 1593–1597.

Varlamov, A., Khalifa, N., Liddle, P., Duggan, C. & Howard, R. C. (in press). Cortical correlates of impaired self-regulation in personality disordered patients with psychopathic traits.

Wallace, J. F. & Newman, J. P. (2004). A theory-based treatment model for psychopathy. *Cognitive and Behavioral Practice*, *11*, 178–189.

Index